Real
Oxford

Other Titles in the Series:

Real
Oxford

Patrick McGuinness

SERIES EDITOR: PETER FINCH

Seren is the book imprint of
Poetry Wales Press Ltd
4 Derwen Road, Bridgend, Wales

www.serenbooks.com
facebook.com/SerenBooks
Twitter: @SerenBooks

Text and images © Patrick McGuinness, 2021
Series Introduction © Peter Finch

ISBN 978-1-78172-620-4

A CIP record for this title is available from
the British Library

The publisher works with the financial assistance
of the Books Council of Wales

Printed by Bell & Bain Ltd, Glasgow.

CONTENTS

SERIES EDITOR'S INTRODUCTION

Real books are not simply guides, travelogues, histories, biographies, recollections, inventions, literary manipulations, tales of wonder nor tales of belief. They are all these things. Psychogeography is a word that often gets appended to this now popular, often quite learned, and lengthy series of volumes covering many of the UK's conurbations. But psychogeography is not quite it. I was asked once how to walk a city as a psychogeographer might. Do the streets in alphabetical order was my reply. But there's none of that in Patrick McGuinness' *Real Oxford*. He might have a familiarity with the playful strategies of the situationists and the wonders of the *dérive*[1] but in the present volume he keeps such avant garde activities well under control.

Oxford Town, Oxford Town sang Bob Dylan in 1962. He meant the Johnny come lately Oxford in the State of Mississippi rather than the home of the oldest university in the English-speaking world over here. But Dylan is the exception. Ask most people right across the globe and although they might suggest that Birmingham is in Alabama and have never heard of Cardiff, they'll know about Oxford.

This is a small city with a population of not much more than 150,000. Industry, car building, canals and, to quote McGuinness, places where things were 'melted, smelted, burned, and hammered' might account for much of its topography but it is the University that provides the core. The city persists, suggests our author, while the university dominates, as it always has done. There is more extant history in the central square miles than in virtually any place world-wide outside of perhaps Jerusalem's Temple Mount or Tutankhamun's tomb. Reale OxnaForde would have made a viable prospect.

Walk the streets and you'll encounter examples of every style of architecture from the late Anglo-Saxon to hi-tech modernism. The extensive suburbs can offer Swindonian blandness but the central area restores faith with, among many other wonders, Georgian crescents, Nicholas Hawksmoor's Bodleian Library, the Saxon military tower of St George, the Radcliffe Camera, Christopher Wren's Sheldonian Theatre, and an Anglicised replica of the Bridge of Sighs.

In this place you'll find University College which has a founding date of at least 1249 (although some suggest Alfred the Great actually set it up in 872) along with BMW's ex-Morris car plant at Cowley which still turns out Britain's world-beating Mini. For a brief stretch here the Thames, that ancient river, is given an even older name, Isis. It joins with the River Cherwell right where those ancient Oxen made their ford. Or maybe they didn't. Rivers move and get realigned. That crossing of the waters might have been near Magdalen College, or north by the flood plain of Port Meadow or somewhere to the west on the current Botley Road. History moves about. No one is quite sure.

As in most University centres town and gown rarely mix well or even at all and that's pretty much the case with Oxford. Our psychogeographer author, however, readily melds the two. His city encapsulation, exploration and exposition is one of the most readable in the entire Real series. Being a Fellow at St Anne's gives him entrée. Being a poet allows him to report the city's workings with veracity and vision. Being a prize-winning novelist gives him the ability and the range. A liking for pubs provides the common touch while his status as a natural inquisitive means barges, swing-bridges, pubs, eco-warrior battles, 1996 VOTE MCGUINNESS posters, jam, the Anglo-Catholic revival, Harry Drinkwater's brewery tower, the Mound hillfort, Oxford of the politically uncomfortable, the ballet of cranes, the hard pizzle of the water supply, rats the size of your shoe, and the ghost of St Ebbe's. All these Oxfordian diversions feature.

Real Oxford joins a list of Oxford-centred literary masterpieces. This place is a very literary city. Writers perpetuate its fables and myths. Hardy's City of Light, Colin Dexter's city of crime, Evelyn Waugh's city of privilege, Philip Larkin's Oxford of working class survival, Philip Pullman's place of fantasy and Dust.

Broadening this present work Patrick McGuinness' own Oxford poems join a long list of Oxford realities celebrated in verse – Keith Douglas' city of the young, Gerard Manley Hopkins' city of towers, W.H. Auden's city of knowledge, along with the fine Oxfordian poetry created by Matthew Arnold, Philip Larkin, C.S. Lewis and many others. Poetry permeates this place. The present Professor of Poetry is Alice Oswald who succeeded Simon Armitage in 2019. Oxford University Press sets a gold standard for poetry in print. Verse here is a world force.

McGuinness takes his subject to be everything contained by the Ring Road which gives him a fair area to cover. Over time he walks it all to report back on just how real he finds it. McGuinness is right on the money giving us his version of the 'Home of lost causes, and forsaken beliefs, and unpopular names, and impossible loyalties.[2]' Expect a vibrant mix.

Peter Finch

Notes

1. Situationist Guy Debord's 1958 insistence that (and I paraphrase here) the best way to visit a place is to drift through it, to let yourself be drawn by the attractions of the terrain and the encounters you find there. Climb the hill because it is there rather than because there's something significant at the top. Follow your spiritual sense not the road sign. Track the lost river. Look under stones. Be encouraged by sensation.
2. Matthew Arnold, *Essays in Criticism* First Series, 1865.

INTRODUCTION

'*Real* where?

'What next: *Real Narnia?*... *Real Disneyland?*... *Real Middle-Earth?*

When I told people I was writing a book called *Real Oxford*, the jokes were predictable. On the face of it, the City of Dreaming Spires is about the last place we might expect to find the real, or anyone who knew much about it – though some might have glimpsed it from the window of a passing train or an airport bus.

This city of 150,000 inhabitants is the term-time home of 45,000 students from two universities, and is visited each year by 7,000,000 tourists. It's a good bet that neither the students nor the tourists have come for the 'real' Oxford, but for the mythical Oxfords they've seen in films, read about in books, or been encouraged to apply to study at. As for the remembered Oxfords which may be even less real than the imagined ones – *alumni* groups in more than 100 countries cater for hundreds of thousands of people nostalgic for the place they briefly lived and learned in.

I'm nostalgic for Oxford, and I'm still here.

All this by way of saying that 'real' Oxford has a great deal of competition from the other Oxfords. This book tries to even the balance. When I first arrived, in 1991, I was barely aware of how Oxford the city persisted, often against the odds. The university dominated. Its tendrils stretched up to and beyond the ringroad, with its science parks, student halls and technology centres, its arms-length businesses that swallowed up the city almost as fast as the developers built housing of Swindonian blandness. Oxford's second seat of learning, Oxford Polytechnic, became Oxford Brookes in 1992, and has grown fast, extending its footprint in East Oxford and Headington. Oxford is the highest-ranked city in the UK for student population (25%), 30% of its population was born outside the UK, and the house price to earnings ratio is an eye-watering 17.3 to 1. Oxford has low unemployment and a high rate of jobs growth – the latest statistics show that there are 1.25 jobs per resident of working age. For every one of us working, there's a quarter of a job not being done. It also has the UK's highest rate of population turnover, with almost a third of its population leaving and being replaced each year. Cistern-city: each flush different, each flush the same.

The universities are international – my typical day in college involves talking to people in fields ranging from thermofluids to ancient philosophy, and who come from all four corners of the world. The names on plaques or on prize medals, in newspaper articles about new vaccines or world-leading research into everything from sustainable growth to the History of Empire, are international. Whenever I feel the world is narrowing, the outlook shrinking, I go into work.

It took me a few years to realise that behind all this success, this dynamic present and this prestigious history, there was also a city called Oxford. It went mostly unnoticed by students and academics, and the universities themselves paid scant attention to it.

I realised that Oxford was a large, vibrant, diverse, once-industrial city with an identity of its own, that was always remaking itself. It had no choice. It didn't just have its own history, it had its own present too. But it was squeezed between the unfettered expansion of the universities and the dead-eyed rapacity of developers. That continues today. I felt that there was something endangered about it: industrial Oxford, working Oxford, its people and its places, were always the first to go, the last to be defended or preserved. They had the wrong sort of past for the historians to notice, and the wrong sort of future for the economists to bother with. It's no coincidence that they were the wrong sort of class too. I write about this Oxford as well as the Oxford of honeyed stone and Brideshead myths.

To be in Oxford is to be in several places at once – several eras too. These places and eras merge and overlap and rebecome distinct, often in the course of a single walk. I've tried in this book to create a sense of lateral Oxford rather than linear Oxford – not just the 'then' behind the 'now' (that's easy enough), but the 'now' that continues behind, beneath, and to the side of all that 'then'. I've also sought to make Oxford more polyphonic about the stories it tells about itself, and more diverse about the stories it's ready to hear about itself. The city of light and learning has plenty of darkness.

In practical terms, what I write about can be seen on foot: from pavement, towpath, traffic island, bridge, muddy bank, river, edgeland, and all the places in-between. The one constraint I imposed upon myself turned out to be a liberation: everything (except what I've invented or remembered, which is a good portion of the book) can be visited or looked at without paying. That's no small feat in an Oxford that's becoming pay-per-view.

As *Real Oxford* joins the family of *Real...* books, I want to give the reader a similar sense of this over-envisioned, endlessly-written, extravagantly-poeticised, exhaustively-photographed, idealistically-painted city. Here in Oxford, where everything has been seen so many times, we can be the ones who notice.

CENTRAL

STATION

Arriving in Oxford by train, the traveller could be forgiven for thinking they'd disembarked at Swindon. I did, and I'd never been to Swindon, merely knew it as a byword for subtopia. Edward Thomas called this approach to Oxford 'the most contemptible in Europe'.[1] Over the years I've watched the tourists line up their wheelie-cases, adjust their rucksack-straps and raise their eyes in anticipation the way I did when I came. This is one of the world's most famous cities, home to the legendary university. They've seen the movies, got the postcards, read the novels. Culture-vultures bound for the Ashmolean, Harry Potter addicts, Alice in Wonderland fans, Tolkien aficionados, shopaholics heading to the Westgate, students embarking on their first term: all arriving with their own Oxfords in mind.

Judging by their faces at the ticket barriers, none of them is this one: they're expecting something grand like Newcastle station, old-fashioned and cosy like Hereford; or the miniature cosmopolitanism of Marylebone. But no. Oxford station looks like the shell of a bankrupt garden centre. Tacky glass doors and blue PVC fascias, and toilets that are small and rank, the air inside them untroubled by any form of ventilation. Take a moment to observe the gender inequality of public convenience design: women waiting in queues while the men lumber in, flies azip, then breeze back out wiping their hands on their trousers. Welcome to Oxford.

Knowing what the station might have been like makes it worse. As with all towns and cities, there are past Oxfords and virtual Oxfords, and I imagine this one – the 'real' Oxford I've lived in for nearly thirty years – flanked by the Oxfords that were and the Oxfords that might have been. They aren't necessarily better, but once you know about them it's difficult to unknow them. Actually, they probably are better, but nostalgia gets you nowhere and it's impossible to live in a place that doesn't exist. This doesn't stop many of us from trying, however, and some might say this is what Oxford is all about. As for this book, it may be my attempt to do just that.

The station is a good place to think about these Oxfords, because the city's railway history is a microcosm of its relationship to the world: arrogant but also insecure, high-minded yet petty. Oxford was offered a branch-line in 1837 with a station near Magdalen Bridge at the bottom of Cowley Road. It was rejected by landowners and by the City Corporation, who feared its Abingdon road tolls would dry up. The second proposal came a year later. This time the university killed it, fearing students would fall prey to London's evil influence: 'improper marriages and other illegitimate connexions'. The Chancellor of the university, the Duke of Wellington, had a more general concern about rail travel: that it might encourage the lower orders to 'move about'. With today's rail fares, he needn't have worried.

It's ironic to think of Oxford University being afraid of its students bringing in unsavoury and immoral ways from the outside world. Looking at today's politicians, and considering the blustering, entitled, ineptocracy of a ruling class that Oxford has exported over the last few generations, it's the outside world that should be afraid.

Oxford's first station, at Grandpont to the south, was, for a time, a happy compromise: for the city because students still had to pay tolls at Folly Bridge, and for the university because its security staff had the right to patrol the station. An agreement was reached with the company that students would only be sold tickets to 'suitable' destinations. Grandpont was opened by Brunel, but lasted barely thirty years – small, flimsy and badly-sited, it was a victim of competition in a golden age of industrial engineering. The city went from no stations to three stations in less than a decade. So strong is the cultural and economic pull of London and the South East today that we forget this about Oxford: while the university pointed at

London and Cambridge, Oxford as a South Midlands city pointed towards the industrial powerhouses of Birmingham and Wolverhampton.

This is still reflected in the travelling habits of town and gown. London and Birmingham take roughly an hour each to get to by train and cost more or less the same. For the gown, Birmingham is remote, northern and far away, and many students and staff have never set foot there. But for Oxford people, Birmingham is a quick and easy destination for everything from concerts to shopping, by way of superb Indian restaurants and the kind of old-style pubs Oxford got rid of in the 1990s. The Oxford-Coventry-Birmingham-Wolverhampton line is as much part of Oxford's outlook as the Oxford-Reading-London line, and discovering Birmingham has been one of the highlights of my time in Oxford.

GHOST-STATION

When I came here in 1991, there were two stations. This one, on top of its little embanked mound, and another, fifty yards downhill, called Oxford Rewley Road. Closed to passengers since 1951 (freight still rolled in until the 80s), it belonged first to the London and North Western Railway and finally to the London Midland and Scottish Railway, which is what's marked on the frontage in all the old photographs. It was also a stop on the so-called 'Varsity Line', the line that linked Oxford to Cambridge via Bletchley, closed in 1968 but looking likely, as I write, to be restored.

When I knew the station its name was 'Tyre Services and Exhaust Centre', but the building was intact, lending itself nicely to the role of garage and MOT centre. All the main structure was used – station-master's office, waiting room, engine-sheds – and the forecourt had cars and trucks in various states of dismantlement that reassured me that, in between and underneath the dreaming spires, normal people were doing normal things. They were using what was there, absorbing the industrial past into present rhythms of life and work, give or take a few Goodyear stickers and Michelin Men. That's the Oxford I saw first.

My grandfather on my mother's side was an 'ouvrier' in the Usine Camion, a metal factory in Bouillon, Belgium. I spent many hours with him in his 'remise', a little outhouse where he kept reams of disconnected machine parts, old tools, and different kinds of handles, moulds for keys and hinges and things I didn't know the names of and still don't. He'd lay them out on grey sheets in the courtyard and swap them with people who, like him, exhibited rather than used them, on boards hung with little nails or in frames and glass cases. It looked like an autopsy room for robots. Many of his friends had sheds that were tiny museums to what had once been their livelihoods. I noticed they often raised these items to their noses and breathed them: they smelled of machine-oil, paraffin or polish, and further back along the chain of memory they smelled of meals together and table-beer and nights in cafés playing cards, of days when work was secure and communities were built around it.

One reason smells and tastes in literature get such a bad press is that, thanks to Proust and a few others, they're the province of the easeful and the rich. They needn't be, and my grandfather's bits and bobs opened up a world as resonant and connected – and also as painfully gone – as Marcel's *madeleine*. One of the best things about being a student here in the 90s was knowing Malcolm Bowie, a great critic and Proust scholar, and Marshal Foch Professor of French at All Souls College. He lamented in an essay that nostalgia was a cop-out, that 'we allow ourselves to be caressed by a past that has had its claws removed'[2]. That made a lot of sense to me: I think the past should hurt. It should bite and scratch. Here in Oxford it often does.

Oxford is rich in industrial pasts, though they are often blanked out in the glare of the university's prestige. They're also flattened – literally as well as metaphorically – in the inexorable development of shopping centres, office blocks, and residential buildings that pay scant attention to any history that isn't marinaded in medievalism.

To me, born after my grandfather's factory had closed and long after he'd been laid off, these machine-parts smelled of the St Eloi 'fête' we had every December 1. St Eloi was the patron saint of metalworkers, and the people he blessed are gone or almost. The work they did, like the factories they did it in, has disappeared. What remains exists, like my grandfather's tools, in the unvisited heritage museums of neglected towns. Or landfill. Saint Eligius himself, however, still keeps busy: he's also the patron saint of vets, goldsmiths, horses and those who work with them, taxi drivers (the machine-incarnation of the previous category) and the British Army's Royal Electrical and Mechanical Engineers. He has a varied portfolio. When you're a saint it's never too late to re-skill, which is probably what saved him from the fate of so many of those he watched over.

But the smell of Rewley Road Station/Tyre and Exhaust Centre was familiar as I lugged my suitcase past it on October 1 1991. It was the same smell – give or take a world of differences – I remembered from Bouillon. So I start this book where I started with Oxford: with some car-parts laid out on the forecourt of a ghost-station.

INDUSTRIAL OXFORD

Rewley Road station was a Victorian prefab, and dates from the same year as the Great Exhibition of 1851. It was made by the same contractors too: Fox, Henderson, who used similar cast-iron components for this small two-platformed station as they used for the Crystal Palace. Both buildings were due to open on the same day – 1 May, 1851 – but Rewley Road was delayed by two weeks. An inauspicious start for a railway station, but, as anyone who has travelled on British trains will tell you, not an unfitting one. It was pretty basic: two lines and two platforms, linked to a railway swing-bridge which took the trains over the 'Sheepwash Channel'. The swing-bridge, remnants of which are rotting with indignity between slabs of identikit new housing nearby, was necessary because the canal was and remains a working one. The day I visit it to take photographs, there's a barge covered in blue plastic tarpaulin moored beside the fragment of swing-bridge. A bike is locked to the roof and some herbs grow in a wooden planter. There's been a lot of rain – across the tracks the waters in Osney are licking the pavements and the barges are almost level with the parked cars.

The Oxford Preservation Trust is making valiant attempts to get the swing-bridge fragments protected, so it's fenced-off now, pending – I hope – restoration. I can still see the engineering of it, the wheel which needed to be turned to align the rails with the lip of the next bank. Beside it are two modern iron railway bridges and one arched footbridge. They all cross over the same narrow pass of water. We're only a few yards from the station, but the trains out are already going fast, picking up speed, heading north. The trains in are slowing to a grind, and from the footbridge I can see the passengers on their phones, on their tablets, at the doors, fingers hovering over the release buttons. I can guess their texts: 'Just getting in', 'stuck at the lights', 'get me a cappuccino xxx!'.

Rewley Road Station had quality, harmony and function: small, dignified and with a sturdiness belied by the grace of the ironwork. It was built at a time when pragmatism and elegance were not just compatible, but extensions of each other. It's a feature of this part of Oxford, drab though it at first appears, because it's one of the areas where people made things, mended things, brewed things, received and dispatched things, lugged them on and off trains and carts and lorries, half a mile but a whole world away from the colleges and their towers. John Ruskin, who at the time was involved in a much grander Oxford construction – the Museum of Natural History – has a great essay entitled 'The Work of Iron', where he fulminates against the way iron is mass-produced to build railings to keep people out. Iron deserved better, he claimed: such a noble material, beautifying our structures, underpinning our networks. It rusts, says Ruskin, which means it lives. I think of the magnificent pillars of the Museum of Natural History, with their embossed leaves and green and gold paint, and those of this cheap and cheerful prefab, this ghost-station, as cousins: related not just in the material they use but in the collective mind that makes them possible. It's the Victorian mind, which built for ever and built for all.

Rewley Road Station was Grade II-listed, which didn't stop it being taken down in 1999. It's now at Buckingham Railway Centre in Quainton, restored and repainted, and though I'm glad it still exists, it has the air of a pristinely-embalmed corpse, perfect in every respect but life's. I preferred it as a tyre centre because it projected over the whole of Frideswide Square something untidy and transient and alive. There was a burger shack outside, made out of what looked like pieces of railway shelter – an old signal box, I think – that made the best burgers in Oxford: Bret's Burgers. It burned down one night and never returned.

In his 1948 book *Oxford Replanned*, Thomas Sharp, a brilliant and polemical town planner, wrote 'Oxford stations have come to be spoken of with the kind of joke that people make to keep them from the black despair of hope continually deferred'.[3] The Great Western Station would have disgraced, as he put it, 'a small Lancashire industrial town'. Yes, OK, I can go with that. But Rewley Road, he said, looked like it belonged to 'a small and decayed prairie camp'. It's true that it wasn't worthy of a city like Oxford, but it had its place, and its place was the bustling commercial Frideswide Square quarter.

Sharp is as good as his name, and his book is a big, bold reimagining of the city's space. Oxford was Hitler's favourite English city, and he instructed that it be spared from bombing. The canvas here was therefore considerably less blank than, say, Bristol or Swansea or the East End of London. Thomas Sharp imagined both stations torn down, with Rewley Road replaced with a bus station, to make 'Station Square' into an integrated transport centre. A 'hub', to use today's parlance. Sharp was replanning townscapes that had been blighted by the Blitz, but since Oxford was spared one, he intended to provide his own: swathes of demolitions to produce a road linking the station to Cowley Road via the back of Christ Church, cutting through the meadow, slicing its way behind Merton College and replacing Magdalen College School on The Plain with a bridge. Whatever the merits of his plan, he would take a dim view of what stands in the old station's place: the Saïd Business School, named after Wafic Saïd, arms dealer, friend to Syria's Assad dynasty, and enthusiastic donor to Margaret Thatcher and the Conservative Party. It's now the first thing you see when you arrive in Oxford.

I wouldn't blame you for turning round, heading back and buying a ticket to Birmingham.

PLAQUE OVER PLAQUE

When the garage packed up, the station became the site for one of Oxford's first environmental protests. Eco-warriors squatted in the building and occupied the trees. After a desultory siege, police and private security guards yanked them out and dragged them off the premises into vans. The trees were cut down immediately and the logs carted off. All that was left was a bed of sawdust patrolled by men in uniforms. I confess I'd never noticed the trees until there were people in them, but the Battle of Rewley Road now seems like a harbinger of things to come: not just the bulldozing of industrial heritage or the buying-up of Oxford by the university and by developers, but global warming, habitat-destruction, the corporate state. What was a few hippies in treehouses in the grand scheme of things? Some things disappear for good – like stations. Other things come back looking different, and it's our job to recognise them. That eco-battle of the 1990s felt like the last stand of hippiedom. Today, as students and schoolchildren lead the way in climate rebellion, it seems like a different version of the now. The archaeo-contemporary.

The Business School added a new wing in 2013, a squat little appendage tucked away behind the taxi rank: the Thatcher Business Education Centre. Finally, the university that refused her an honorary degree accepted a building named after her. One of the first things the Business School did once it secured the right to use the Oxford name (sorry – *Brand*) for its degrees, was extricate itself from the university's fees system and set its own. The MBA there costs £63,000. For that price you can get four Masters in Classical Archaeology and one Masters in Film, and still have enough left over for a Postgraduate Diploma in Applied Theology – worth it just to find out what they mean by 'applied'.

Easily missed underfoot as I scuttle past the business school on Frideswide Square is a brass plaque to the old station. On the other side of the building is another plaque – more info-panel, this – reminding us that before the era of station-masters and commuters, MBAs and 60K fees, there was a Cistercian abbey here. Built in the late thirteenth century, it was a victim of the dissolution of the monasteries in 1536. It's all gone now, though some of its stones were used in other buildings. Recycling has always been with us, and one of its arches survives in an old wall in Jericho: Jericho, Oxford, that is, not the biblical Jericho of the famous battle. Come to think of it, Oxford's Jericho, on the other side of the river, has its own battles, and we'll cross that bridge – how nice to write that and mean it literally – when we come to it.

We've barely arrived in Oxford. We're still just a few yards outside the station, and already we're standing on a piece of land that has been an abbey, a station and a business school. Each incarnation was a product of its time and its beliefs: God, machines, and money. This is how it's going to be here. Every square metre of Oxford has been so many things that even the plaques are crowding each other out: plaque beside plaque, plaque over plaque, plaque to a previous plaque.

FRIDESWIDE SQUARE

Saint Frithuswith (650-735) was Abbess and founder of St Frideswide's Priory, now part of Christ Church Cathedral, which houses a beautiful stained glass of her by the Pre-Raphaelite artist, Burne-Jones, a Brummie and one of Oxford's 'Birmingham Colony'. She's the patron saint of both Oxford city and Oxford university, and as such symbolises a unity that maybe only exists in the symbol.

Frideswide deserves a better square than this, but it was always going to be a planner's nightmare. Oxford was never designed for so many people and so much traffic. It was never designed. When it was planned, as with the transformation of nearby St Ebbe's, the planning was geared towards cars rather than people. Even in the 1940s it was felt that the High Street and Broad Street were unmanageably congested.

In 1996, I was the local Labour Party council candidate for Oxford Central. A key policy was closing the city-centre to private vehicles, pedestrianising Cornmarket, and creating a one-way system. They say today is the era of political abuse – that social media means new outlets for old hates. But as a failed local politician I can attest that people were pretty handy with the old technology too: pen and paper, typewriter and telephone. For the VOTE MCGUINNESS literature we took a photo of me standing in front of some bikes on a congested St Aldate's, near where Frideswide's remains are buried in Christ Church, mixed in with someone else's after they were desecrated and her tomb vandalised in the Reformation. When we got the leaflets back from the printers, I saw the bikes behind me had also been vandalised. It looked like I'd just kicked them in myself, a message to the electors about what to expect if they didn't vote for me. My campaign-manager was one of a breed of New Labour technocrats, and he did everything right except register me with the returning officer by the deadline.

I had to abandon my candidacy, told people vote Green (they got in), and went back to the real world, which in my case was the ivory tower, to finish my doctorate on avant-garde theatre. My supervisor, Alan Raitt, FBA, FRSL, Commandeur des Palmes Académiques and Oxford United season-ticket holder, told me it was probably better for my academic career. He added, 'and also for Oxford'. My campaign manager went on to work for Tony Blair's New Labour, who were elected two years later. I like to think his débâcle with me gave him the kind of on-the-ground experience no focus group prepares you for.

Cornmarket and Broad Street were eventually pedestrianised, while the High Street, St Aldate's and Queen Street were closed to private vehicles. It helps a little, but by the time you get to Frideswide Square, it's a log-jammed free-for-all again. It has to function as a *hub*, not just for the station but for the roads west to Botley, the ringroad, Swindon and Bristol; south to Abingdon Rd; north to Jericho, Summertown and eventually the Midlands; and east down the High Street towards The Plain and on to London. All these roads are narrow – it's a traffic system made up entirely of pinch-points. And that's before the bikes and the buses. The buildings are grimy, the businesses feel temporary. Even the ones that have been here for years look like they're about to decamp somewhere more savoury.

We might be tempted to head straight up and into the city centre – towards the colleges and shops, or take the canal path to Jericho, where Inspector Morse solves an early case. Station quarters have their own aura, and this area has an aura of scrappy transience, as if it's encouraging us to leave as soon as we can. Which doesn't make it uninteresting – it just means we'll have to look a little harder than usual. Five minutes walk uphill and Oxford will suddenly storm our eyeline with grandeur and beauty. We'll be peering over fronds of selfie-sticks. We won't register the modest, the unlooked-at and the undervalued. So let's make the most of Frideswide Square and look around. We won't be the first to do so, but we might feel like we are.

STREET OF WHEELS

Stations create eco-systems, a term coined in 1935 by Arthur Tansley, Sherardian Professor of Botany at the university. To get a better view of this eco-system I'm watching life through the window of Dhosa Park, a South Indian eatery facing the Business School. A few doors down is the universal Domino's Pizza, niftily positioned on the corner so its delivery mopeds can hit the roundabout like roulette balls. There's a dhosa, some pickles and a cucumber lhassi in front of me – this is where I come when I'm off a late-night train, but today I'm having a rare daytime Indian meal. The pavement is wide, so it feels set back from the traffic, and there are deep planters with a screen of struggling greenery. In the summer there are tables outside so you can watch your food develop the same sooty sheen as the buildings. To my right is The Oxford Royal Hotel, built in 1935 for well-heeled commercial travellers. It's been struggling to adapt for decades – the ground floor is now a Sainsbury's Local, and before that a sequence of unsuccessful restaurants and cafés. It's too close to the roundabout to cater for more than budget visitors today.

Park End Street and New Road used to be known as 'Street of Wheels'. It's not a reference to the thousands of wheelie cases being dragged from Airbnb to Airbnb, but to the garages and car dealerships that sprang up in the 1930s, purpose-built and with nice art-deco touches. They're minor variations on what Ruskin wanted for Victorian industrial architecture. No-one looks at them now: the tourists, 'randy for antique' as Larkin put it, want the Sheldonian Theatre and Magdalen Tower, and they're too cavernous and draughty for office buildings, the world of watercoolers and hot-desking. The Cantay warehouse was three floors of books when I first came, where I bought a first edition New Directions Pound's *Cantos* for a fiver. It was built in 1901 as a furniture depot to supply the British Empire's civil servants with home comforts and office equipment. It now houses a high-end hi-fi shop, a.k.a. an 'Audio Consultancy', a night club, and one of Oxford's many English Language schools. Its modern descendant, the office supplies company Staples, closed down in 2019, but occupied the old Hartwell garage, with its stucco pillars on the façade and its mosaic with the H medallion at the entrance.

BECKET STREET, ST THOMAS THE MARTYR, FLOATING CHAPEL

I settle the dhosa bill and walk down Becket Street. It's named after Thomas à Becket, but suits Samuel Beckett rather better: boarding houses from whose rotten-framed bay windows you can imagine one of Beckett's characters misanthropically gazing. There's something deeply unpromising about taking this direction and that makes me curious. It's how I've walked Oxford over the years. As a response to the place's endless visual stimulation and the grandeur and beauty even of my humdrum route into work – Iffley Road, Magdalen Bridge, High Street, Radcliffe Camera, Bodleian Library, University Parks ... you get the idea – I started to seek out places that didn't care whether you looked at them or not. Here's one of them.

There's a long track of fencing abutting the rail-line to Didcot and London, then Oxford Business Centre suddenly happens. And 'happens' is putting it strongly. It doesn't build up after some tapering edgeland, but begins suddenly: printers, rent-a-car, more printers, Mallett's wholesale newsagents. Prefabs again, but modern ones. It's a relief to see they're totally unremarkable; it saves writing about them. And so I stop there and look around, enjoying the way my eye slides off everything. Nothing catches it. Relief. Eye-muscles relax, the mind stops turning stuff over. I want some bland please, visual vanilla. This will do nicely. The park is being developed into student flats, so the few remaining businesses are watched over by cranes that hang like Damocles's entire sword collection. On the other side of the track, and on the other side of the river, the same is happening in Osney. Further west, it's the same again in Botley.

Facing the station car park which was once the Hanley Brewery maltings, the faded letters of Furey's Hotel faintly show through. Such a thrusting name, such muted letters. Behind it, a twelfth century church, St Thomas the Martyr, still serves a loyal flock but looks marooned as the neighbourhood around has been flattened for roads and apartment blocks. This part of Oxford, St Thomas's, was expendable: like much of working-class Oxford, it had its buildings razed and its people moved, but unlike St Ebbe's there's just about enough left for me to be able to imagine what it was like. The church is a tiny island of peace – an island within an island, because it's surrounded by a small graveyard with lopsided headstones. At rest in the graveyard is Olive Gibbs, who appears several times in this book, and who represented St Thomas's ward as a councillor. This church was a key player in the Oxford Movement, and like many of Oxford's church buildings, it hosts different denominations now. When I go in today it's being used by the Romanian Orthodox Church, and a row of icons has been set up around the altar. A priest sits in the back and local Romanians are queuing to speak to him, confess and have their new babies blessed.

It was from here that Oxford's first floating chapel set out in 1839. The Boatman's Chapel did God's work on the water until 1868, when it sank. Oxford's canals are full of detritus of old boats, sunk or scuttled or simply rotted into murk and sludge, and there's a man further upriver in Jericho who still lives as a kind of water-tinker, scooping out old bits of boat and drying them out on a raft made from discarded plastic barrels. It's hard today to file the canals and waterways of Oxford under anything other than 'lifestyle and leisure'. But they were Oxford's third thoroughfare after road and rail. Livelihoods depended on it. Oxford's crest – an ox 'fording' three wavy lines of water (see page 13) – was a reality before it became a symbol.

Frideswide's, or, as Thomas Sharp had it, 'Station Square', has one of Oxford's treasures: Frank Cooper's marmalade factory. Designed by Herbert Quinton in 1902-03, this it's where Cooper mass-produced marmalade to his wife's recipe. A blue plaque to her is on 83 High Street – the site of Cooper's original grocery shop. The factory was purpose-built, and constructed by Kingerlee, a local builder who remain major Oxford builders – their logos and billboards are all over the city. In the first illustrated *Alice in*

Wonderland, there's a pot down the rabbit hole; there's a jar in a breakfast scene in *From Russia with Love*, and The Museum of Oxford has Captain Scott's jar, found among his things in the Antarctic. Englishness in a jar. The building is known as the Jam Factory, but you can tell its major purpose was marmalade by the stone carvings of oranges in the façade. They're so detailed I can see the pores on the rind.

Production was moved to Botley Road after World War II, then out of Oxford in 1967, when the company was sold. When I came, the ground floor was an antiques market, and the first floor was workspaces for people who didn't like offices that looked like offices. Every detail of it is perfect, down to the ribbing of the windows, the patterning of the bricks. Its courtyard is dominated by the chimney and gives a perfect view of it: vertiginous and up-close. The best way to admire it is with a pint of Cotswold Brewery beer in the Jam Factory pub and restaurant that opened in its ground floor, and which now uses the courtyard as a beer garden.

Cotswold beer is nice and local, but until recently this area would also have been a great place to drink something even more local: Morrell's Brewery just across the road only closed in 1998. Bought by an 'entrepreneur' who sold the land and buildings to developers then closed the brewery and its pubs, it was one of Oxford's institutions.

We're at Oxford's main intersection-point: where the trains and the cars, the boats and the carts, unloaded the oranges and the sugar, the malt and the hops, the tourists and the students. And from which, after whatever processes and transformations they underwent, they left again, headed out into the world.

THE BREWING QUARTER

Many Oxford buildings, including the Examinations Schools, the Town Hall and the workhouse on Cowley Road, served as hospitals during both world wars. In 1915, a history don called C.R.L. Fletcher wrote *Oxford: A Handy Guide* to raise money for the soldier's tobacco fund. He was a cheerleading imperialist, anti-democrat and reactionary conservative, but explained the workings of the university in refreshingly democratic terms:

> Most of you, I suppose, entered Oxford from the railway station in the western suburbs, and a guidebook ought, therefore, to begin with a description of the things you will see coming up Park End Street, New Road, Queen Street [...] But I gather that you were usually so much occupied in abusing the uneven surface of these streets, while you were being jolted to your Hospital, that you had little chance of admiring the County Jail, the Assize Court, or the Canal Wharf, which were the main things you would see before reaching the top of the High Street at Carfax...[4]

The jolting cobbles are long gone, the Assizes Court moved in 1986, and the County Jail is now a Malmaison hotel, presiding over the 'Castle Quarter' of bars and eateries. The Canal Wharf was filled in and turned into a bus station and later a car park. Lord Nuffield – William Morris as was – bought the wharf buildings and demolished them for Nuffield College. He thought the western edges of Oxford an 'eyesore'. He wasn't the only one. Thomas Sharp called the area between the station and the centre of town a 'slum', and that view became the orthodoxy for a long and destructive period in Oxford's development.

We'll get to that. First I finish my pint and cross Hollybush Row, to where some busy men in shirtsleeves are doing high-tech, hot-desk, blue-sky thinking behind the ornate windows of an old Hall's pub. They've got their shirtsleeves rolled up and look like they're about to deliver a TED-talk *a capella*. It's now an office called 'Latent Logic'. When I last drank there it was The Honey Pot, and before that The Albion. I've no complaints about the Cotswold

lager I've just had – these are the days of micro-breweries and relaunched pseudo-heritage brands – but it's a shame not to be having a pint of Hall's a few yards away from its own brewery. The Hall's sign – a hare flanked by some hops and barley – is still there by the door. Hall's Oxford and West Brewery Company had pubs everywhere, and you can still map the city by the tiles of doors to what are now homes or offices or flats. Ghost-pubs require ghost-pub-crawls, and in the Oxford beside this one we're already a few pints in. Our lift home is sorted too, though we'll be waiting a while: Latent Logic turns out to be a tech company researching driverless cars. It's still Street of Wheels after all.

If the disembarking soldiers were in good enough shape, they'd have followed their noses towards a different Oxford skyline from the one in postcards: the chimneys of Oxford's Brewing Quarter. There's only one chimney left: Morrell's. This is a strange area because it is – in population terms – dense, yet I rarely see people walking around. It's full of old corner shops that are now consultancies or architects and brewery buildings that are luxury flats. The breweries around here needed the water and the power from the water, and there were water-wheels and malthouses, and even a horse hospital for the dray horses.

I take a photo of the Morrells chimney, built in 1901 to a design by the ironically-named Harry Drinkwater, a Victorian industrial architect who specialised in brewery buildings. Octagonal with yellow brick shaft red brick edging, the tower is so tall and the new streets around it so narrow that I can't stand far enough back to get it all in. I'd need to climb a wall or fire escape. At the base today, there's a grey cat sunning itself. A passer-by tells me his name is Dopey and he's often here so it's known as 'Dopey's Tower'. Nearby, the entrance to the brewery is an iron arch and the developers have kept enough of the buildings' shape and façade for the place to be imaginable.[5] There's a plaque to the Morrell's war dead just on the inside of the gate. I make a mental note to check the price of a flat here – it won't be any less believable than the existence of driverless cars.

WOODIN'S WAY

It's named after Mike Woodin, a Green Party councillor and tutor in Balliol who fought every good fight, and with whom I worked when I was in the Labour Party. We organised academics against student fees, a group which crossed the political divide – old Labour, old Tories, Greens, Liberals and a scores of academics from the ranks of non-aligned boffinhood. In the Sheldonian, we lost the vote in Congregation, the university's parliament, and the rest is higher education history. Mike died of lung cancer in 2004 aged 38. At his funeral, his coffin was towed by bicycle, accompanied by a convoy of cyclists. He was instrumental in the Green Party's national rise, and contributed more to Oxford politics than any of us from the traditional parties. His deep scepticism about the Euro, and about the hard, capitalist, monster-bureaucracy of the EU, was ahead of its time in the way it articulated an ecological left-of-centre unease about its totalising projects. I didn't know him well and I didn't agree with him on that, but I still think about him because so many of the things he cared about – sustainability, air quality, fossil fuel emissions – are part of our lives today. I'm glad the city named a street after him, and I'm glad it's a pedestrian one.

A hundred years ago, I'd be standing here watching the dray horses leaving the brewery gates, smelling the hops, hearing the clatter of wheel and heel and hoof. Multiply that by four or five for the other breweries here, the maltings and the chimneys, and add in the smell of horseshit, burning coal and boiling oranges, and I'd have the West Oxford nose-scape in a bottle. Because of Hollybush Row, a modern road with endless traffic, this area feels amputated now and just smells of cars. I head towards Paradise Square and St Thomas Street, and there are small terrace houses, all that remains of a large spread of Victorian housing stock. It's student accommodation, parked bikes, makeshift curtains.

On the corner of Osney Lane and St Thomas's are Christ Church Old Buildings which, despite the name, are much newer than most of Christ Church. It's where Olive Gibbs was born – a few yards from where she's buried. Olive Gibbs is a magnificent character, and she and Frideswide would have had plenty in common. The plaque begins 'Olive Gibbs 1918-1995', and goes on to list as many of her achievements and distinctions as can fit without the plaque feeling like an opticians's eye test. I'll note just three: 'Defender of Oxford's urban landscape, Tireless champion of social causes, National Chair of CND'. I was proud to be in the same party as her, and much later discovered that she was instrumental in saving Jericho, one of Oxford's hidden, and now, alas, unaffordable, gems from the same fate as St Ebbe's and St Thomas's. The Jericho so magically reinvented, yet realistically rendered, by Philip Pullman, exists today because of Olive Gibbs and people like her.

St Thomas's is a warren of interesting little streets, but they all end abruptly. The feeling here is of truncation: topographic, urban and social. I follow a street or a row of houses with my eye and suddenly it's lopped off or blocked, bollarded-in or walled-up. Or it's just traffic. The pedestrian area is unsatisfying because no walk lasts very long. I cross a footbridge and spot an old wheel, an old flagstone quayside, and one of the many streams that flow underground and then suddenly emerge from under a chain-restaurant or a car park, then disappear again under the same. These would have been the open sewers that fed the diseases that made the old city centre such a prime candidate for the slum clearances. Henry Acland, the Regius Professor of Medicine, published a study of the cholera epidemic in Oxford in 1854 by examining these very streets and waterways – ten minutes' walk and a whole world away from All Souls, or from the Museum of Natural History which he helped to found.[6]

OXFORD PRISON, 'A POUND FOR A MOUND'

At the Quaking Bridge I check on the shopping trolley upended and snagged in weeds like an abandoned lobster pot. It's been here so long it could become a landmark. Across the water, between houses and flats, I can see the crowds heading up to the city centre on the main drag. I'm in the margins of the city, a little fish in the tourism slipstream. I'll join the tourists later.

Past Quaking Bridge I reach the Castle Complex via 'The Mound'. The castle was Norman, built by Robert D'Oyly in 1071. Most of it – bar the tower – was destroyed in the English Civil War by Parliamentary troops. The site was used as a prison until 1996, and Malmaison Hotels have done a nice job turning the cells into luxury rooms. The system of *passerelles* and iron staircases in the middle – classic prison design – is all still there. I see what attracted Piranesi about imagining prisons: the chance to create lines and angles in a world of chaos and overhang. There are good bars there too, where people sit and make *Daily Mail* style jokes about prisons being like hotels these days. Which is exactly what someone is doing when I visit. The staff have heard it all before, and smile along, stolidly.

The prison might be picturesque to look at, especially with the fluffy pillows and crisp bedsheets, and the smartly-dressed East European staff, polite and over-qualified, but it became untenable after the prison reports of 1986 found it inadequate. It was meant to close in 1991, but it had a five-year respite. When I was a student, freed prisoners – they'd 'graduated', went the joke – had two directions to go in: down to the bus or rail station and back home, or up to Cornmarket, to the pubs and shops.

The Mound alongside the prison is an uncharismatic bump in the ground, but there was a hill fort here and it was, in its time, a vantage-point. On Tripadvisor, the modern age's gripe-archive, someone complains about paying £1 to go up there. 'I'd sooner throw a pound down the drain than climb the mound again' says J.N. Brooks of Melbourne, telling us to save our money and climb Carfax tower instead.

It's a mound, J.N., a MOUND! – what did you expect? Snowdonian vistas, cities on plains, the hanging gardens of Babylon? Anyway, it's not a bad view, and reminds us of how people saw the world when the places they looked out from weren't very high. I'd pay a quid to be reminded of that.

THE WEST GATE AND THE WESTGATE

Where the medieval West Gate of the city stood is the Westgate Shopping Centre. It's the second incarnation of its kind. The front has a row of pigeon-proof spikes where the pigeons perch undeterred. The old Westgate was dreary and ailing, the new one is dreary and buzzing. It's designed to be open to the elements. Apparently it gives the place a bright open air feel. I know that it's to speed up the footfall, make it harder to dawdle, and discourage homeless people from sheltering. There's no seating. It's criss-crossed with little alleys and roads that have *olde worlde* names and replicate, in a parody of commemoration, the small streets that were bulldozed to make way for it: Trill Mill Lane, Bridge Street, Leiden Square. The latter was opened to celebrate Oxford's longest-standing city twinning, dating from 1946. Staying with the theme of European reconciliation, Bonn Square is opposite the Westgate entrance, where Jehovah's Witnesses preach and the drinkers drink, laugh and fight slowly around benches. The busking is poignant, occasionally desperate. Oxford is a polarised city, and it's no surprise that the street music is also: it's either students, schoolchild prodigies and amazing gypsy accordionists, or hopeless one-chord tunesters with toy mikes and Bontempi keyboards.

The Westgate is designed to kill the *flâneur*'s spirit, so I tell myself to pass by and ignore it. But that's a cop-out. The prince of *flâneurs*, Baudelaire, would take this place as a challenge. He'd come at an angle not just to the traffic but to the ethos of the place. He liked glass, watching the window-shopping, or the window-licking – *lèche-vitrine* in French. He'd enjoy the fact that so many things we can't afford are right there, just on the other side of a thin, easily smashable windowpane. Yet we don't smash it – what does it say about us? That we see so much that we can't have, yet still love seeing it? Baudelaire would arrive around 5.30, one drink in, maybe two – just enough to put an ironic glaze on things, to see the place in inverted commas. The shopping crowds would be thinning. Artificial light would be starting to replace natural light. There'd be a different clientele now – post-work drinks types heading for the bars and eateries on the top floor, or the multiscreen cinema. Baudelaire – or as my students call him, 'Charlie B' – would hang about on the edges of the Westgate, where the bins loiter and the deliveries come and go. He'd be drawn to the numbered bus-stops near the few remaining houses of St Ebbe's that lie amputated and outscaled like those farms you see in the Pennines, lodged between opposing three-lane lines of motorway. Inhabited traffic-islands.

I'd take Baudelaire up the escalator to the cocktail lounges and show him, down below, the gardens of those lingering houses of St Ebbe's. A few parked cars, some rusting barbecues, a trampoline. A tiny row of seventeenth century houses and their 1970s successors.

Live branches on the trunk of a dead tree. One of the gardens has a pole and flies a ragged England flag.

Baudelaire would write a prose poem about life in the interstices of capitalism and set it right here, then head downstairs to poke about among these strange last-street-standing bits of Oxford. They feel pickled: that is to say, preserved like body parts. I'd leave Baudelaire to it, because I'd be heading to UNIQLO, where I buy my shirts. What I resent most about the Westgate is that I shop there.

The old Sainsbury's has held on, and half of it is in the shopping centre, the other half opens out onto a scrappy humdrum square with a dead pub – another place whose customers now live too far away. There's the ubiquitous planning permission notice in the cracked window. I don't need to read it to know it's more flats. Last summer I was in the Sainsbury's for the first time in a decade and witnessed a superbly-choreographed piece of shoplifting. It was hot and the disposable barbecues were stacked up at the door. One man ostentatiously swiped one, setting off the alarms, and when the store detective gave lumbering chase, another, already inside, ran out with a bag of steaks and a bottle of red wine, grabbing another barbecue for good measure. All that was missing was the salad. The disposable BBQ is a staple of summer in Oxford, and the area around the Westgate – St Ebbe's, Paradise Square, etc – has various shelters for homeless people and assisted living. Baudelaire would have written about that. I teach Baudelaire a lot, but I've yet to take students on a Baudelaire field trip here. If I called it that I might get my college to pay for it. My experience of purpose-built shopping centres is that they're the first thing in a town to go out of date. They go from spanking new to used-up without any of the intermediary benefits of ageing: that weathered look, a durable aura, a sense of absorbing time rather than dissolving in it. Nor can anyone recall exactly when the transition took place. It's because every shopping centre is the result of money imagining a future. The more money there is, the less future it can imagine. So they knock down houses and buildings that have stood three hundred years and replace them with structures that are lucky to last thirty. If you don't believe me, take a look at the Clarendon Centre, a few yards away on Cornmarket. Half the shops there are closed or pop-up, low-rent junk-mongerers selling vape liquid or wrapping paper. Even the security guard there is part-time. She's Albanian, and today I have my bike, which is not allowed, so she shoos me out, pointing at the sign saying 'No Bikes, No Smoking' etc. I know her from the number 3 bus – Rose Hill to the City Centre. She orders me not to make her laugh because she's just had dental work and it hurts. Someone sells pale sweets from boxes on a trestle table. Another sells phone cases and half-price calendars for a year half-gone.

That's the Clarendon Shopping Centre: where the future came, took a look around, and went somewhere else.

The New Shopping Centre

The cranes have gone. The Westgate after rain
gleams under a pigeonspike tiara.
Today they fit the cash machines,
the shelves, the final plexiglass vitrines.

A van unloads a charnel-house of mannequins.
A box of heads with faces closed; a box of hands
of which half beckon, half refuse. Then infopanels:
'Learn about the vanished suburb of St Ebbe's'

and 'Trill-Mill Lane in History'. They've kept the names.
That's nice. The places? Landfill. Archaeo-yesterday.
Money, like the rain, will always find the shortest way.

The verb *to vanish* fills the holes on which we stand.
The corporate Ozymandias surveys
His honeycombing galleries of brands.

THE OXFORD CRANE BALLET

My favourite thing about the Westgate was that for months beforehand we saw the cranes building it. Dramatic, beautiful things, balletic in their grace. It didn't matter where you were in Oxford, you could see them. One midsummer night they were especially magnificent. I left a retirement dinner in Pembroke College with my colleagues and we sat on the bristly parched lawn to watch the cranes. We were almost alongside them, in a tiny quad that started as a medieval hall. The cranes looked shaky and precarious. Even with no wind they swayed. Up close they looked somehow gangly, not fully grown – teenage runaways from the Eiffel Tower family. Later I went to read up on the names of crane parts: the lattice, the sheaves, the booms, the jibs, the load-chains and the catenaries. The little lights at the top and the end of the boom so planes and helicopters can see them. Like ships, cranes have oversailing rights, and the buildings below them can refuse to be 'oversailed'. Many do, which is why, when we watch cranes, they keep turning back on themselves to reach a point they were only a few metres away from in the first place. It's a choreography of 'Air Rights'.

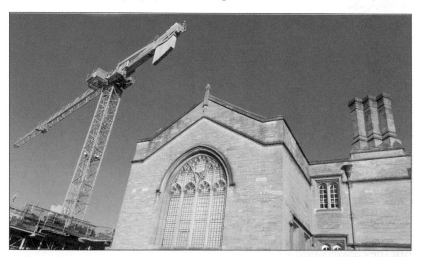

Another time I watched them in a summer storm, but from further away, closer to the station, and without the medieval magic of a college quad. Now they seemed different, sturdy, hunkering down in the lightning that came and went in the time it took me to go into the station, buy a coffee, then come back out. Then the storm went and the sun returned, and there was no trace of the rain and thunder and lightning except that the cranes shone as if they'd just been licked.

The Oxford skyline is protected, as are the 'viewing cones' from which it can be seen. 'Air rights' of sorts. Oxford formulated its first 'views policy' in 1962, and the city now has ten protected views which prevent high-rise buildings and development.[7] But the Oxford air ripples with temporary skylines, cranes stalking the gaps between spires and towers, and often higher than them. In all the years I've looked at Oxford from hills or mounds in the city or on the outskirts, it has never been crane-free. When I was a student at Magdalen, a friend had a ground-floor room in the Daubeny Building, a nineteenth century chemistry lab adjoining the Botanic Gardens. We would climb out and stargaze in the hot summers. The cranes against these beautiful skies, the streaks of purples and reds, were like spaceships. Best of all, I liked the powdery electric night-blue until someone explained the effect was caused by pollution.

Whenever I see cranes in the city I think: where next? Literally, *where can they possibly go next?* There's no space, there's nowhere left. But they always find somewhere. Like the fair, the circus or medieval travelling theatre, the cranes leave town, head elsewhere to drill for car parks or skewer the clouds with the bones of high-rise blocks.

I started a poem I never managed to bring off entitled 'The Oxford Crane Ballet', and it began like this:

> As if this choking city could be mined
> for more horizon to build on, drive to, shop in;
> more tourist-tossed, franchise-crammed,
> zero-houred, gig-economic under-toil...
>
> Still, when we see the cranes square off the sky
> we think it's time to try a different air
> and climb them with our eyes to where
> the Oxford Crane Ballet plays a season on the skyline:
>
> Meccano ballerinas with their leading men,
> at work on the shopping centre behind Westgate.
> Nijinsky and Fonteyn, they shiver, dip and rise
> against the cyclorama of the city's spires.

Then it went to pieces. I'm not sure what I was trying to say: there's a point in every poem, every piece of writing, where – a bit like operating a crane – we need to decide what it is we're building and why, and how to adjust our jibs and our booms and our weights. This poem didn't know: was it a comment on change? was it just admiration of the abstract beauty of it? It couldn't just be an attempt to keep, in language, that one evening in Pembroke where the mix of sun and rainsheen on the Westgate crane looked like the most beautiful thing I'd seen. It had to be more than a special-feeling poem, and it probably wasn't. I couldn't finish it.

Where was Baudelaire when I needed him?

THE GHOST OF ST EBBE'S

Gas stations are probably only admired by people who don't have to live beside them, but the gas station at St Ebbe's was another addition to the Oxford skyline much-disliked by the well-to-do. If the classic Oxford skyline is the canonical one, and the crane-skyline the unofficial one, then the industrial one is the counter-skyline. The occasional chimney still pokes out, a middle finger raised to the planners and snobs who razed the old suburbs to the ground and shunted their populations to the outskirts. St Ebbe's was a predominantly working-class community. Called The Friar's by its people, the area, like St Thomas's next door, was considered poor and scruffy – slumland ripe for clearing.

On Trill Mill Lane in the Westgate there's a panel inviting us to 'Find out more about the vanished suburb of St Ebbe's'. The West Gate of Oxford was full of businesses, artisanships and small industries. In that sense the shopping centre is still doing the work of its medieval and renaissance antecedents, as well as its eighteenth- and nineteenth-century predecessors. The old St Ebbe's was an architectural calque: some buildings were ancient, some were seventeenth- and eighteenth-century, some were Victorian terraces. It's still just about possible to see the different strata. From the 20s and 30s onwards, its days were numbered. St Ebbe's is mentioned as a problem area by successive planners, not just the flouncing aesthetes and the dead-eyed pragmatists, but the Victorian social reformers and the inter-war progressives who designed new council housing for Oxford's growing industrial population. The term 'social cleansing' didn't exist then, but the practice was being fine-tuned in the mandarin minds of planners. It was eventually carried out in the 1960s, the populations rehoused on the outskirts of Oxford – Barton, Rose Hill, Blackbird Leys.

So this should temper my nostalgia. But I can't help imagining St Ebbe's preserved. Today it might be a larger and more beautiful place than Jericho: mixed city-centre housing with an eco-system of local businesses, a market, bakeries and shops (probably quite *chichi* by now, more sourdough than Mother's Pride), with its own riverbank and bridges, at the heart of a connected city. It could even have been the connection itself, as it once was.

In corporate info-panel parlance, St Ebbe's *vanished*.

In search of its ghost, I exit the Westgate and head towards the complex of little houses I've just pointed out to Charlie B from the rooftop terrace of clinking cocktail-goblets. I'm struck by the name, Turn Again Lane. I think of T.S. Eliot's *Ash Wednesday*: 'Because I do not hope to turn again'. Eliot is talking about religious conversion, and about how it's never too late. But it's too late for St Ebbe's. I more dimly remember another poem, more to my purpose right now, by Orwell. But I can't recall the lines, so I put it aside. I remember it has cranes in, but that's because I have cranes on the mind. I'll look it up later.

Turn Again Lane is 40 metres long and consists of seventeenth-century cottages with timber frames cheek by jowl with the Westgate. Nearby is a wall that marks the original medieval town wall and recycles some of its stones. From Westgate to West Gate. The street was saved by the Oxford Preservation Trust which in 1971 bought them and turned them into its offices. This thwarted the developers (and the council) whose principal argument was their disuse. A very genteel and very Oxford version of the environmentalists occupying Rewley Road Station.[8] The Oxford Preservation Trust is a remarkable organisation to whose ingenuity, vigilance and grit we owe a great deal of what remains of the characterful city.

Turn Again Lane is its old name, but also its new one – I keep seeing cars that have erred into St Ebbe's finding themselves bollard-bounded and forced to reverse – to turn again – to find their way out.

I get home and look up the Orwell poem, 'On a Ruined Farm near the *His Master's Voice* Gramophone Factory':

> There, where the tapering cranes sweep round,
> And great wheels turn, and trains roar by
> Like strong, low-headed brutes of steel –
> There is my world, my home; yet why
> So alien still? For I can neither

Dwell in that world, nor turn again
To scythe and spade, but only loiter
Among the trees the smoke has slain.[9]

Here I am, admiring cranes and trains, the very brutes of steel
Orwell so ambiguously condemns. It's a profound poem because it
knows that we're always in between, that there is no turning back –
only the cranes can turn and turn again.

PROGRESS AND 'PROGRESS'

In 2017, MAO, Modern Art Oxford a few streets away, hosted a
moving show by the artist Rachel Barbaresi, which consisted of
images of the old St Ebbe's and reminiscences by the former
residents. The book, *urbansuburban,* is an ingenious visual and
verbal narrative, with old photographs and maps, and images of
demolitions that are properly heartbreaking. Rachel's own prints
merge geometrical shapes, old photographs and handwritten
memories of St Ebbe's to powerful effect.[10]

The question is: what had to go so this could come? My
companion here is James Stevens Curl. Not in person, I'm sorry to
say, because judging from the turns of phrase in his book *The
Erosion of Oxford,* he'd be lively company. Curl was the founder
and first president of the Oxford Civic Society, and he too laments
the St Ebbe's that could have been. Not least because it already *was*
what it could have been – it just needed looking after. He accuses
the developers of falling prey to the illusion of 'progress, that
doctrine, as Baudelaire observed, beloved of idlers and Belgians'.[11]
As a Belgian myself I feel bound to qualify Curl's condemnation:
the young *bourgeois* state of Belgium produced *art nouveau* and
industrial architecture on a grand scale – subtle and joyful and
humane. It was the same *bourgeois* idea of Progress that knocked so
much of that architecture down and destroyed whole swathes of
Brussels in the 1960s. *Bourgeoisie* giveth and *bourgeoisie* taketh
away.

I share Curl's and Barbaresi's dismay at what happened here,
not just architecturally but in terms of population – a working class
pushed out of a city centre which it underpinned and kept moving:
fed it, heated it, supplied it, served it and drove it. For decades
after, the council invited the inhabitants of St Ebbe's for a tea party
in the Town Hall – municipal guilt, perhaps – where the residents

could come back and walk around the place that was once their home.

We're at the very centre of Oxford. Dead Centre – just because the money is moving around it doesn't mean the place is alive.

CARFAX

The name bastardises the Latin *quadrifurcus*: four-forked. To stand there is to see why: at the centre of the cross where Cornmarket meets the High Street, St Aldate's and Queen Street, Oxford's major thoroughfares fuse. Carfax Tower is actually St Martin's Tower, all that remains of St Martin's, Oxford's city church between 1122 and 1896. Demolished and rebuilt in 1820, it was demolished again in 1896 to make room for traffic. I'm talking coach-and-horse traffic, but the car was only a few years away. A few yards too, because in 1902, at the eastern end of the High Street, on Longwall Street, William Morris took over the disused stables that produced, ten years later, his first car.

Also gone – relocated intact in 1787 – is the baroque water tower, Carfax Conduit, which took water from a well-house on Hinksey Hill. According to a 1686 account, 'water passed into the body of the carved ox, and thereby the city is supplied with good and wholesome water, issuing from his pizzle, which continually pisses into the cistern underneath from whence proceeds a leaden pipe out of which runs wine on extraordinary days of rejoycing'.[12]

Revealingly, the lead pipe that carried the water had two apertures: the upper part catered to the colleges, the lower one to the city. Even the water supply differentiated between town and gown. It's still pizzle-water: Oxford is sixth in the UK for water hardness. It tastes metallic and sour, and produces a lid of scud on your tea unless filtered.

Carfax has a symbolic role in the academic community, and anyone who works or studies here knows it from the university regulations: that students and fellows must 'reside' no more than six miles from Carfax. With property and rental prices here, it's increasingly difficult, so colleges have been expanding to the east, building student halls in residential areas of town. A planning law was passed to protect Oxford's skyline stipulating that no building could be taller than Carfax Tower's 74 feet. In 2018 the rules were relaxed. Oxford is growing in every direction, and that includes upwards. The project which so terrified people in 1962 that the skyline rule was put in place was a 25-story concrete pagoda for the zoology building near University Parks. From the models I've seen, it would have looked delicate and airy, and is definitely on my list of Oxford's best might-have-beens.[13]

Carfax has been a place of noise and bustle for centuries: town and gown have always met here, eating and drinking, banking and buying, banging, bitching and brawling. Taverns, shops, slaughterhouses, inns and brothels existed cheek-by-jowl with colleges, quads and chapels. This is where the market stalls were before they were moved to the covered market in 1774. Animals were slaughtered here until Edward III forbade the practice within the city walls. The blood would have slicked downhill, towards the West Gate or Fish Street, *aka* St Aldate's.

Oxford city centre can still be navigated using John Speed's 1605 map. I try it using a print-off I've downloaded. Around here, underfoot Oxford sticks close to its old self, even when the streets have changed their name. Gropecunt Lane for instance. Now Magpie Lane, it's one of the shadier passages off the High Street. Literally shady: it's like one of those streets in Naples where people dry their washing balcony-to-balcony because the pavements haven't seen daylight since Boccaccio's day. In Speed's time it was the prostitution zone, and prostitution remained one of Oxford university's best-kept secret anxieties until the early twentieth century. All of this area of Oxford is doing what it always did, what everyone does when four roads meet. Minus the prostitution, which has moved, in response to city zoning and car ownership, to the outskirts and the suburbs. Impossible to kerb-crawl by bike.

Carfax and Cornmarket are always busy. Some parts of Oxford close down at night, or seem half-shut in the daytime. Here the activity is constant. The horse and carts that served pies and capons have been replaced by kebab vans catering to the post-pub, post-club straggle. Even kebab vans have been gentrifying: stone-baked pizza or Japanese food vans and mobile crêperies. There's a sometimes amusing website called 'Overheard in Oxford'. Here's one for their archive: 'Yeah, had a heavy night – stayed out til 2 then stopped for a spinach crêpe'.

FIVE PUBS AND A HARDWARE SHOP

If the eateries are recent, the drinkeries tend to be old – ancient if not always venerable. What does that say about us? That the tavern and the saloon bar, the café or the boozer, put down deeper roots than our restaurants? Go to any town or city, anywhere in the world, and the oldest establishments after the churches (and sometimes before) are the places where people drink. To misquote Tolstoy, we all eat differently, but we all drink in the same way. Take The Old Tom opposite Christ Church: it's a classic Oxford pub, real ale, scholars and locals, university works people – carpenters, plumbers, electricians – and academics. Hundreds of years of rubbing together. Students and choristers fresh from singing or playing in concerts. It's always had its own eco-system, an unjudgmental place to drink and be yourself, whether you wanted Stella or the latest bitter that tasted of eggs and leather and old men's dogs. These days, it has teamed up with some Thai chefs and the kitchen has been transformed from a conduit for frozen lasagne and sausage and chips to excellent Thai food. It's the same pub as ever, just differently the same. Gowns, overalls and aprons, all at the bar together. It's one of those pubs, like the Lamb and Flag on St Giles, where college staff, maintenance people, electricians, porters, stop off after their shifts.

Off Cornmarket is The Crown, an old pub where I used to play darts and which was frequented by freed prisoners in the first flush of their discharge grant. It's here that I teamed up with a fellow student, a classicist, to take on some of the pub's regular pairs in 1993. The problem was that my friend was called Cedric, which didn't look too good on the blackboard where we wrote our names and scores. So we became Pat and Sid. I go in for a drink, twenty-seven years on and alone. There's real ale and what looks like decent food, so that's a change. A panel outside wittily advises 'Don't cry over spilt milk – it could have been gin'. The original pub, dating from 1364, was across the courtyard from this one, which used to be the stable block. Shakespeare is supposed to have stayed there. It's McDonalds now.

On Carfax crossing itself, in the wall of the Santander Bank, is a plaque to a pub I'd have liked to visit, though not with Cedric. The Swindlestock Tavern '1250–1709' is where a deadly riot exploded on February 10 1355. It began when students and priests complained to the landlord about the wine. He responded to this customer feedback with 'stubborn and saucy language', and a student threw a beer pot at his head. Townspeople were summoned to arms by the bell of St Martin's, and a three-day brawl ensued. Student halls were attacked and 62 scholars killed. St Scholastica's Day Riot remains Oxford's deadliest spate of unrest. Say what you like about Tripadvisor, but no-one dies.

The St Aldate's Tavern was resolutely Town, but has recently been 'refurbed' by a company that owns another classic Town pub, The Grapes. It bestrides a courtyard which used to be a stables and now stables 001 taxis. The old place isn't so different after all. The Bear Inn on Blue Boar Street is mostly students and tourists, and has the peculiar décor of ties, endless ties in glass cases. It was a tradition started by Alan Course, pub landlord, *Oxford Mail* cartoonist, and general Oxford character. His 'thing' was to chop off a segment of his customers' ties in exchange for half a pint of bitter. When he ran out of wall, he used the ceilings. It's a Fuller's pub, so I decide to stop for a drink. One of the reasons I became an academic was to avoid ties. I'm not the only one, and a pub like this would need a new *schtick* if it wanted to start today: baseball-cap vizors? earpods? Covid-mask strips?

From The Bear to The Wheatsheaf on Wheatsheaf Passage is a charming little walk: Christ Church walls on the right, and more little courtyards on the left, dark and narrow and cool in the hot summers. Oxford gets really hot. All that stone, all that brick, storing the day's heat and keeping it going for hours after the sun's gone down. Catch it at the right time of day and you can be alone, or almost, and watch the people hurrying down the twin highways of St Aldate's and the High Street. Up ahead, Oriel College has its own square, while away from all the bustle the tiny Corpus Christi, and the larger Merton College, share a cobbled street that is hell to cycle on. It's classic *Morse* filming territory, and if you live in Oxford and watch the continuity you'll see how Morse only ever seems to walk or drive from listed building to listed building, except when he's interviewing 'Townie' suspects. There it's dingy or vulgar, and the beer goes from real ale to Carling. In the real Oxford you get both, the continuity lies precisely in discontinuity, and it's all the better for it.

I promised a hardware shop but I'm afraid we're too late. Gill's Ironmongers in Wheatsheaf Yard was a long narrow shop that had everything. It was staffed by people who knew what you needed and where it was stacked, racked or filed. None of that 'have you checked online?' crap. Wherever I'm travelling to, I seek out the hardware shops, because they're the canaries in the coalmines of cities. Where they're central and part of the day-to-day run of shops, it means that however rich or prosperous or crowded the town is, there are still normal people who live close enough by to walk in and buy nails or pots of undercoat. There are landlords who aren't upping the rent just because they can. Just off Hadrian's Square in Rome, there's a buzzing hardware shop; in Paris, there's one on every other corner; in the centres of Venice, Barcelona, Copenhagen, Santiago, Dresden…. Not in the centre of Oxford any more. Gills closed in 2010. It had been open in and around Cornmarket since 1530. When I look up the *Oxford Mail* article about its closure, there's a photograph of the manager holding the handle of a gardening fork. In the foreground, there are four blue candles sticking up out of a box. It's an allusion to an iconic hardware-based moment in British comedy: The Two Ronnies' 'Four Candles/Fork Handles' sketch. Ronnie Barker, Oxford man: lived in Cowley, went to Donnington School and Oxford High School for Boys, and got his first job at a bank on Cowley Road. Maybe he got the idea here at Gills.

HIGH STREET

I once invited the French poet Gilles Ortlieb to Oxford, at All Soul's College on the busy High Street. All Souls has no students, only academics, and even then it's not always clear the place is inhabited: past the vast oak door with its tiny entrance portal, it's like scholarship's version of the world after the Neutron Bomb. Ortlieb has a line in a poem I'd like translated into Latin and worked into the university crest: 'Le réel, éternel vainqueur aux points': 'Reality: always the winner on points'. But All Souls gives reality a run for its money – this is the home of the 'Mallard Ceremony', where a Fellow of All Souls is chosen as Lord of the Mallard and carried around the college while the 'Mallard Song' is sung. The tradition requires them to climb onto the college roof and sing the song loudly enough for the town to hear. That the ceremony takes place only once every hundred years is, therefore, the least of its oddities.

On the other side of its walls is Oxford's busiest street – the main drag, pavements riveted with bus stops, a road pocked with traffic islands. And right outside the college, one of Oxford's most peculiar objects: an atmosphere detector measuring air pollution. It's a grey metal box covered by a square metal cage, tightly-meshed, in which you might expect to see some exotic bird. Instead there's a platform with a reinforced glass bulb and a sort of ear-trumpet open to the elements. They've been there for at least as long as I have, measuring the city's lungs. Beside them, some picked-clean chicken bones and a plastic fork from one of the fleet of kebab vans have been pushed through the mesh. It looks like an altar with some ancient propitiatory offering to the gods of carbon dioxide or global warming. The High Street's own Mallard ceremony.

THE COVERED MARKET

A delight to walk through at any time of day. The mix of shops is a microcosm: butchers and bakers, fishmongers and vegetable stalls; then pie-shops, cake shops, snack bars and coffee and tea merchants; then come shoe-repairs and key-cutting, framing shops and florists. Finally the luxuries: scented candles, soap shaped like fruit, cookies, milk shakes, jewellery, baby-clothes with slogans on. Where the old grumpy left-wing bookdealer had his stall, it's beard oil, leather rucksacks, shaving bowls and Converse All Stars.

Look past the current incarnations of these shops, and they're all versions of things that were there four hundred years ago. In descending order of necessity: grooming and luxury; lifestyle and comfort; basic needs. An anthropologist could walk in now and trace the place back to the fifteenth century. Here the nose has even more to get on with than the eyes: the high smell of hanging meat one moment, the next a camembert in the October of its days; then some lavender candle-waft riding the smell of ice-water impregnated with fish-juice; baking dough, then a fresh box of roses dropped so hard you can smell it in ripples a few metres away; roasted coffee and cobbler's glue.

It still has a happy scrappiness at the north end – butchers, fishmongers, bakers, fruit and veg, and cheese stall. Salad leaves underfoot, spots of blood, feathers, toothpicks, crushed flowers, crumbs. There are days I feel I'm in the eighteenth or nineteenth centuries – the lorries come in as the carts used to, delivery-boys cycling supplies to colleges or restaurants. The bins outside gestating refuse until the binlorries come.

The two best times to come. The first, very early when the deliveries come in. The day is fresh – like I've just opened a can of it. The second

is around 5pm. There are two little bars ensconced in some empty units, one doing beer, the other wine. I have an hour to watch people close their stalls down and take a few sips of the beer they've ordered as they wind shutters down or peg the tarpaulins over their displays. It's 5.15 so I permit myself a little Grüner Veltliner. There are barrels and taps and a discount if you bring your own bottle, like in Europe. The guy from the sports shop comes for a beer, which he takes sips of as he closes his shop in stages. Lights, a sip of beer and a chat, rubbish out, sip of beer and more chat, shutters down, sip of beer and a chat, this time sitting down. I like that, making the closing as well as the opening into an occasion, something to be done slowly, a little gift of extra time, courtesy of the dailiness of things.

At Christmas the market is Dickensian in a good way, and feels like a costume drama which ends well, despite the hanging carcases and the bloody sawdust on the ground. Nash's bakers does old style cakes: no croissants or pains au chocolats here thank you very much. Have some Battenburg or Lardy Cake instead. There's Brown's Café, an Oxford institution, that looks unchanged since the 1950s, and is owned by Portuguese people who, as well as making English food, have a line in crispy home-made *pastéis de bacalhau*, salt cod fritters. I buy the last three to take home.

There's also a wonderful shop specialising in cakes: the day I visit there's a cake resembling a Gucci bag and one replicating Santa's workshop, in which the big man and his elves wear Covid masks. They're made to order, so they'll be commissions: football fields,

golfing greens, Morris Minors. I make a mental note to order a Westgate one for my colleague in St Anne's, the Professor of Spanish and our Westgate Senior Fellow. There's a special pleasure in seeing people doing skilled work, and the big windows allow us to admire it: the detailing of the marzipan figures, the colouring of the icing, the calligraphic nozzle-skills as they write the messages and names.

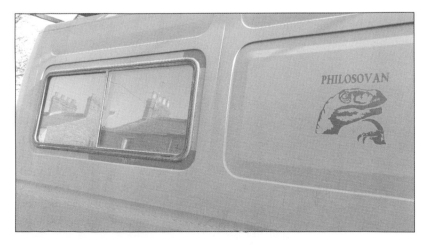

THEODORA AND ADRIAAN

There's a couple, identically-dressed in high-quality Barbour coats and jumpers, cord trousers and brightly-polished chestnut shoes. They have matching umbrellas and leather cases, also of exceptional quality. They may not be here when you come, so I want to mention them and put them in the *Real Oxford* of my words. They look like they've just arrived from the late nineteenth century. They smoke roll-ups and hold each other's hands, stroke each other's arms, with a love that isn't dulled by having become instinct. They're homeless, and spend their days either by the bus stops next to Lincoln College or on a bench near the Ashmolean. But they don't like that so much – it's where the tour buses stop and disgorge fumes and tourists.

Adriaan and Theodora are Dutch. They've been in Oxford for fifteen years. They lost their money in a property scam, though they're keen to say that they aren't broke. They're obsessed with Tolkien, and have plans to illustrate a new edition. They don't use the homeless shelters because they don't want to be separated. Where do they sleep? 'Back there', they say, pointing eastwards and over their shoulders. I ask them what their favourite part of Oxford is. It's the meadow opposite Magdalen, on the other side of the river which marks the start of East Oxford. Fastidious in their dress, their talk, they're always together. I've watched them many times: from the top deck of the bus, from a café, from the bus-stop, they hold hands and talk and laugh and point things out to each other, and roll their cigarettes. She has the tobacco, he has the papers, and each cigarette is crafted jointly. Just before I leave I realise what it is that snagged my attention when I first saw them years ago and keeps me looking time after time: when one of them speaks, the other strokes their hand and leans in to hear. 'We are one', says Theodora, and they are.

CORNMARKET

Cornmarket is, if not the heart of Oxford, certainly the bowels. It's the could-be-anywhere high street. McDonalds? Check. Boots? Check. WH Smith? Check. Burger King and KFC? Check and check again. Souvenir shops with dodgy names like Oxford Campus Stores, named after the one thing Oxford doesn't have: a campus. They seem to be the only businesses that grow around here. In the early summer mornings I walk through Cornmarket and the ground is sticky underfoot: soft drinks, alcohol, ketchup spillage, kebab shreds, macerated kerbside splatter and various *disjecta* poaching in binjuice. It must resemble the old smells, give or take a few changes of diet, so I while I don't exactly linger I don't rush past either. It's an ancient confluence of people and goods: the clue's in the name.

Cornmarket shows how small the centre of Oxford once was. Here, on the corner of Ship Street, is St Michael's at the North Gate – the city's church. Its tower dates from 1040 and is attributed to the same lord, Robert D'Oyly, whose tower I passed on the way from the station. The church is of particular significance because the Bocardo prison once attached to it is where the protestant martyrs – Cranmer, Latimer and Ridley – were held before being burned a few yards away on the intersection of Magdalen Street and St Giles.

On George Street I tick off the Jamie's Kitchen (shut down), TGI Friday, two kinds of burger bar, Bella Italia, and the History Faculty, which is housed in the old High School for Boys. It has an enticing garden set back from the pavement, but the new entrance is at the back, rather than at the splendid front. It's understandable: George Street is pub-crawl and chain-restaurant itinerary, so the tourists wander in and people use the gardens to relieve themselves. But it's OK, Oxford historians take the long view.

RIP BOSWELLS, 1738–2020

By the time you read this, Boswells will be gone. Seen here in its death throes, the carcase of this decrepit high-street behemoth is as I write being picked clean by the hyenas of late-capitalism: bargain-hunters. This venerable old shop, founded a few doors away at 50 Cornmarket Street in 1738, has occupied this building since 1929, and is – will have been, to use the future perfect, the tense of those whose days are numbered – the second oldest department store in the world. It's now another skull in our roving catacomb of businesses.

Everyone loved Boswells. It was a trip into the 1950s, not just in terms of stock – doilies, teacosies, ramekins (Boswells is where I learned the word *ramekin*) – but in terms of staff, who seemed so

shaped by the age of rationing that they found it hard to sell you things. It was a place to go if you wanted to hear the last vestiges of the Oxford accent in the city centre. Boswells was a resolutely local employer, and people who worked there were part of the old Oxford. They also had a tendency to direct you to other shops, and my main memory of shopping there is being told to go somewhere else.

I said everyone loved Boswells. I never said everyone shopped there. That's because it was easier (and certainly cheaper) to love local and shop global. We thought: Boswells has lasted this long without us, why not another century? We'd go there and buy bin liners once a year, a teapot every five or six, and expect it to survive. All that staff, all that misjudged stock; those inconvenient stairs, those shelves of terrible teacosies. We'd browse the kitchenware basement then order online. We'd feel a bit guilty, but we'd tell ourselves that Boswells would be OK. There was bound to be someone coming in later who'd buy the Pyrex dish full-price, along with a twelve-pack of doilies, an electric blanket and that mushroom-coloured bedding set, wasn't there?

Wasn't there?

Reader, there wasn't.

MARTYRS' MEMORIAL: THE DEATH OF THE TRADITIONAL WAIT

Opposite the Broad Street entrance to Boswells, where they sell university-crested sweatshirts, caps, union jack cushions, Frank Cooper's 'Oxford' marmalade... is a small ancient island amid the roar of traffic. It consists of a graveyard, a church, a monumental spire and underground women's toilets. The church and graveyard are surrounded by railings with tethered bikes. I pass them every day but have never been in. Today that changes. It's a High Church place, ancient of course like so much else around here, and smells of incense. In the tenth century, it was on the outside of Oxford city walls – the North Gate being on Cornmarket in the old Oxford. It's an impressive place, restored in 1842 by the young Gilbert Scott. It has famous bells, and, in an Inspector Morse novel, Morse's love interest is a bell-ringer and church caretaker. Morse's love interest never works out, either through his failure of nerve or because she turns out to be the *who* that *dunnit*. Spoiler alert: in this Morse, it's the latter.

Behind the church is Martyrs' Memorial: to Cranmer, Latimer and Ridley, protestant victims of Queen Mary. They were burned close by, just outside the city walls. A cross in the tarmac of Broad Street marks the spot. But here is where they are remembered, though not by any of the people who sit and drink there. Nor by me, much of the time. That's the thing about memorials – few people remember them and even fewer notice them. The monument was also designed by Gilbert Scott three hundred years after the martyrs were burned, and looks like the steeple of a Gothic church that sank underground. The three martyrs are sculpted on the sides, serenely at prayer. Beneath them, it's less serene. Mornings and daytime, it's drinkers, often with dogs; in the afternoons and evenings, it's language school students. In the old days they had ghetto blasters, but now it's i-Pods with bluetooth connections to minuscule but powerful speakers. Tourists rest here, consulting apps and maps.

In the days before mobile phones, we'd meet here from all corners of the city before deciding where to go. Technology has killed that species of place, and that species of time, where hanging about happened: intermediate zones and intermediate durations, always on the way to somewhere else, to some other moment, to what we called 'events'. Waiting is different now; it's a mishap or an obstacle. Oxford is full of places I used to wait at or in which I now pass, destination-fixated because all my arrangements are being made in 'real' time. What other time is there? (Lots, actually, but that's a different book.) I've forgotten most of these meeting-places, but I remember this one because it's where I'd wait for my faculty to open – the Taylor Institution on the other side of the road – so I could give my 9 am lectures on *Waiting for Godot*. In true method-acting style, I'd prepare different kinds of waiting in order to show that the play, and what it conveyed, was first of all rooted in experience, in how we live. Only then did it start to have abstract things like symbolism. I'd ask volunteers from the audience to demonstrate the difference between waiting and waiting *for*. I think they learned more from doing that than from my academic books.

In 1995 I organised a poetry reading and invited Donald Davie, who read in St John's with Seamus Heaney and James Fenton. Davie informed me by letter that he wanted to meet at the Martyrs' Memorial so I waited here, phoneless and expectant. I thought it was just a convenient meeting-point, but for him it was more. He put down his bags and bowed his head. A staunch protestant footsoldier, Davie talked about the martyrs as if we could still smell the burning.

I make Davie sound fierce and maybe he was, but I was an atheist and I spent quite a large part of my twenties trying to be the sort of person I wasn't in order to measure up to him. He was kind to me and encouraged me when there was no need to. I admired his work, and cared about him deeply. He read that night with amazing power. It was August, hot and sticky. I didn't know it but he was dying. I was due to visit him in late September, but he died the week before in that unexpected-expected way of cancer. I sit on the steps of the Martyrs' Memorial and have a memorial wait. I've brought the copy of *To Scorch or Freeze* he gave me – his reading copy, with his little annotations, references, anecdote-prompts. I love many of his poems, but these are the lines I read out now:

> 'Do you believe in a God
> who can change the course of events
> on earth?'
>   'No, just
> the ordinary one'.

A laugh,
but not so stupid: events
He does not, it seems, determine
for the most part. Whether He could
is not to the point; it is not
stupid to believe in
a God who mostly abjures.[14]

It's not so different from Godot. And the 'God who mostly abjures' is the kind I could believe in.

Beside me now are two men, on the cusp of what the law used to define as vagrancy, sharing a 4-pack of cider. One of them has the last can, which still has the four plastic rings attached, 'yokes' they're called in the drinks trade. Whenever he takes a sip he seems to be looking out through enormous spectacles.

At the base of the stairs, underground, are the women's toilets. I never went in here, but I often used their Gents counterparts across the roundabout, in the traffic island that was a taxi rank. They were a perfect example of thoughtful Victoriana: efficient, spacious and naturally lit by glass ceiling bricks. You went down the stairs like Alice down the rabbit hole, and found proper high ceramic urinals, cubicles and elegant tiles. The women's toilets remain open, but the men's are being converted into holiday accommodation. Quality, Harmony and Function. In Sheffield Town Hall I visited a fancy cocktail bar called 'Public', built in (and of) the Gentlemen's toilets in the basement. That's the greatest compliment we can pay the Victorians: that over a century on, we're eating, drinking and sleeping in their toilets.

MAGDALEN STREET, THE RANDOLPH AND THE MORSE BAR

Magdalen Street is one of Oxford's busiest walking streets. It's narrow enough anyway, but the bus-stops, cashpoints and supermarkets are here, so pedestrians throng the pavements and spill out into the road. I'm surprised there aren't more accidents. Because so much of Oxford looks like a pedestrian zone but isn't, tourists wander across busy roads, vague as cattle. The European language-school students, drunk on freedom and often just drunk, dart in and out of the bus lanes. I used to know a bus driver, Billy, whose route was the number 2 to Kidlington. We first met in The Three Goats Heads and he'd give me free rides up to Linton Rd, where I lived briefly among the likes of Iris Murdoch and the Bishop of Oxford. Billy couldn't wait to change jobs – he'd even go to Swindon, he said, not something people say lightly in Oxford – just to get away from the knuckle-whitening stress of driving buses here. One day he'd gone, so I assume he found his Swindonia. The traffic has increased but a bus-driver's pay hasn't. A recent plan by Oxford Bus Company was to build dormitory-cum-halls-of-residence for its drivers, most of whom now come from the old Eastern Europe. Oxford depends on people who can't afford to live here – in that respect it's a typical south east of England town rather than a Midlands one.

Opposite the number 2 bus stop, there's a little alleyway called Friar's Entry. It's a louche little place, grimy and unaired, and though totally modern still carries the dodginess of a cut-throat lane from the *Beggar's Opera*. It's piss-sticky and detritus-strewn, the walls graffiti'd and flyposted with ads for demos and club nights. There's a shisha bar down here where I sometimes have coffee, but suddenly it's closed – repossessed by creditors. 'Suppliers please direct enquiries to…'. It must be impossible to run a stable shop or café here, and it's one of those places in Oxford – every city has them – which simply has bad business juju. Nowhere lasts, though the Turtle Bay Jamaican restaurant and the little organic vegetable shop are holding on. Further down, the White Rabbit pub alludes to Alice in Wonderland and, I like to think, Jefferson Airplane. They're luckier, because their yard opens onto Gloucester Green, and there's an eight foot by three-foot strip of astroturf with 'Beer Garden' marked ironically above it. This is the rat run down to Gloucester Green and the station, the dirty little counterpart to the two grander streets – Beaumont and George Street – on either side.

We're just a few feet away from the jewel in Oxford hospitality crown, The Randolph Hotel. It still projects an air of classy entitlement but it's bulky and dark. I've never stayed, but I've been into the rooms and found them drab and the corridors musty. In a world of plush boutique hotels and luxury Airbnbs, it trades rather too obviously on its past. But what – but who – doesn't around here? The one time I ate here, the food was colder than the welcome, but it's always a pleasure to drink at The Morse Bar. Created in 2001, it's where Colin Dexter used to drink while waiting for his walk-on parts in the TV adaptations of Inspector Morse. There are pictures of him and John Thaw on the walls. Would Morse have drunk here though? Looking at the prices, I doubt it.

UMBERTO ECO, INSPECTOR MORSE AND THE COLLEGE CREDIT CARD

I used to bring Umberto Eco here when he was Professor of Comparative Literature at my college. I was new to St Anne's, and was in charge of entertaining our visiting professors. After his lectures across the road in the Taylor Institution, he would enjoy a dry martini or two here. I was, for those precious occasions, holder of the college credit card, and Umberto knew how to put it through its paces. He was a garrulous, friendly man, always interested in things, and talked to students in the same way he'd have talked to Calvino or Barthes, *i.e.* at great length. He puffed obsessively on some contraption which I now know as the ancestor of the Vape. In Vape-evolution terms this thing was Cro-Magnon Man. It had a battery and a little orange bulb at the end. It was trying to look like a cigarette, unlike vapes today, which look like a cross between a bugle and a handgun. The best thing about Oxford, he told me, was my imitation of Sean Connery – whom he met during the filming of *The Name of the Rose* – asking for the directions to the station in Italian. *Scusi, dov'e la stazione?* Try it in Sean Connery's accent – you know the one, he had no other. Eco would ask me to do it at the end of every evening, and when he had visitors, I was invited along to perform it for them. If *Real Oxford* becomes an audiobook or gets an App, I'll record it here in The Randolph in Umberto's memory.

When Dexter began his novels, Morse was based in Kidlington (he'd have taken Billy's bus from outside Debenhams), drove a Lancia, and liked the cheap topless shots in the tabloids. The murders he solved were grotty, suburban, and had little to do with the dreaming spires. But they were still complicated. In the early Morses, Jericho was a rough place and the backstreets of Cornmarket were dangerous. People got killed in Cowley or Rose Hill. Then the Lancia became a vintage Jag, Kidlington police station moved to St Aldate's, and the plots began revolving around the university. The Morses became stylised, slightly obvious, set in grand buildings and quadrangles. The murderers were Sanskrit profs and flop-haired university boys with willowy girlfriends.

These novels had begun a little dirty, like Simenon, in their fixation with the black that's implicit in the grey, and finished up as spires-and-gowns, high-tables and rare books lifestyle porn. I walk down Beaumont Street when I have a twinge in my mouth – I'm passing the dentist where I had root canal treatment in 1992. The dental equivalent of what happened to St Ebbe's. In April 2015, I was outside my faculty when I smelled burning. A fire in the Randolph. A beef stroganoff that got out of hand – 'too much cognac' in a flambée-pan. To this day, Beef Stroganoff is off the menu. Traditions have to start somewhere, and Oxford is constantly inventing new ones.

BROAD STREET: EXTRAS IN THE FILM OF OURSELVES

This stretch of town is the Oxford of Sebastian Flyte and Zuleika Dobson, of honey-coloured stone and gilded youth. It's what I saw when I watched *Brideshead Revisited* in 1981, in Raynes Park. I didn't at the time 'get' that it was about nostalgia and its lures, and I didn't 'get' the satire on wealth and the peculiar species of toxic innocence that privilege brings. Now I like to think I see things in a more just light – that is to say, both the things and the shadows behind them.

Some clichés made their *débuts* as truth and have remained so. It's a cliché that Oxford is a place of beauty and privilege, and that the education it provides – one-to-one and small-group teaching, unparalleled access to libraries and laboratories, and all the benefits that age and money confer on a university – is world-class. But it's also true that however hard we've worked, however much we 'deserve' it, we're still lucky to be here. Yes, there are the wankers and their dining clubs, the dimwits who have surfed here on a wave of privilege. They too are clichés, and they too are real. They exist – look at our politicians. I'm not someone to whom institutional loyalty comes easily, but while I know there remains plenty to be done, I also know that Oxford is trying to change.

Oxford University has no campus, but the street where 'The University' looks most itself is Broad Street. I start on the small cross where the martyrs were burned, and head east. Balliol College and Trinity on the left, Turl Street with Jesus, Lincoln and Exeter tucked away on the right. Blackwell's bookshop gives off old-school airs but it's a ruthless business: in summer they replace the ground-floor DVD section with two walls of Harry Potter merchandise: plastic broomsticks, globes, wizard's hats. They do 'Oxford Walks' that are cliché bingos, which are of course always full. Much fuller than my 'Real Oxford Walk' would be.

I pass the Sheldonian Theatre, scene of votes we've mostly lost, cross the Bodleian quad and cut into Catte Street, where the Bridge of Sighs links two parts of Hertford College. It's all beautiful, so of course it's full of people taking photos, trying to snap the students crossing the bridge. The Radcliffe Camera in a courtyard of cobbles and surrounded on all four sides by splendour: St Mary's University Church, Brasenose, the Bodleian, All Souls. I walk by twice a day, though it's been years since I used the 'Rad Cam' and I'm rarely in the Bodleian. Of all the old buildings, this is my favourite. This Oxford, the less 'real' Oxford, is where one person's daily life is someone else's film, where our ordinary is someone else's fantasy. So I try to stay patient with the selfies and the group shots, the slow walkers and the rubbernecking. I've seen people poke cameras attached to selfie sticks through the open windows of student rooms, and tourists buy students' gowns as they return from exams. Merchandise is available from souvenir shops, but maybe we're becoming the merchandise ourselves. How many of us who live in Oxford are in the backgrounds of photographs on faraway walls and shelves?

I know I am. In 2010 I met a couple from the US who came here in 1993 on honeymoon. They were back seventeen years later with children, and called out to me across the road. 'Me?' I mouthed across the traffic on The Plain. 'Yes' they mouthed in reply. They were showing Oxford to their teenagers, re-enacting the old photos. They showed me one from Magdalen Bridge: there I was – there I am – sitting on the parapet, smoking, in a red T-shirt.

Filming for *Morse*, then for *Lewis*, and recently for *Endeavour*, has been a constant feature of life here. I've enjoyed spotting, a year or two later, the scenes I walked past during filming: the actors smoking or getting their faces re-done between scenes, the cameras on little rail-tracks, the vans with food and drink for crew. Every student wanted to be an extra, and one of my friends managed it. When we all gathered with her to watch the programme, it turned out they'd cut the slither of film she'd been in. I've seen them all now, John Thaw, then Kevin Whately, and recently Shaun Evans playing the young Morse in *Endeavour*.

1970s and 80s Morse would have been a great walking companion, much better than the 90s version he became, haunting the old quads and chasing begowned killers who use museum artefacts as murder weapons. But Oxford changes us all, makes us all think we've all got a shot at starring in the film of ourselves. And failing that, we can always be extras in the centuries-long film that is Oxford itself.

The strangest effect of living and working here is the suddenness with which I can escape the crowds and the traffic and the noise by opening a college gate and letting it close behind me. The cars and buses are banked up on Banbury Road. Parks Road is clogged up in both directions. The back gate of St Anne's snaps shut. It's like putting on noise-cancelling headphones. It cancels more than just noise. Oxford gives us world-cancelling headphones. But only until we leave again, and however long we're here – three years or thirty – we always have to leave.

Notes

1. Edward Thomas, *Oxford* (London: A & C Black, 1903), p. 21. For a witty account of the train ride between Didcot and Oxford in the 1940s, see Edmund Crispin's detective novel, *The Case of the Gilded Fly*, in which we are introduced to his English don sleuth, Gervase Fen.
2. Malcolm Bowie, 'Remembering the Future', *Selected Essays of Malcolm Bowie. Volume 1: Dreams of Knowledge*, ed. Alison Finch (Oxford: Legenda, 2013), p. 13.
3. Thomas Sharp, *Oxford Replanned* (London: Architectural Press, 1948), p. 158.
4. C.R.L. Fletcher, *Oxford: A Handy Guide* (Oxford: Oxford University Press, 1926), p. 7.
5. Another way to discover Oxford's industrial heritage while getting exercise is with a copy of Liz Woolley's *Oxford's Working Past: Walking Tours of Victorian and Edwardian Buildings*, (Oxford: Huxley Scientific Press, 2012).
6. Acland's cholera maps of Oxford can be found on the Bodleian Library website: https://iiif.bodleian.ox.ac.uk/iiif/viewer/e290f1f9-ef2c-4779-a326-42f79f69a992#?c=0&m=0&s=0&cv=0&r=0&xywh=-1650%2C-255%2C10280%2C5585
7. For an outline of the 'Views Policy', see: https://www.oxford.gov.uk/info/20064/conservation/876/oxford_views_study
8 The Trust's own account can be found here: https://www.oxfordpreservation.org.uk/content/saving-8-10-turn-again-lane
9. https://www.orwellfoundation.com/the-orwell-foundation/orwell/poetry/on-a-ruined-farm-near-the-his-masters-voice-gramophone-factory/
10. The book, along with Rachel's St Ebbe's-related art, can be seen here: http://rachelbarbaresi.co.uk/?page_id=490
11. James Stevens Curl, *The Erosion of Oxford* (Oxford: Oxford Illustrated Press, 1977), p. 130.
12. http://www.oxfordhistory.org.uk/old_oxford/carfax/index.html
13. The March 2018 issue of the Oxford Civic Society's newsletter contains a brief article and a picture of the model of the proposed building: https://www.oxcivicsoc.org.uk/wp-content/uploads/2018/03/201803_visions.pdf
14. Donald Davie, *To Scorch or Freeze* (Manchester: Carcanet Press, 1998), p. 55.

EAST

MAGDALEN BRIDGE

Like Istanbul's Bosphorus Bridge, Oxford's Magdalen Bridge is where the East begins. The east of Oxford, but also the east *in* Oxford: the Cowley Road. This is where Oxford comes for Indian, Bangladeshi, Nepalese, Korean, Japanese, Persian, Thai, Palestinian, Lebanese, Greek, Syrian, Indonesian, Jamaican, and African cuisine. It goes without saying that there are at least three places for Turkish food too. Then there's Eastern Europe, the Polish, Romanian, Ukrainian and Baltic shops. Have I left any out? Probably – that's the speed things move at on the B480, as the SatNavs call it.

Apart from two numb years in North Oxford, I've always lived here. I bought my first house in 1998. I wanted a place in Jericho, but Princes Street was all I could stretch to. If I were starting today – first job, single, no savings – I couldn't even afford to live at the tip of the eastern front of Cowley Road. The late 1990s and early 2000s here were the gentrification-thermometer of Oxford. It started just after Magdalen Bridge. Tyndale Road, Jeune Street, Stockmore Street... so many notches as the mercury of money rose. Crown Street, Bullingdon Road, Bartlemas Close... Princes Street was only six streets up Cowley Road. It felt far. A North Oxford-dwelling senior colleague asked: 'Cowley Road? – you had the jabs?'

It's called Cowley Road but it's more than a road. When you say it's where you live you're giving more than an address. Cowley Road isn't a state of mind exactly, let's not exaggerate, but a few steps in and it already feels different from the rest of Oxford. That isn't difficult. Around here, all it has to do is be normal, which is exactly what it is. In cities like London, Cardiff, Glasgow, Manchester, Birmingham, and in most decent-sized towns, there are dozens of streets like it. Here in Oxford there's only one, so it stands for all our multicultural elsewheres.

Today's Cowley Road has only been part of Oxford since 1889. It's iconic because it's a reflection of social and political change in a city that has invested so much of its identity, and garnered so much of its cultural and financial capital, from ignoring change. Cowley Road even feels different from the two roads that flank it. Iffley Road is largely residential, and though St Clement's is busy, it's too short to feel like anything other than a waiting-room. It barely gets into its stride before it's lopped off by traffic lights, a crossroads, and bus stops taking you away as soon as you've arrived. St Clement's is a street of blur; nothing stays for long: the people are in transit and most of the businesses too. Except the pubs, which feel like poles in fast-moving water – The Half-Moon, an old Oxford Irish pub with often spontaneous Irish music, The Angel and Greyhound, The Old Black Horse and The Port Mahon. St Clement's is for the coaches to London, Heathrow and Gatwick. The hospitals too: John Radcliffe, Churchill, Manor, Nuffield, Warneford.

If you're on Iffley Road you're going home; if you're on St Clement's you're going somewhere else. But if you're on Cowley Road then you're going to Cowley Road.

There's been a bridge here since at least 1000. The current one dates from 1774 and was designed by John Gwynn. It's been widened several times since, notably for Oxford's short-lived horse-drawn tram company, which linked the top of Cowley Road to Rewley Road Station. It ran from 1884 to 1914 and today's Oxford Bus Company is its direct descendant. Both city and university opposed the electrification of trams, not wanting the overhead wires spoiling 'The High'. Meanwhile, the 'motor-omnibus' had begun its reign. There's no trace in today's underfoot Oxford of the tramlines that used to cut down Cowley Road, along the High Street, through to the station quarter, and then north to Martyrs' Memorial and Banbury Road. In 2015, plans were revived for a new European-style tram system, the 'Oxford Metro', linking the city centre to its ramifying outskirts, providing carbon-neutral transport for the tens of thousands of people moving in. I'm not holding my breath. Actually, maybe I should – air pollution levels on St Clement's and the High Street are a whopping 50% higher than the European Union legal limit.

THE PLAIN ROUNDABOUT

The Plain is so-called because when they demolished the tiny twelfth century church of St Clement's in 1828, the place looked... plain. Today's roundabout was voted the UK's second most dangerous to cyclists in 2017. The mound it encircles is a *memento mori* in urban planning. In 2007, Oxford Archaeology carried out a watching brief during roadworks, and found bits of the old church, sixteen graves, and 'a small assemblage of human bone [...] recovered as charnel'. They concluded that the 'quality of the coffin remains and coffin fittings are consistent with the historical information that described the population of St Clement's parish as poor and of low status'.[1] The coffins are better these days, thanks to Colourful Coffins of Crescent Road in Cowley, whose range of coffins includes rattan, eco, cardboard, as well as 'classic'. As for the designs, my favourite is the cardboard one with a pair of motorcycle handlebars riding into the sunset. It's called 'Destination Unknown'.

Cambridge has a monument called 'Reality Checkpoint'. It's a lamppost on Parker's Piece where, so the legend went, the city begins and the university ends. When I came to Oxford, I felt this place – the clock on the Victorian water-fountain that replaced the toll booth that replaced the turnpike at the roundabout that replaced the churchyard – had the same function. Built in 1897, the fountain celebrates Queen Victoria's sixty years on the throne. The water ran out years ago and the clock is one I consult for my periodic reminder of Time rather than any specific information about *the* time.

Anyway, who needs a clock when we can read these words, one in each panel of its octagonal roof: LYMPHA CADIT RUIT HORA SAGAX BIBE CARPE FUGACEM?

The Plain

The fountain on The Plain beside the roundabout
about which there's nothing much to say except

it used to be a tollbooth that used to be a church
that used to be a cemetery whose bones

still pick their way back up each time the council
digs for pipes or cables. That fountain.

With the water that ran out when.
And the clock that's always then.

The nervy weathervane that shows
you where the wind's just been, not where it blows.

The Latin motto says the only time you need
to know about is the kind that rhymes with tide:

LYMPHA   CADIT   RUIT   HORA
SAGAX   BIBE   CARPE FUGACEM

The water sinks   the hour flows
the wise drink   seize what goes

DORIS, OLIVE AND CLIVE: A COWLEY ROAD STORY

My plan was to walk the Cowley Road according to the dishes on
offer. 'Voyage Around My Table' was the section I most looked
forward to. But I don't want to write a gastro-trek that overlooks the
realities of the place, and of the OX4 postcode which once
designated Oxford's poorest and most marginalised area.[2] It still
does, despite the ferocious pace of gentrification. Besides, the
culinary tour has been done, in Martin Stott's excellent *Cowley
Road Cookbook*.

The world's changes feel far away. We read about them online
and wonder what they have to do with us. So we switch off, take a
trip to the Albanian tailor or the Pakistani pharmacy, get seen by the
Moldovan doctor and served by the Ukrainian waiter at the
American burger joint opposite the Korean supermarket that's next
door to the Lebanese café with the Polish manager. I often have my
lunch courtesy of the Syrian man running 'Aleppo's Falafel' on
Marston Street. It starts as turmoil on your TV somewhere on the
other side of the world and finishes up as a dish on your menu.

Walking home from St Clement's via East Oxford Community
Centre on Princes Street, I like to check on my first house. Today, a
young couple is moving out, loading a van. I ask if I can pop in and
look around, explain I used to live here. I feel some part of us still
lives everywhere we've ever lived but I don't say that because I'd
sound like a weirdo, preaching the nostalgist's *droit de seigneur* to
people driving into the future. The place is bright and shiny. Fitted
kitchen in an extension with skylights, flame-effect gas-fire,
spotlamps set into the ceiling.

When I first arrived on Cowley Road, academics and London
commuters priced out of Jericho and North Oxford were moving

in. The developers were too. Small-scale to start with – buying two or three houses at a time, doing them up and selling them, banking half the cash and starting again. Areas like Jericho, affordable up to the mid-90s, were out of range for young academics or first-time buyers. East Oxford became our territory. The place glowed with dinner parties seen through newly-installed sash windows. You could smell the asparagus steaming. *TLS*s and *LRB*s poked out of the recycling. There was the buzzing of drills and electric saws (either that or a lot of Stockhausen), and the domino-ripple of loft conversions street by street, skip by skip. It's still going on. The worst of it was that the people I peered at through the windows in the soft-lit rooms with such contempt were people like me. Those weren't windows, those were mirrors.

In my defence, I've never converted my loft and I've never hired a skip. When I moved here, the challenge was to put things into the house not throw them out. An hour after I walked into my brand-new Princes Street home, my neighbour came to welcome me. Doris was 92. Born in the house she lived in, she had that beautiful Oxford accent I hardly hear any more – imagine two parts West Country to one-part Midlands. She told me I'd be happy, that people here weren't nosey, just looked out for you. She and her cat Tracey lived on Doris's pension from the British Potato Board in Cowley, where she had worked all her life. Doris was in the early stages of dementia. She sometimes asked me to buy things for her then eyed me suspiciously when I brought them. Tesco was two streets away, but the rush of Cowley Road confused her. When she set out we kept an eye on her. She was never far, but all places are far from home when you're lost. The illness took over fast. Dementia went from 60 to 0 in a few weeks. I moved in in October and by February her old self was intermittent, like a scattered radio frequency I had to chase with my dial. But she was right about the community. People rallied to her: everyone, it seemed, but her own family, who lived in Reading.

Her closest friend was Olive. Twenty-three years on I've lost touch with her, but when I pass her old house on Cross Street I don't recognise the curtains (wooden blinds now) or the windowsill ornaments. Olive called on Doris twice a day; brought food and did her shopping. Olive did one thing Doris abominated – took her to church. It was a kind but predatory Christianity. Every Sunday, Olive and a few Sunday-bested chaperones came for Doris, who would shout: 'I don't want to go to your shittin' church' and 'I don't care about your bastard god'. There'd be a gentle tussle, and Doris would be guided out, dragging her feet, shaking her fists. A couple of hours later, she'd be back like some Old Testament figure, fuming, haranguing her maker and his church with fabulously inventive imprecations. It was salty, scatological stuff. Doris sounded pretty on the ball then.

Doris died in pain and confusion. 1999-2000 was one of the coldest winters for decades. She caught gangrene from an untreated cut. The odour started gamey and sweet, and when I half-caught it, not knowing what it was, there was something compelling about it, like exotic vegetation on the turn. I hazarded a fuller inhalation, took more of it into my nostrils. Then I knew. When she finally got into hospital for an amputation, she was too fragile to operate on. She caught 'flu and died. She left her house to Olive, who fought a successful but wearying battle with Doris's absentee family, who questioned her will and soundness of mind. Doris's nephew appeared wanting her house, taking photos. I saw him once peering in through the window, an armful of estate agents' brochures, eyes bulging with imagined £££s: the *Daily Mail* incarnate.

Olive won and sold up fast. The house was bought by a builder-developer, Clive.

Not a company or a flashy millionaire, just someone who bought houses, did them up as he lived in them, then sold them on. He was local and knew the housing stock. 'Only one rule: always buy a crap house in a good area, never a good house in a crap area'. Clive dug up the garden for his extension, finding the buried bodies of thirteen cats. Doris's lifetime in pets. Their grey skeletons, some still leathery, skin like beef jerky, some so dry they exploded when they hit the skip, joined the pizza boxes and empty tubes of *No More Nails*. Clive was good company. We drank together over the fence and once went to the pub. I found his politics unpleasant, he found mine hypocritical. But we got on. He liked people on a one-to-one basis, but didn't think much of humanity as a whole – a trait I've noticed on the political right. That was a change from the middle-class left like me who liked the idea of humanity in the abstract but somehow found that individuals never measured up.

Gentrification is middle-class bad faith, monetised. We lied to ourselves and we knew it. We pretended that what we loved about East Oxford was its character, its difference, its authenticity, even as we changed it to make it less like itself and more like us.

'Real' Oxford? *Oh yes please, I'd love some – can I have mine decaff?*

We liked the idea of living in East Oxford, but wanted to change it all into what we already knew: corner shops into Delis, bakeries into patisseries, pubs into wine bars. In other parts of Oxford, like Jericho, everything uneven, surprising, irregular, rough-edged, unpredictable, was being smoothed out and sanded down by gentrification. By us. But Clive, who came from Oxford and went to school down the road, didn't bemoan it. It was change, 'and where there's change there's money'. Clive wasn't prone to bad faith. It dulled his instincts for getting rich.

In summer 2000, I moved to Cardiff to join my partner, selling up to a Welshman who owned a diving business in Belize. He was buying two houses in East Oxford with money from one in Summertown. A garrulous, sociable chap, he'd pop in during the interminable weeks of house-sale and take me to dinner or drinks with his friends. I looked him up recently to see what he was up to. He was found in his flat in the island paradise of Ambergris Caye in 2015, in a state of decomposition so advanced it was impossible to tell how he died. Local papers and websites tended towards conspiracy theories and contraband-related explanations. As I stand in my old house, I remember him describing how his company created artificial wrecks to drop onto the seabed for rich divers to 'find'. But what I most remember is his joke, made several times in any one conversation, about how Oxford was a bit like that too.

At the end of Princes Street is the East Oxford Community Centre, once the boy's school Clive attended. There's a Chinese

Centre now, Yoga, Pilates, a music and poetry club called 'Catweazle', life-drawing classes and various theme nights based around East Oxford's various nationalities and cuisines. Today a Romanian flag flies above the old school door. It's the Romanian presidential election and there's a queue outside. Parked round about with their hazard lights flashing are Ubers and taxis.

Doris and Olive, Clive and Peter, are the past. This is the present. I'm somewhere in-between.

BARTLEMAS LEPER'S CHAPEL AND THE EXCELSIOR CAFÉ

I'm sceptical of psychogeographical writing, with its search for urban leylines, its ponderous *flâneries* and its self-celebrating fascination with 'sensibility'. That's because I'm inclined that way myself. The term 'leyline' was coined by Alfred Watkins in the 1920s and has become shorthand for a mystical, hippie-ish attitude to landscape. I knew what a line was, but I didn't know what 'ley' meant. It turned out, prosaically, that it was just because the places Watkins did his primary research in had 'ley' in their names, from the Old English *leah*, meaning clearing.

This cues me up nicely for talking about the Cow*ley* Road in exactly the way I'd promised to avoid. The area between the Warneford hospital at the top of Divinity Road, the Leper's Chapel on Bartlemas Close, The Church of Saints Mary and John on Cowley Road, with the mosque, the homeless shelter and the health centre on Manzil Way, and the Excelsior Café, has its own distinct energy – recurring patterns that mark its history. The words I'm looking for to describe the place's aura are on the Parish of Cowley St John's website: 'a remarkable history of welcome to the afflicted and rejected'. Behind the main drag of Cowley Road, on Magdalen Road, Helen House Hospice cares for ill children and teenagers, and the St John's Home looks after the old. The All Saints Sisters of the Poor have a convent here where they do charity work in Oxford's most deprived wards, and The Porch is a day centre for rough sleepers or the vulnerably housed. On Manzil Way, Icolyn Smith, who arrived here from Jamaica in 1965, has been cooking and serving food to the homeless for over thirty years. Her charitable foundation supports the Oxford Community Soup Kitchen, where she can still be found, now in her 90s, twice a week.

We've passed the upscale tapas and sushi places, the Italian deli, the bistros and the retro burger joint. Here it's more takeaways, kebab shops, and Asian grocery stores with amazing produce arranged in gravity-defying piles on upturned crates outside. There's a nosescape here too: coriander, melons, close-packed fruit and vegetables, bus and car fumes, spices fresh and dried, the base-gravy being cooked for curries in four or five different restaurants, cigarette smoke and the vapour off the odd joint, after-shave and perfume. All of it constantly stirred, and coming in different combinations depending on weather and time of day. There's a shop run by people who don't drink which sells the most amazing range of beers I've seen outside Belgium – including the most local of all beers, Orval, brewed by Trappists near my home town of Bouillon. Its distinctive taste comes from the yeast, *Brettanomyces bruxellensis*, named after the modest little river Senne that flows through Brussels – a letter and a world away from the grander Seine in Paris. Orval was my grandfather's favourite beer, and remains the beer of choice for the *bouillonnais*. Buying it here gives me a bittersweet sense of the global village in action. This is the Cowley Road's Cowley Road.

I'm at Bartlemas Leper's Chapel. It's April 24 2020, and the day

I'd set aside to take notes is week five of Coronavirus lockdown. On my way I see people delivering food in masks, leaving shopping bags at doors, ringing doorbells, stepping away. People talk through windows: literal windows and Zoom and Skype windows on their phones and laptops. The little window through which the lepers watched communion is suddenly an ordinary thing. I don't even need to do what I usually do in the face of things that seem far-off or unimaginable or lost in time, which is bend my mind into the required frequency and try to tune in. I'm tuned now. Like everyone else on the planet. We're still the same people: covering our mouths, afraid of our bodies and of the unseen germs in the air around us. We listen to rumours and set fire to 5G masts. We're in medievo-modernity. If Chaucer or Villon came here now they'd poke about with my phone for a while then turn around and ask 'OK Prof, so what's new?'

The graveyard of Saints Mary and John offers brief, occasionally can-, bottle-, or syringe-strewn walks among the overgrown graves, little desire paths of tramplings between Leopold Street and Magdalen Road. Like all graveyards, this one has a good cross-section of nineteenth and early twentieth century East Oxford. All of life is here. The church's architect is buried here, and there are tailors, college cooks, a 'lunatic asylum attendant', a family that died in a harrowing murder-suicide in 1909, and someone with the splendid job title of 'Inspector of Nuisances'.

A few doors away, The Excelsior Café, which closed in 2014, was a Cowley Road institution. The homeless and the hostelled, the sick, the addicted, the alcoholic, in-patients and out-patients – it was their *home from home*. Or, strictly speaking, their *home from home from home*. People in various kinds of dependency or dereliction, wracked, toothless, bruised, hurt, but coming here because the coffee was good, the food was affordable and the rarest of all commodities came free: they were treated like human beings. You could be who you wanted here, and you could also be yourself, which wasn't always the same thing. The tables were formica-topped and chipped, stained with the burns of unattended cigarettes. It used to be called The New Excelsior Café, but somewhere along the line the Cypriot owner took off the 'New'. Maybe it gave the wrong impression. The house special was Moussaka, where the chef released all that remembered Mediterranean sun. The coffee and their toast – fat, white slices of ordinary bread slathered in ordinary butter – were the best in town.

When smoking was banned, the clientèle simply stood outside or sat on the benches on the pavement, creating a special Excelsior corridor of tobacco and coffee fumes as their buttered toast congealed inside.

MAGDALEN ROAD

If I could take the DNA of my favourite street and clone it for the benefit of humanity, I'd choose Magdalen Road. It's Oxford's anti-High Street, the opposite of its near namesake, Magdalen Street in the city centre.

It's an eccentric little street where you could be born and die and happily fill the life in between. From the Iffley end, it starts with a fine-dining pub and a theatre. So far, so Iffley. From the Cowley Road End, it's very Cowley: a huge raucous 'pub and sports bar' and the Christian Life Centre that started out, in 1937, as The Regal Cinema. In my time here it has been a bingo hall, a night club and a music venue. In my day (a phrase I use more and more), 'Past the Bingo Hall' had the same ring as 'beyond the city walls' in medieval times. Back in the 1930s, when The Regal was built, these really were the outskirts of Oxford, and it retains a sense of what academics call the *liminal*.

The Magdalen Arms is a gastropub with superb food and beers that range from local ales that taste of eggs to micro-brewed gum-tingling hipster specials, by way of the mass-produced lagers many of us secretly prefer. Everything is seasonal and sourced with minimal mileage – the food economy being so distorted that something flown in from Namibia costs less than something pedalled over from Kennington. That's what global capitalism does: first it destroys the local, the pub, the shop, the fishmongers, the butchers, then it sells it back to you as lifestyle, at twice the price, and served by men with beards and check shirts. Take the Magdalen Arms 'Flea Market' on Sundays: it's basically John Lewis with a veneer of stripped veneer. Still, I eat there as often as I can afford to because it's so good. Wild garlic soup, English octopus, table-sized pies.

As I said earlier: that window I'm looking through is a mirror.

A few doors away, at the Pegasus Theatre, the emphasis is on local talent, community and experiment – it caters to the Oxford that exists, rather than the Oxford the world thinks exists. It's not all arty or bohemian here. Opposite the Pegasus are the offices of the Oxford Samaritans, and, further down, 'Best Buys', an Asian supermarket. They sell samosas by the till, and every time I've been they've been warm and still crispy. Best Buys has a small fruit and veg display set back from the pavement. By the door is a wooden serving trolley belonging to a 1970s dining set. It's used for the convenience store equivalent of the day's catch: today there's a ziggurat of toilet rolls, and mangoes and watermelons. After Covid, we'll never be able to look at toilet paper the same way, it will be some kind of once-precious commodity, like tulip bulbs or frankincense. Best Buys has full-frontal, woodlouse-carapace roller-shutters: in the daytime it's all overspill, noise, parked cars, deliveries and pick-ups, people milling about, bits of fruit and veg, papery onionskins blowing about and vegetable shavings all over the place. At the end of the day it's seamlessly closed from awnings to pavement, and totally silent and still. The graffiti on the shutters fills out, the taglines take shape and even though I was only here this morning I wonder if it's ever been open, if it'll ever open again.

On the corner of Best Buys is an arrow pointing to 'Interzone House'. It's the urban version of Alice's 'Drink Me', so in I go. I don't see a house, but that's OK – it's the Interzone I've come for. There are serviced offices including a physiotherapist and a care-home staff recruitment agency. Magdalen Motors garage and Shonk recording studios, run by a founder-member of The Candyskins. When I was a student, they were part of the Oxford scene, along with Radiohead and Supergrass. There's a small fragment of Britpop history lodged here.

A house near the church now occupied by The Porch is aburst with colours and decorations: gnomes, enamel butterflies, fairies. Urban grotto. A decomposing Citroën DS worth a fortune just in terms of its increasingly spare parts. Further along, Dave Seamer Entertainments does disco hire, karaoke, DJ and lighting services, bubble machines, glitter balls etc. There's a shop called The Goldfish Bowl: 'Everything for the Fishkeeper'. They mean it: aisle after aisle, tank after tank of them, from three-foot carp to tiny, lighting-fast striped fish that look like underwater fireworks. It's a library of aquatic life, a free zoo, which is what many of us use it for, bringing our children to look at the piranhas or the frogs and turtles. When we've seen all the creatures, we move to the second part of the shop, which sells aquariums and accessories. That's where I always think of Peter Jones the diver – looking at ceramic shipwrecks or castles on coloured gravel at the bottom of £300 aquariums.

At night, the shop's four huge windows light up in blue, illuminating life-size models of turtles and sharks. The restaurants and pubs include a legendary Thai restaurant, Oli's (book months in advance) and The Rusty Bicycle pub. The Tibetan pop-up food-stall I know from Gloucester Green market has just moved in and started a restaurant here, next door to the Magic Café and Wild Honey, an organic foodstore, thus adding further lustre to the street's gastronomy.

On Howard Street, and in my mind included in the Magdalen Road cluster of Oxford's best places, is the Everest Nepalese restaurant, which is also the Donnington Arms pub. A local pub in danger of losing its custom as the demographic changed, it was bought by a Gurkha family who turned one half of its cavernous space into a restaurant, and kept the other half looking like an old people's boozer. Approaching it from outside, I see both: on my right, a 1950s bar with bitter-pumps and beer-towels, dartboard and old men, on my left, a crowded eatery served by staff wearing Gurkha uniforms. Approaching it on a dark evening, it's like looking at a split-screen documentary about a changing country.

On Hertford Street, Gibbons bakers made old-style bread in a world of focaccia and sourdough. It looks like Gibbons closed decades ago, but it's only been three years. It could be from Pompeii, its cracked lettering giving it the feel of an unearthed mosaic. The community notices are still in the window – lost cats, small things for sale, upcoming events now long-past, caught on some strange branchline of time between the tenses. The long-finished and the recently-ended are hard to tell apart here at W.T. GIBBONS, BAKER, ETC, though they mean the same thing to the dead shop, the retired shopkeeper, and the neighbours who move in and never knew.

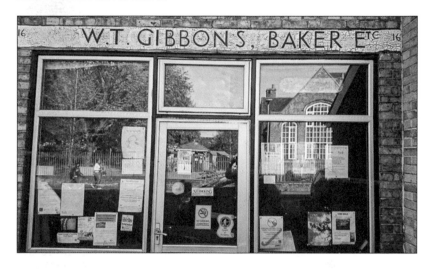

Today's trip isn't down memory lane, but to Silvesters hardware store. I'm buying bulbs for my garden, as I've done since I moved here. I've bought roses too, and garden twine, paint and paintstripper, brushes, screws, teapots.... The works. I can still buy royal wedding cups here too – that's Charles and Diana's. After 110 years, Silvesters should be listed. In my head, it is. The owner is Stuart, but his parents, Bert and Gwen Silvester, ran it when I arrived. There's a photo of them on the wall behind the counter, and Bert was still working here into his nineties. Stuart is like them: he remembers people, what they came in for last time, what screw they needed. It's a place of happy clutter – a long, narrow curiosity shop, a hardware wonderland. The smells change as I go through: bulbs and gardening materials, pet food and birdfeed, oils and lubricants, plastics, paints, varnishes, and then at the end, the smell of steel and iron. It's a Pitt Rivers of hardware.

What else can I say? Go there and buy things. Now.

THE WARNEFORD

The 'lunatic asylum attendant' I mentioned earlier walked this way to work: up Divinity Road to the place everyone knows as 'The Warneford'. Opened in 1826, it was endowed by Samuel Warneford, whose rich wife, plagued by mental illness, died young and left him her money. Strictly upper-crust sufferers. A 1935 advert offers 'treatment and care, at moderate charges, of mental patients belonging to the educated classes'.[3] An asylum was originally meant for the Radcliffe Infirmary on Woodstock Road, but building it here, at the edges of nineteenth century Oxford, is consistent with pushing mental illness to the margins. The location was semi-rural – farmland and meadows, with therapeutic walks, and designed with discreet entrances and exits so sufferers could come and go without being observed. Much harder to be discreet in the Radcliffe, overlooked by that world-famous observatory. The Warneford had 'airing courts' segregated not just according to gender, but according to class, like cabins on luxury liners – first, second and third.

On the north wall there's graffiti – the date, 1854, and CvG IS LINc. Or that's what I think it is – someone's initials? Lincoln College? More puzzling is a series of scratches on the soft Headington stone all along the north wall. I'm not sure what they mean, but they resemble days etched into cell walls. These are purely heritage walls anyway. The real walls are inside: green mesh fencing and high-security turnstiles. The fire-escapes are enclosed. For the old sound-effects of rattling keys and squeaking locks, substitute the *beep* of fobs and keycards, which is what I hear now – a doctor emerges, removing his lanyard with one hand and loosening his tie with the other.

I walk around the back of the chapel, or 'Sanctuary', to see the stained-glass window. I like the back-of-the-tapestry feel – a sense of the intricacy and beauty inside, but here on the 'wrong' side it's scrambled and bitty, the roughness of the lead, the dark bits, the flaws in the glass, the outer mesh protecting the window from vandals. I'm poised for the non-epiphanic epiphany, which is the kind I prefer anyway: the epiphany-shaped hole which somehow magnifies the ordinary without denaturing it. At this very moment a small porous square of sunlight is opening the bottom left of the window, flaring up blue-green and gold. On the other side, the edges will be bright and hard, the shapes clear, the colours radiant; on this side, they're furring indecisively into each other like watercolours on wet paper.

Behind me, built into the outer wall, is the old mortuary, another late-Victorian building with low-key decorative finials, a carved arched entrance with double wooden doors, and a modest gothic window above. The side-door is narrow and unadorned – as if this tiny building were making a statement in stone about entrances and exits. It's now a storeroom.

SOUTH PARK: DREAMING SPIKES

It's a long slow sunset. The dreaming spires again, the classic view, seen this time over the spikes that mark the boundary of Warneford Park. I try a photo – purple-and-orange-shot sky with enough clouds to rift it so it looks layered. This is where the small patch of colours I've just seen in the sanctuary window comes from. That was the translation, this is the original. I think of Thom Gunn's line: 'What captures light belongs to what it captures'. Oxford's towers and spires are echoed by the prongs of the railings and across the overflowing bins. Cans, cardboard crates, plastic four-pack tinny-rings, empty wineboxes, disposable barbecues…. It's all part of the last-of-the-summer, season's-end decadence that takes hold of Oxford at the end of September. The city's last blow-out before the universities move in for the term.

The barn beside the Warneford was part of Headington Farm, later known as Cheney Farm (Cheney School is opposite), and was a working farm until the 1930s. That gives me a sense of how much countryside there was not just around Oxford but inside it. It's a listed building now, and features in a painting by J.M.W. Turner of the Oxford skyline. It's now TOAD: The Oxford Artisan Distillery. It's their last day running the bar before they close for the season. There's a small mellow crowd sipping fine shots of gin and vodka on trestle tables outside. The sun is now almost at eye-level and I join them to drink in, and *drink in*, a Turner view.

WARNEFORD MEADOW AND HOSPITOPOLIS

I'm at a roundabout with a small estate of modern houses: Demesne Furze. Two words I only know from books. The university's 'Old Road Campus' is on my left, on my right a sudden wilderness: little paths, streams, pools covered in bright green algae, thick muddy puddles, dense trees, and then, eventually, a wide-open field with joggers and dog-walkers. I had no idea this place existed. Overlooking it is the vast and expanding Churchill Hospital. I'm in Hospitopolis: speed-bumped roads, residential pockets of pastiche Victorian houses, short-let flats for NHS staff, ambulances, cars, buses and inter-clinical shuttles.

Farmhouses, demesnes, furze, meadows... all this rusticity evoked in names on signs in Oxford's hospital quarter. Once I'm out of the edgeland-undergrowth, Warneford Meadow spreads out in front of me. It's huge, or feels it: 20 acres of dun, sodden grassland. It was bought by the hospital in 1918 for the benefit of patients, and forms a secret green link between medical Oxford, which I barely know, and streets I walk every day. I realise the little lane off Hill Top Road I always assumed was someone's drive leads here. It's a secret wilderness between Headington and Cowley. Developers have their eye on it.

LYE VALLEY AND THE SLADE

For a place so unexpected and so magical, it's easily missed. I know – I spent twenty years missing it. It doesn't look like much, but East Oxford is full of places that don't look like much but turn out to be rather a lot. In the vein of *Alice in Wonderland* – an unprepossessing threshold onto something completely unexpected – Lye Valley is entered via what looks like a path between garages off the side of a long, unremarkable road called The Slade. This delicate, ecologically unique 8000 year-old haven constitutes 1.5 of the UK's 19 last remaining acres of tufa-forming fenland. I'm not sure what that means in theory, but in practice it makes this area unlike anywhere else in Oxford and like very few places anywhere else.[4] On the other side of The Slade there's Rock Edge, the remains of one of Headington's limestone quarries, full of fossils and coral from the Jurassic age, when Oxford was sea. Just off The Slade is a street called Peat Moors. In terms of cityscape, this part of the city is pretty average. In terms of landscape and habitat, wildlife and geology, it's full of hidden treasures. That these places are wedged between dull housing and duller roads only adds to the sense of freedom, the contrast-thrill of the secret threshold as I enter.

The path through Lye Valley is winding duckboard. In the summer it was alive with colour, plants and flowers so high and bushy the duckboards were sometimes hard to see. Today – autumn descending into winter – the plants have died back, anonymous. The Lye Stream threads its way through here, and joins Boundary Brook, the stream that starts in Headington, passes under the Churchill hospital, and continues out to Barracks Lane, through Cowley and Iffley and to the Thames. The streams and the rivers, the brooks and rivulets have their own routes. On either side of me the water glints, aquatic plants and reeds spearing the undergrowth, insects skating over the pools. In the spring, it's full of frogspawn, thick as jam – fat jelly bubbles with black eyes staring out in their thousands. Whatever the season, the water is always so clean and pure you can see down to the bottom. I spot a few walkers, people joining the path from little entrances off the streets above us, using fallen tree-trunks as bridges over the streams and pools. We're overlooked by houses and there's a line of little home-made, unofficial-looking gardens where the residents have built treehouses or mini-allotments across the road from their homes.

HORSPATH DRIFTWAY

It sounds like a band. As in: 'Yeah – I saw them when they were supporting Radiohead back in '93'. 'Horspath Driftway' is on my list of Oxford band names that never were, along with 'Lewknor Turn' and 'Botley Interchange'. 'The Driftway' to their fans. I imagine them as Psychedelic Folk, but my friend Jake insists they'd be Prog-Rock, which just shows how they resist being pigeonholed. The dictionary tells me a driftway is a broad route along which livestock were driven to market, often across fens and marshes, both of which we have right here, underfoot. Today it's a broad route along which thousands of cars are driven over tarmac to supermarkets and offices. This is one of Oxford's most urbanised environments, yet I've just walked through millennial fenland and looked at some coral from when we were under the sea – the far-off past that may also be the future. I've walked through a wood and found myself at the rim of a ringroad that takes tens of thousands of cars a day to London and the South East. I tell my students to pay attention to street names, because that's how they can reimagine what was there before: Peat Moors, Town Furze, Quarry High Street, Horspath Driftway... so many names out of Thomas Hardy or the Brontës. So I stand on the driftway and imagine farmers driving their livestock and their goods past the quarries, over the fens, through the soggy marshland, down to the city to be sold in St Ebbe's, St Aldate's, Cornmarket. Then I imagine them returning at close of day, the sun setting behind them, to their farms and smallholdings which are now houses and apartment blocks, Aldis, Lidls and Homebases.

PLANT OXFORD AND THE MINI

The Minis are lined up in a vast pen in front of me. The car plant that celebrated its centenary in 2013 has belonged to BMW since 1994, and hasn't been called Morris since 1984. As a child of the 70s, my knowledge of British carmaking is strikes, takeovers and closures. Our Morris Marina was an entire industry's death rattle. It's in every list of the world's crappest cars, from *Auto Express*'s 'Worst Cars Ever' Top Ten to the website *www.theworstcarsofalltime. com*, where I discover it's also the UK's most scrapped car. Crap to scrap. That's exactly what my parents did, then bought a Lada. Not something you did lightly at the height of the Cold War, especially when, like my father, you worked for the British government.

If anywhere represents the allure of British carmaking at its peak, it's here, where the Mini that saved Oxford as a motor city is produced. This was also where our Marina was assembled, so there was a lot of saving to do. The plant still employs around 4000 people, and at its peak 28,000 worked in or around Oxford's car

industry. Today's Minis are not to my taste – they look like toys with
their Union Jack lights and cartoonish dashboards. Too much
Italian Job BritNat nostalgia for my liking, and the car has become
more self-consciously British now that it's owned by the Germans.
This would have been anathema to Lord Nuffield, himself a
staunch believer in English self-sufficiency, who rejected the first
plans for Nuffield College on the grounds that they weren't
'English' enough. As he said, complaining about his taxes: 'If we do
not alter our ways, the foreigner will soon beat us in the world
markets'.

NUFFIELD OBELISK

If I wanted to make a memorial so banal it was really just a prompt
to amnesia, I'd come here, to Oxford Business Park, built on the site
of Morris's car plant, and learn from the masters.

'Nuffield's Needle' stands in the middle of a roundabout on
Garsington Road. The pavements here are purely ornamental, like
plastic fruit in furniture shops. Signposts stuck into dead roadside
grass offer units to let; a sign bent around a lamp-post points
ambiguously at the city centre; there's a petrol station, the last
before the ring road, with a fridge full of pasties; brick and glass
buildings of companies whose names give no clue about what they
do, and whose offices, judging by their lobbies and staircases, may
be empty anyway.

The area feels like it was flattened in a hurry, then rebuilt in
another. In the middle of it all is a mound of unkempt grass with a
pale futuristic obelisk in memory of William Morris, Lord Nuffield.
It has an air of Italian fascism, but is in fact modelled on the Morris
Minor badge – at its base is an ox on the water, with the front grille
of a car on either side evoking wings. I have an old Morris Minor
badge with me. I cross the road, which is busy – no-one comes here,
but everyone seems to come past here – and hold it up under
Nuffield's Needle.

The Morris car plant had three sites. Only the Mini plant, where
the Pressed Steel Factory stood, is still in use. Where I'm standing
was Morris's first factory, which began production in 1913. It was
demolished, along with its counterpart on the other side of the
Bypass, in 1993. I didn't expect the husks of the car industry to be
here, aspicated for my post-industrial antiquarian benefit. Unlike

Victorian industrial buildings, most of their twentieth-century descendants weren't built to last. But I'm surprised at how little has been made of the Cowley Works. This blandtopian anywhere-place was once Europe's largest motor manufacturer. It defied the Great Depression. I know that across the Bypass there's more by way of life, but this – this dead cordon of urban filler – is not where I'll find it.

The challenge of writing about places is that occasionally I come across somewhere that's neither interesting to write about, nor dull in the kind of way that gives me an 'in' to writing about its dullness. This is unusual for Oxford. Even the sewage works on Grenoble Road and Oxford Science Park, hitherto my benchmarks for nothing-to-say places, hold some interest. Not just for the amazing things I imagine happening behind those windows and in those pipes and filter-beds, but because of the abrupt little fragments of countryside that break up the futuristic façades and the empty, silent electric shuttles that dart around like traffic in a Ballard novel.

But this… no. It's dead. So, in my mental cinema, I screen a filmreel.

Everything starts at the jagged, jerky pace of silent movies, crackly with black and white flecks: Military College demolished, new factory built, Morris cutting the ribbon, assembly lines fleshing the skeletons of the cars, cars emerging, destined for stations, docks, depots and showrooms. The soundtrack of industry changes as I go through the decades, the workers clocking in and clocking off, the strikes at the Pressed Steel, Abe Lazarus and the Welsh socialists who came here for work and demanded union rights... I change reel, colour film comes in, robots are replacing people; now I can see the reds and the blues of the cars, not just the piss-poor Marina, but the Princess and the Mini and the Allegro, parked in the drives of ordinary houses in suburban Britain, cruising streets across the globe in the fading British Empire...; then the less and less, the fewer and fewer, the new strikes and the new demos, the burning braziers and the redundancies; then the silence... Next reel: the bulldozers and diggers, coming to close the circle.

Welcome to Oxford Business Park.

INDUSTRIAL ACTION

Before the car, Oxford's working class mostly serviced the university, directly or at one or more removes. When I was a junior fellow, some of the college staff were second or third generation. It wasn't uncommon to be served at table by siblings, or by a parent and child. Some lived in college-owned houses with rent docked from their wages. Paternalist welfare, it was also a way of locking people into work and ensuring a steady stream of future college servants. There are still dynasties of servants. Class politics in Oxford colleges are different from the class politics of more straightforward workplaces, but they exist and deserve to be studied in their own right – it's where the *Titanic* of class theory founders on the iceberg of personal relationships.

In the 1920s, the university city with the rustic hinterland found itself with an industrial working class. Morris Motors sucked labour from across Britain. People came from the countryside or left jobs in colleges, but the car industry needed more. These industrial changes created cultural shifts similar, in their way, to those that took place decades later with the Windrush generations, the arrival of immigrants from former colonies, and most recently migration from the European Union.

One of the most durable changes to Oxford's demography was the influx of workers from South Wales. By the mid-30s there were two thousand Welsh workers in Cowley, of whom about twenty per cent came from a few square miles of the Garw valley. They arrived with the highly-developed political culture of the unions, putting them on a collision course with William Morris, a Fordian capitalist with Fordian politics. The Pressed Steel Factory was known as the 'Red Factory', and Morris enquired of the Home Secretary if it was possible to stop the Welsh from migrating to the industrial Midlands. Their demands for employment rights and unionisation gave the Welsh a bad name. Many were turned away from lodgings, refused service in shops, and treated as criminals. Florence Park, built in the early 30s, was known as Little Rhondda. The *Oxford Mail* preferred to focus on Welsh musical talent than their firebrand Socialism: a cartoon from the 30s shows a wholesome male-voice choir. 'You can't stop them singing!', goes the headline. The Cowley Welsh Choir started as an octet in The Cape of Good Hope pub on The Plain. Named 'The Party' after the political leanings of its founders, it changed its name in 1931 to the Oxford Welsh Glee Singers.[5] The choir competed at the National Eisteddfod and is still going strong.

BLACKBIRD LEYS TO GARSINGTON: THE TWO ENGLANDS

When I want an alternative to the *focaccia* and croissants, I cycle to Blackbird Leys for a late breakfast at Nash's bakery, on the shopping parade between Evenlode Tower and Windrush Tower. The towers opened in 1964. By London or Birmingham standards they're not much – fifteen floors each, sixty flats per tower – but here on the outskirts of Oxford they loom. The parade is sheltered by a footway connecting the flats above, so Nash's have tables and ashtrays out in all weathers. I come here for the Lavazza coffee and the egg sandwiches. Before I go, I choose a few 'fancy cakes' for the children. The window is full of brightly-coloured delicacies, all at child's-eye-level. Who wants a croissant when they can have an ice-cream cone filled with marshmallow and sprinkled with hundreds and thousands?

Blackbird Leys estate was all over the news when I arrived in 1991. I'd see the odd police car, hear faraway sirens, but as far as I was concerned I was in a different city. Except I wasn't. I lived on Longwall Street, where Morris built his first car, the Bullnose Morris. At the other end of Cowley Road, where I went for my

curries and my pints, were the car works – derelict but not
demolished. I began on the Morris leyline, the *Cow*leyline, and have
stayed there ever since. If I wanted to know about Blackbird Leys,
all I had to do was keep walking.

   The end of British car-making was a complicated, long-
drawn-out crisis. Here in Oxford it was an urgently present reality,
but the people to whom it was reality were people we never saw.
There had been trouble brewing in Blackbird Leys for years – the
kind that happened everywhere when the anger of neglected
communities boiled over. In summer and autumn 1991 Oxford was
the home of urban unrest, dubbed 'City of Screaming Tyres'. The
parade of shops where I am now, wiping my fingers on a paper
towel, was the centre of clashes between youths and police in full
riot-gear. The press photos show batons, shields and armoured
vans. It was all about cars then too – as one observer put it, where
the parents had once made cars, the children now stole them. It was
an exaggeration, but Blackbird Leys became famous for 'hotting'
and 'displaying': cars were stolen and driven around in 'displays'
that become crowd-pulling events, usually in the early hours of the
morning. When police gave chase, they were stoned, cars set on fire,
there were injuries and arrests.[6]

What I'm after today is the Blackbird Leys/Garsington axis. I walk there by roadside, slivers of pavement, and flat muddy meadow, turning to check the towers are still visible behind me. Got it: Mini Plant, towers and Garsington sign. It may not look like much, but I've crossed worlds: from the urban overbuild of industrial Oxford to the rich, green, privatised countryside of Home Counties England. But why am I here?

At the same time as the working-class were building industrial Oxford, with their factories, housing estates and unions, the 'Bloomsbury Set' were disporting themselves here in Garsington, two miles from Cowley. Ottoline Morrell and her circle included Virginia Woolf, Bertrand Russell, Lytton Strachey, and Augustus John, and Garsington Manor became a byword for debauchery, aestheticism and the drawing-room radicalism of the upper classes. 'It is England – my God it breaks my soul,' wrote D.H. Lawrence after a visit to Garsington, 'this England, these shafted windows, the elm trees, the blue distance ...'.[7]

Standing here, I wonder if that England ever paid much heed to the England on the other side of this field, to the people who made the cars, fought the wars, went on strike to join unions. I wonder if Bloomsbury and Cowley ever noticed each other across Lawrence's 'blue distance'.

I once planned a radio docu-drama interspersing extracts of Garsington-Bloomsbury letters and diaries with oral histories and recordings of Cowley's political and social life. My plan was to narrate the programme while walking this territory, slightly breathless as I am now, incorporating the sounds of country and city as I went.

ROSE HILL CEMETERY, HENRY TAUNT, CHURCH COWLEY

I'm looking for Rose Hill cemetery, where the pioneering photographer, Henry Taunt, is buried. Taunt created an extraordinary record of Oxford in all its variety, from the 'slums' of St Ebbe's to the grandeur of the High Street. Born in 1842 to a poor family in St Ebbe's, near Trill Mill Stream, Oxford's most polluted waterway and the centre of Oxford's cholera epidemics, Taunt never shied away from depicting the city as it was.

When he died, thousands of his negatives, on glass plates, were either thrown out or cleaned by a local builder and used for greenhouse glazing. But thousands more were saved, and constitute a unique record of Oxford life. Taunt's success was tied in with the boom in Victorian tourism – photography, souvenirs, coffee-table books, and the postcards in newsagents and gift-shops on the High Street or Broad Street are the descendants of his.

Rose Hill Parade has two of my regular eating-places: Café Spice, a Bangladeshi restaurant and takeaway, and Polish Kitchen. Today, I'm booking a table at Polish Kitchen. I come here for the sour rye soup, the dumplings and the 'Brigand's Stew' with potato pancakes. It's the ultimate comfort food. The décor is chunky wooden tables and chairs that belong in log cabins, posters of forests, and old cartwheels on walls and windows. The owner, Alicja, has picked up all the old-school English endearments and is as generous with them as with her portions. I already know what I'll have, the only matter up for debate is which of her spectrum of vodkas I'll take as a *digestif*. Polish Kitchen is a good place from which to observe how the different communities eat. Café Spice is hugely popular with the takeaway crowd, not just Deliveroo or after-work pickups, but catering-size meals for whole extended families. Cars pull up with thermos boxes and fill two or three at a time. At Polish Kitchen, there's a steady stream of people coming in for takeaways, or builders, carpenters, tradespeople stopping for quick soups or stews. I know these places as restaurants, but to their communities they're culinary consulates.

The route to Taunt's grave takes me to Westbury Crescent, where the side of a whole house hosts a Ship of Fools mural of Conservative politicians on a sinking galleon. Theresa May, Boris Johnson, David Cameron (with a pig on his head, an allusion to an act of porcine necrophilia he performed as a student), Michael Gove and Jacob Rees-Mogg. Every one of them studied at the university down the road, and it's a reminder of how my institution has for centuries pumped out this ruling-class *bacilli*. Up here, far from the hallowed colleges with their quads and seminar rooms, debating societies and dining clubs, the people who live in the other Oxford think they're chancers and vandals and liars. Sadly, we're also on the ship of fools, and while they prance about on deck, the country itself is locked in the hold.

The cemetery is enclosed by houses and gardens. This is still Rose Hill, but very soon I'll be in Cowley. I can already see, on the other side of the mossy, lopsided graves, the old houses of Church Cowley, Cowley's original village. I peruse the noticeboard outside the church. Parish notices, council minutes, Rumba, coffee mornings. It's like Woodstock or the Cotswolds. Thatched cottages, stone houses, mullioned windows. The clatter of horseshoe on flagstone. I half-expect a film crew for *Midsomer Murders*. The vibe is suddenly Betjeman, the detail Pevsner. Oxford isn't just surrounded by villages, but full of them.

CHURCH COWLEY TO TEMPLARS SQUARE: BETJEMAN TO BAUHAUS

Downhill on Beauchamp Lane is another condensed, contrastive little Oxford walk. I see a whitewashed cottage on the edge of a main road. The house is tiny but the thatched roof is huge – like someone small wearing an enormous hat. As I approach it, urban Oxford emerges and rustic Oxford recedes. The parish notices and horseshit are less than a minute and more than a century away. It's Pets at Home, Poundland, Asda, Sainsbury's, JD Sports... I've reached the old border that's also the new border, named after a local field, 'Betwixt The Towns'. It was once High Street, Cowley, but became Between Towns Road in 1930. There's a lot of betwixtness around here.

Opposite the cottage are the narrow concrete ribs of Castle Car Park, connected to Templars Square Shopping Centre by a bridge of sighs over Crowell Road. Six storeys, 470 parking spaces, never full. Templars Square, a once state-of-the-art shopping centre, is right opposite the new retail park. The two slug it out on facing sides of Between Towns Road. It's a good car park; very satisfying on the eye. There's something of the Bauhaus about the way its tonnes of concrete look so light and clean. The staircases are especially fine, and built on the outside of the building's carapace. I used to enjoy climbing up to the top for the views. Today they're blocked off with padlocks, fence-panels and DO NOT... signs. Also, the building used to be white. Now it's moulding over, and at its base it looks like the ground is coming up to claim it.

It's greening at the gills, with the same moss and slithering blotches of wet algae as I found on the graves just up the lane. The car park and the graves breathe the same air, live in the same conditions. But the graves are made of porous stone, and become ingrained with the damp and the mould. They wear them well because it's part of what they're designed to do. The car park's concrete and white paint don't – I drag my finger through the stuff. It's like hairy jelly and comes off on my skin. The stone absorbs time, the concrete tries to repel it. There's already one derelict car park behind Templars Square, and this one feels like it's on its way. Development plans hover over it and the shopping centre next door, now drab and full of poundshops and closed units. I'm betting the car park will go first – this bit of future got misfiled under 'PAST'. Maybe by the time you read this, it will have been condemned to demolition. For what? The usual: something Swindonian on the eye and Londonian on the pocket.

Outside, there's a skip. The Oxford skip, the skip of ubiquity. It should be on the city's coat of arms: Skipford: a skip with three cranes and a £ sign rampant.

TEMPLARS SQUARE

I like it (he said, defensively). It's named after the Knights Templar, who were here in Temple Cowley for 101 years between 1139 and 1240. Maybe they heard the Norman church in Iffley being built, the sound of chisel on soft stone. The Knights Templar are long-gone. Luckily for them, they're remembered here in Templars Square Shopping Centre.

I like the proper shops and the no-airs cafés. I get my eyes tested here, go to Cagney's, a characterful diner with booths and American 1950s décor, and I go to Wilko. Today I'm buying a thermos. Inevitably, I also buy more Wilko notebooks. As I near the till, I decide I need light bulbs, a couple of seed trays, and new towels for visiting Belgian family, so round I go again.

By the time I leave, I've also bought seed potatoes, firelighters, a rake and some barbecue-cleaner, and am loaded like a mule. My bags

stick out to my side and the rake protrudes. My passage is awkward, and I've still got a fair walk home. Outside Wilko is a beautiful mosaic of Oxford and Cowley, representing the two towns through their buildings and their shared histories. It's a fine piece of public art, and I love the way it's right here, beside Wilko. In fact, it's so beside Wilko that there's a Wilko panel stuck into the side of the mosaic.

I'm looking at it for the umpteenth time when I hear what my students describe as 'Scenes' in front of the frozen food shop I've just passed. Two security guards are manhandling an angry and very articulate man. His girlfriend is berating them. The shops are trying to close, people are trying to get in or to reach the tills and they're being turned away. It's a Friday, people have had a few drinks – just enough to remember they forgot to get dinner, but not enough to forget to buy dinner altogether. The worst of both worlds. A quick, jerky little fight. A finger-jab is interpreted as a punch. Things escalate. The shopping centre's piped music is super-mellow, chill-out classical, and very slow. Meanwhile, in front of me, people are jostling and shouting and pushing each other. I double back and head down the escalator. There, still to the same slow soundtrack, I see the flashing lights of two police cars outside the William Morris Wetherspoons under the shopping centre. There's a lot of snarling and fist-swinging, but the instrumental overlay is shopping-centre Morricone, or one of those climaxes in *The Godfather* films where grisly murders are choreographed to serene music.

HEADINGTON QUARRY

There's no better place to grasp Headington's distinctness than 'Quarry'. From the thirteenth to the eighteenth centuries, Headington provided the stone for many of Oxford's buildings – from the bell-tower of New College and the Bodleian Quadrangle to entire colleges, notably All Souls and Christ Church. The stone was carted down (gravity helped), and by the mid-seventeenth century several rich colleges owned quarries here, which functioned as their own personal builders' merchants.

It still feels like a small rural-industrial town. The quarry can be felt underfoot and undertyre. The land dips and rises, the houses are built on slopes or in hollows. On Quarry Road, the Methodist Chapel, built for the quarrymen, overlooks its neighbour, a modern house several metres below street-level, like those Balkan churches built in holes so their steeples don't reach higher than the Ottoman mosques. There are dozens of alleys and footpaths, winding up and down, around and along, according to a landscape still shaped by an industry that had mostly been replaced by the 1890s. The Mason's Arms pub testifies to that, a building so perfect it looks like it's been taken from a model village and blown up to life-size. Quarry Primary School is still the local school, the old bell in its belfry behind pigeon-proof netting. It's bourgeois here now, but that sound I hear is the same sound I hear each time I head out from the city centre and walk more than thirty minutes: the Bypass.

The relationship between Headington stone and Oxford university is the relationship between the raw and the cooked. The university city depended on local farms for its food, on local mills and breweries for its bread and beer, on dynasties of local populations for its servants, and local quarries for its stone. I'm imagining the journey – literal, but also metaphorical – of Headington stone. I, like millions of students and tourists over the years, have walked past it oblivious to where it came from; who quarried it, how it got here, who built it into such magnificent halls and churches, who sculpted and decorated it. I'm what's known as the 'end user': always at the dreaming spires end of things. But however much it pretends otherwise, this great international institution that is my university is rooted in the local; in a few square miles of people and place.

'THE OTHER WITHIN'

Betjeman wrote that Oxford was the city of 'the two William Morrises': William Morris the artist and social reformer, and William Morris the car manufacturer.

I'm adding a third Morris: Morris Dancing. It's why I've walked to William Kimber Crescent, one of Oxford's most unpromising roads – in keeping with the city's habit of naming its dullest streets after its most interesting characters. At the end of the small path that passes a row of red-brick terraces behind Headington Community Centre, is Magdalen Quarry Nature Reserve, also known as the Workhouse Pit. The last of the working quarries, it closed in 1949. It's now another island of greenery just off the Bypass. Headington is full of these pockets of escape, little routes out of the city, some, like this one, so small you can spend years passing them without noticing.

William Kimber captures Headington and the kind of England that surrounded both the university and what Betjeman called Motopolis. Born in 1872, Kimber was the son of a quarryman Morris dancer, and trained as a bird-scarer before becoming a builder. The quarries were becoming an anachronism, but not as much of an anachronism as the folk traditions of its population, which were anthropological *curios*. The antiquarian and folklorist, Percy Manning, persuaded the Headington Quarry Morris dancers to regroup and paid for their equipment. Even in the 1890s, Morris dancing, like folk songs, was becoming an object of study – a sure sign its days were numbered.

The Morris revival began here by chance: Kimber and the freshly-re-equipped Quarry Morris Men were performing on Boxing Day 1899 outside a cottage off London Road, making ends meet while building work was scarce. They caught the attention of Cecil Sharp, a leading scholar of the folk song revival. There's a plaque commemorating the encounter on the wall of Horwood Close. Sharp asked Kimber to come back and play the tunes so he could transcribe them. Sharp died in 1924; Kimber in 1961. In the old photos, Kimber looks pagan, his postures hieratic, his body muscular and lean, his face dark and heavily moustached. He's channelling something primal, as ancient as the oak trees in Headington Park and the stones and fossils under my feet.

Kimber built his own house on St Anne's Road, and died two years after the Headington-Rose Hill segment of Bypass was built, half a mile away. Think about the co-existence, on this stretch of ring road, of the Morris dancing, the concertina-playing folk traditions of Headington Quarry, and the breakneck speed of industrialization at the Morris car plant. It's a short walk between these two Englands, overlapping and flowing into each other, while down the hill the university that ignored them both was also made of them both.

The Pitt Rivers Museum has an evocative name for its English folk collections: 'England: The Other Within'. Manning's folk collections are in there with the Egyptian sarcophagi, the totem poles and the shrunken heads, and you can see the costumes, the bells and the ribbons worn by Kimber and his troupe, in the glass cases not far from the Samurai armour or the Yup'ik clothing of the Alaskan Inuit.[8]

I didn't need to go to the North Pole to find a world of ancient customs and strange clothes, just the Northern Bypass. Morris Men are a regular fixture of today's Oxford. I watch them on May Day, notice that strange intensity they have; the way people look at them first in mockery and then with a kind of fascinated awe as they feel the countryside coming back to haunt the towns, the past coming back to jangle its bells at the present. That's the spirit of William Kimber, here to remind us of the Other Oxford within.

C.S. LEWIS, RISINGHURST, THE KILNS

Five minutes from Kimber's house is the graveyard of Holy Trinity Church, where he rests beneath a headstone carved with his trademark Anglo-Concertina and a pair of Morris Dancing bell pads. The grave is neglected, pocked with lichen and moss so the lettering is almost illegible. Even the carvings are hard to make out. His near-neighbour, in death as in life, is another resident of Headington Quarry now lying under Headington stone: C.S. Lewis, who lived across the Bypass at 'The Kilns'. Lewis's grave, however, is clean and tended, and there's often someone in front of it.

In the church, I'm more impressed by the Narnia Window than I expected. The image itself is predictable – a lion, a wingèd horse, children being transported by phantasmagorical animals, mountainous peaks, towers and galleons cresting waves. But because it's made of a mix of clear glass and frosted glass, it looks sculpted from sheets of ice. The world outside the window is incorporated into the design: the dark green of the grass, the brown of the autumn leaves, the grey-blue sky, the red brick of some building I haven't yet seen and hadn't noticed when I came in, a white wall, some chimneys... all of it filling out the shapes in the window, becoming part of it while at the same time drawing out its otherworldly designs. The ordinary and the extraordinary, the real and the imagined, each giving the other texture and dimensionality. I thought it would be a bit cheesy – some kind of twee municipal homage – but it's not. Instead, it's a lesson in how the ordinary and the extraordinary infuse each other, fill each other out – whoever commissioned and designed and executed this knew their C.S. Lewis.

THE MANOR GROUND: OXFORD'S MISSING CENTRE

Old Headington feels like a Cotswold village. Old country church, old country pubs, blue plaques to diverse famous residents. One, Isaiah Berlin, lived behind a high gate decorated with pineapple finials on Old High Street. Another, Tolkien, left Headington for Bournemouth in 1968. It's a short walk to Waitrose, but also to the Manor Road football ground, the home of Headington United, and then Oxford United, between 1925 and 2001.

I enjoy the thought that Tolkien and Berlin heard the football from their studies, and bumped into fans with their scarves and rattles and bobble hats. They saw what I saw as they did their shopping: the iconic arch up the lane to the London Road stand behind the petrol station that's still there, the blue and yellow Oxford United façade and the squeaky turnstiles. Headington became a suburb of Oxford in 1929, but the team kept its name until 1960, when it became Oxford United, to the resentment of Headington people. There's nothing left of Manor Ground – the graffiti was the last to go, runic inscriptions slagging off Reading and Swindon. Beech Road and Osler Road with their detached houses and bay windows ended with a dramatic rectangle of football stand. The roars of the crowds shook the windowpanes. It's now a private hospital, part of the Nuffield Health Trust.

Joining the ghost stations and the ghost breweries, the ghost gasworks and the ghost-suburb of St Ebbe's, is the ghost football stadium. The high-flying League One Oxford United football club that resides at the Kassam Stadium began here. Which brings me to a point I meant to make much earlier. In most cities you know it's a match day because the city centre is buzzing with home and away fans. Banners fly, scarves flap. In Oxford centre you'd never know there was a football match on, because the people who live and work there aren't from Oxford. Is this unique to Oxford? In every place I've lived it's been possible to tell when there was a football match on. When Newcastle United came for a FA Cup match in February, I only saw Newcastle fans in town. Here was a big match, but the home team may as well not have existed. It's not just because the Kassam Stadium is off the ringroad, but because Oxford City Centre doesn't belong to Oxford City. But when I walk the rings of the city, or take a bus to Headington, Blackbird Leys, Templars Square, Rose Hill, Barton, Northway, Littlemore, Risinghurst... I see Oxford United stickers and flags, and the pubs with the fans and the songs.

As far as the city centre was concerned, Newcastle were playing against air.

HEADINGTON SHARK

The Headington Shark is a sculpture-cum-installation on New High Street in Headington. 25 feet long, it depicts a shark crashing through the roof a terraced house. It doesn't merely look like it happened, it looks like it's *happening now*. It bursts with the present tense. It's a landmark and an orientation-point – the buses in from London and the airports go past, and it gives the newcomer a sneak preview of the sort of place Oxford is *not* going to be. To the native, bleary-eyed after a night in the capital or jetlagged on an airport bus, it has the paradoxical effect of being reassuring; homely even: the shark is crashing through the roof, we're almost home, and all is right with the world.

Its original title is *Untitled 1986*. Much less snappy than Headington Shark. Designed by the sculptor John Buckley for his friend Bill Heine,[9] the fibreglass predator was installed on the forty-first anniversary of the dropping of the atomic bomb on Nagasaki. 1986 was a febrile time in politics: Thatcher, the Campaign for Nuclear Disarmament, Chernobyl, US planes using nearby Upper Heyford air base to bomb Libya. The shark symbolised the helplessness of the individual in the face of violence. But it's a very clever object too: a creature of the sea falling from the sky, it says something about how things come at us from above and below in a way that would have been recognizable to any of Headington's medieval denizens: the friars, the priests, the nuns, the lepers – people for whom the precarious life was also just known as *life*. As for today, there's no shortage of world events which can't be usefully glossed by a fibreglass shark crashing through a suburban roof.

HEADINGTON ROUNDABOUT AND THE SUBWAYS

I once thought of Cowley as separate from Headington, which was separate from Marston, which was separate from Summertown and Cutteslowe. And so on. That's because I always approached them from the city centre and walked outwards. I knew Oxford in segments, like individually-wrapped cheese triangles.

By walking Oxford radially, taking longer circular routes, I saw another set of relationships. This segment of Bypass dates from the 1930s, and is Oxford's oldest: from Headington to the top of Banbury Road. The Eastern Bypass becomes the Northern Bypass around the London Road McDonalds, a 1930s tudoresque building that was once the Shotover Arms hotel and housed the last/first petrol station on Oxford's periphery. On one side there's an empty Carphone Warehouse, on the other a parade of shops which includes the Portuguese café I've leapt over traffic barriers and dodged between cars to reach. Nearby is a burrow of subways linking Risinghurst, Barton, Sandhills and Headington.

The most famous subway is under my feet, here on the corner of Kennett and London Roads. 'Headington Subway' was built in 1969 at the London Road shops, and housed a mural (painted in 2002) depicting Headington's local landmarks: shops, cafés, DIY merchants, chippies, churches, Bill Heine's shark, the Manor Ground, scenes from The Hobbit and the Narnia tales. Despite a

5000-signature petition defending it, all from locals, the council pumped it full of concrete and built over it. So when I say it's under my feet, I mean under my feet the way fossils are, or the corallian stone strata in the quarries. There are depressing images on the *Oxford Mail* site of a grey batter of concrete drowning the pictures, though both sides of the mural have been digitally stored and can be seen on the Headington History website.[10]

What's refreshing about Headington is that, apart from a few usual suspects, pretty much everything here is local, small, and international: the Polish mini-market, the Lebanese restaurant, the Turkish barbers, the French-themed café, the hipster eatery where they serve coffee in flanked glasses, the chippie and the bakery, the running shop…. It's a thriving place, wealthy enough and far enough away from Oxford city centre to have its own distinct and characterful high street, which is what London Road has become. So while the subway and its pictures have gone, its spirit lives on.

HEADINGTON HILL HOUSE: OEDIPUS AT HOME

The iron footbridge joining Cheney Lane and Headington Hill to the edge of St Clement's and Headington Hill Hall, the Morrell family seat, was erected in 1877. I'm following the increasingly pungent smell of weed to the huge, golden-stoned Italianate mansion that's now Oxford Brookes's prestige conference centre. There's a young man laid out on a bench, videocalling on his phone, filming the sun, the house and the landscaped grounds from his reclining position, puffing joint-fumes into the air. He gives me a languid nod as I pass. There's no better place to indulge your recreation, whether it's writing *Real Oxford* or smoking a fat joint, than before a Turneresque sunset over a spookily empty stately home marinading in golden light.

It's in fact two houses: one a modest upper-crust family home built in 1824, the other an ostentatious, 51-roomed palace built thirty years later. It's an Oedipal parable in real estate: the first house was built by the father, the second by the son, in such a way as to eclipse the original house. Act III in the Oedipal drama came in 1953, when the grandson sold the place to Oxford City Council, who intended to demolish it and move their council offices here. The first generation builds, the second usurps, the third sells the lot and gets out.

In the late 1950s it was leased to Robert Maxwell, one of Britain's most daring fraudsters, who called it 'the grandest council house in Britain'. Maxwell ran his business empire here, including Pergamon Press, his academic imprint. Later it became his family home and the scene of high-society parties – this lawn has seen many helicopters. At the entrance to the grounds, there's a plaque in honour of the Pergamon Press workers sacked by Maxwell for demanding union recognition. They picketed here between 1989 and 1992. As the plaque laconically puts it: 'His empire collapsed, the union lives on'. The award for most acerbic comment, however, goes to the excellent oxfordhistory.org.uk, who note beneath their photo of the plaque: 'The above is probably his only memorial'.

I walk along the colonnade at the front, peering in: single desks, crested notepads, whiteboards, lanyards… piles of lanyards. I go around the back, crossing a tiny garden with a stunted privet maze and sagging roses. There's a spiral staircase to the roof, and, because it's now an institutional building, health and safety signs are everywhere. The scale of the place is such that I need to get down to the bottom of the helicopter-landing lawn to get it into one shot. But it's disappointing – a big empty toy on a hill. Perfect for a conference centre.

Robert Maxwell used to be one of my teaching-aids. He died the autumn I arrived here – a mysterious accident/murder/suicide on his yacht in the Canary Islands. He'd just defaulted on a £50,000,000 loan and faced a litany of fraud charges. He was a 22-stone, £3 billion debtor who owned football clubs (including Oxford United), publishers, real estate and restaurants – and plenty of politicians. Maxwell came in handy when I was teaching Balzac. There was a lot of Balzac in those days. There's a lot of Balzac anyway, but I mean on the syllabus. When students complained that Balzac's characters, like Dickens's, were 'unrealistic' or 'un-believable', I just reminded them of Robert Maxwell, and they got the point: there's enough that's unbelievable about reality for us to cut fiction a bit of slack. Maxwell was an emanation of Thatcher's Britain, just like Balzac's characters were emanations of Louis-Philippe's France. Today I refer students to Donald Trump, though I use him for teaching Theatre of the Absurd as well. As for the end of Trump's presidency and the storming of the Capitol unfolding as I write, that will help with my lecture on Jarry's *Ubu*.

Another place where Maxwell is remembered – apart from newspaper headlines and the Pergamon plaque – is in the essays of Oxford French students in the 1990s.

LITTLEMORE: BOUNDARIES

The Oxford United/Swindon Town grudge-derby: no crowds in the Kassam – Covid regs – so why the police presence? Oh, I see: in the parking lot, fans stand on wooden pallets attached to their car roofs, cheering teams they can barely see, singing songs and goading opponents. A normal matchday in abnormal times. Oxford lose 2-1, squandering an early lead. To add to the humiliation, the bronze ox statue outside the stadium is graffiti'd with Swindon Town logos. It's damp, cold and bad-tempered, but oddly comforting to see these local enmities adapting so well to today's global challenges.

I pass the cinema and Hollywood Bowl complex, the Oxford United fanshop and the muddy edgeland around the science park. Under a rail embankment, itself embanked with the flytipped contents of a marriage, I'm at Minchery Road, Littlemore.

This is a place of boundaries. The embankment tunnel is wide enough for a single car, and has fluorescent tape along its arch to warn off vans and lorries. On the Minchery Road side I find two boundary markers: a circular iron slab marked GREAT WESTERN RAILWAY 1889, which my walking companion spots and clears with his foot because it's overgrown. A few feet away is the stone marking the HIGHWAY BOUNDARY.

On the railway side of the aluminium fencing, a relationship that reached its own boundary: a pair of huge wedding photos printed onto canvas. They're soggy and mouldy and the wooden frames are warped, but the people are all still visible: bride and groom, groom and father/father-in-law, group shots of the Big Day. They're disturbingly clear despite the ravages. The eyes seem to be following me from the shattered aftermath of a nasty divorce.

In the gaps between houses, I see the smoky-glassed, chrome-pillared buildings of the Oxford Science Park. Those inscrutable exteriors with their hi-tech surveillance and multimillion-pound equipment are pressed up against the backs of people's gardens and loom over the estate. On the outskirts of the science park, on the bus route into the Kassam, is part of a derelict priory that was recently a pub. The stones are turning green, the windows boarded up. It cuts a bleak figure in this futuristic landscape. Nearby, private health and tech firms work on Covid vaccines, apps and testing kits that will help the fans now standing on their cars return to the stands and insult each other at close range again.

In 1525, Cardinal Wolsey closed Littlemore Priory, founded in 1100, and turned it into a farm. The pub, which briefly became Oxford United's most local local, is all that survives of it. There are Youtube videos of fans singing and chanting in its low-ceilinged bar. It closed six years ago but seems to have suffered a century of dereliction. Digs were conducted before the building of a new hotel. Where the church once stood, archaeologists unearthed ninety-two skeletons, including a woman buried face-down and another with her skull staved in. They were reburied in sacred ground, thus spared an eternity at the Holiday Inn Express which now stands there.

CARDINAL NEWMAN

Littlemore is a place of contrasts. At its outer reaches, it's modern estates, council and owner-occupied, some allotments and a vast supermarket. But the centre still reflects the village it began as. It's another place I thought I knew but didn't because I'd never walked it – just driven or taken buses on the way elsewhere. John Henry

Newman lived here, founder of the Oxford Movement, the branch of the Church of England that became 'Anglo-Catholicism'. Hence the 'bells and smells' epithet. The movement's mark is everywhere in Oxford – unsurprisingly, as it was led by powerful academics, clergy and intellectuals. Its institutions include Keble College and Pusey House, named after John Keble and Edward Pusey, and its influence on English culture in the mid to late nineteenth century was deep and lasting. But unassuming Littlemore – even the name sounds like a very modest request: 'please Sir, may I have a little more?' – is where one of the defining moments in English religious history took place.

Newman, vicar of the University Church from 1828, went 'all the way': he converted to Catholicism, and the long, low coach house in front of me is where he did so. It's now called 'The College', and houses a chapel, a library, and hosts religious retreats. On 9 October, 1845, Newman was received into the Catholic church by Father Dominic Barberi. The moment is captured on a bronze relief by Faith Falconbridge, Tolkien's daughter-in-law, on the wall of the Church of the Blessed Dominic Barberi a little further down the road. It's one of Oxford's most striking modernist buildings, half-community-centre and half-spaceship. The front is dominated by a huge clerestory of projecting windows shaped like faceted diamonds. The effect from the road is elating, because the building's base is so unassuming: plain brick inside and out, timber and concrete.

BADLY-SITED BENCHES

The Eastern Bypass flies over Littlemore shops and Littlemore's own Cowley Road, a compressed version of Oxford's: Polski Sklep, Jamaican restaurant, minimarket, hair styling, and a 'Gift Shop' that sells everything. Outside it today are carpet rolls, holographic posters of Jesus (no sign of Newman, but there's a definite Catholic edge to the religious *merch*), shishas, saris, pans, washing-up racks, pedal bins, plastic flowers, high-vis jackets, tartan shopping trolleys, shoe racks and tinsel. Indoors it's the same, only more so.

I'm aiming for the underpass to Rose Hill, hoping to join the path that follows the ring road around the city. The muddy track I mistake for a footpath quickly takes me to the edge of the traffic. There's no barrier. The cars move so fast that I'm at once pushed into the bushes and sucked into the road. I've overshot the underpass, so I walk to a roundabout where someone has painstakingly created an unofficial recreation garden. There's even a notice to that effect, ordering us to respect it. There's a yucca plant, carefully-tended and properly-mulched roses, and a bench facing the roundabout. That's the view. A roundabout. Bench of dreams. Some time ago I began making notes of Oxford's worst-sited benches. This is a classic – a hazard for eye and lung. Another is not far away, on the Rose Hill/Henley Avenue cusp, raised on a stone plinth where the road suddenly steepens. It faces the traffic and a lot of number 3 buses, but it's still popular, as empty beer cans attest. It's is a relic of the time when you could see Oxford from Rose Hill. A memorial to a view.

A TALE OF TWO ASYLUMS

I'm looking between the bars of tall, automated, fob-triggered gates, down the long drive of what was once Oxford County Pauper Lunatic Asylum. Built in 1846 in response to the 1845 'Lunacy Act', and the Warneford's counterpart, sitting three miles outside Oxford like its banished twin. It's now 'prestige' housing and businesses, and the difficulty isn't getting out but getting in.

The asylum is mentioned in Alden's guide as a 'conspicuous object' on the pleasure-cruises from Folly Bridge to Nuneham via picture-postcard Sandford-on-Thames. Today I'm watching

Waitrose deliveries and fresh young couples on flashy bikes buzzing themselves in. Expensive cars are parked at angles, ready to be photographed for brochures. I sometimes wonder if these details are staged, like some pyschogeographical *Truman Show*. The asylum only closed in 1998, after years of decline brought about, apparently, by 'Care in the Community', the 1980s policy that closed 'expensive' mental facilities and turfed out needy residents onto – often literally – the streets. Care in the community to gated community.

Right opposite, in a smudged-mirror-effect, is Littlemore Mental Health Hospital, which replaced it. Much easier to walk around in. Where once you kept the poor out, now you keep the rich in. Privacy is the new real estate. The sun is setting in a blaze and I squint as I cross the road from old asylum to new. There's a lady standing outside in slippers, pyjamas and overcoat. Universal hospital-wear for smokers in the cold. I put my hand to my eyes to shield them from the sun. She mistakes it for a wave, and waves.

Suddenly it's my mother standing outside Tooting hospital, smoking roll-ups and waving to me in that slow, medicalised, semi-recognitive way I'm seeing now. Now I must return the lady's wave – my first one didn't count because I wasn't waving. Now she waves again. I am always one wave behind. I think I might cry. And then I do, and wave again, because this will never end, and because it never has.

Our waves never find their destinations, ricocheting from person to person around the outsides of hospitals the world over. I am waving through her as she waves through me. This is my wave across 20 years to my mother: *Salut maman – 'chuis toujours là, j't'attends. Laisse-moi te dire tout ce à quoi tu manques.* Let me tell you all that you are missing from.

ROSE HILL: LATE OMENS

I've crossed the footbridge over the Bypass from Littlemore. I'm on Lambourn Road, in front of a normal-looking end-of-terrace house decked with crosses: one on the front porch, one on the garage. There are lions' heads stencilled around the walls and garden-centre angels cemented to the gateposts. Some sort of unofficial church? Maybe the garage is a place of worship, hence the big cross

on the roof and the KEEP OUT sign and security cameras. Mixed signals there, but that's religion for you. Maybe the lion is the lion of Judah. I always think, as I pass, 'this is when I stop and knock on the door and ask'. Then I always think: 'another time'.

I'm stopped in my tracks by the sight of a white van with a yellow and pink plastic beer-crate tied onto it. 'MALHEUR'. It's a Belgian beer, and chimes in my head with the Belgian French I've been speaking to my mother since I waved at her through the lady in the dressing gown. She's still speaking to me: that blunt, dread word. A message from the other side – and the other side of the Bypass. *Malheur.* She would tell me to enjoy the surrealism of it, this word blinking at me from the roof of a van in an Oxford housing estate, and to take my dose of darkness with a good long swig of light. *C'est ç'que j'essaie de faire,* I tell her. It's what I'm trying to do.

For a walk as contrastive as Blackbird Leys/Garsington but briefer, it's Rose Hill to Iffley Village. It takes ten minutes. The latter is a classic example of Oxford's moneyed rustic fringes – rivers, locks, towpaths, country houses, pubs, church. The former is a windswept estate pressed up against the ring road, an arrangement of residential streets enclosed by crescents and planned around 'The Oval' (actually a circle). There's an endangered-looking shop-parade that doesn't even face The Oval: supermarket, takeaway, newsagent. The bare minimum. 'Bare minimum' is how the place feels today.

The Oval was designed as a village-green-style centrepiece, but today it's just a place buses turn around in. That's what's happening now: two buses, their interiors overlit in the gloaming, engines thrumming, waiting to take people into town for Friday night revels. I walk to Rose Hill shops, through the 'Corporation Housing', as Oxford called its council housing in the 1930s. They're solid, well-built, made of dark red brick, with proper front and back gardens, square rooms, and plenty of space. The gardens are full of building materials. There's been a DIY bug – old sofas, fridges, ovens, windowpanes, planks, and then more toys, broken stuff, all accumulating until there's enough to order a skip or drive to Redbridge recycling. Our white goods leave through the same door they arrived, like our coffins. Garden after garden. Cement that's set in the rain and taken on the shape of the sack that once held it, creased like an old grey pillow.

I pass a window decked out like a theatre set: dramatic velvet curtains, a vase on one side with plastic flowers, a cat on the other, who may be real but is so still it might be an ornament. Disembodied in the join between the curtains is a child's face, solemnly looking me in the eye. She has very black hair and looks serious. I wave jerkily, feeling pretty discomfited by now. She holds my gaze. Her hand appears and waves back slowly and unsmiling, the way children wave in films that end badly. I want to tell her that if she's an omen, she's too late. This is the walk of waves.

PEVSNER AND PREFABS

Down to Iffley Village, with its mix of architect-built modern houses and old country piles, its upper-crust pubs and the twelfth-century church Newman admired from his mother's house and Pevsner loved so much he used it on the cover of his *Oxfordshire* guide. Behind the Rose Hill Kia garage I follow some unpromising back alleys. Bins and brambles. I know it well, but I still try to err. Today I err into a maze of little lanes that cut up and down and sideways, threading between houses and gardens, a hotchpotch of architectures: handsome old houses, one with a turret, 1930s semis with grand bays and their original windows, cottages and corporation houses. Here I get great sweeping views of the city, part of the old Rose Hill panorama before Florence Park blocked the view. I'm almost at Iffley Village when I see a traffic barrier gating off Tree Lane from Annesley Road.

The 350 year-old tree of Tree Lane died in 1974 of Dutch elm disease, but the village it leads to is still more or less intact. Thatched houses in pristine condition, converted barns, a mill, a malthouse, a manor, old pubs, river walks, locks and a village shop run by volunteers. Listed buildings on every side.

For years I'd walk to Iffley for fresh air and river views, conditioned to ignore the estate that lay at its edges. Ignore it? I didn't even *see* it.

S.P.B. Mais, an *Oxford Mail* journalist, was once a famous travel writer. His 1955 article about Iffley began:

> 'Iffley Village Only' says the sign-post. There is no through road. There are no buses. By some fantastic miracle Iffley remains both in appearance and in character a real old, very old, English village. It has become embedded among its modern surroundings, like a pearl in an oyster, but it has, most surprisingly, not allowed itself to be submerged by them.[11]

The 'miracle' is a secular one: barriers. As for the oyster and pearl analogy, it says something about how social housing was seen by Oxford's middle and upper classes. Off Tree Lane, I turn into Church Way searching for the pearl within the pearl: the church of St Mary The Virgin, a Norman church, built in 1170 in the Romanesque style, and one of the finest in Britain. I'm as thrilled to see it as Pevsner was. The doorways, windows and arches are recessed, the lines of carvings overlapping, so there's a dizzying *trompe-l'oeil* effect of depth. The west doorway is the best-preserved and most decorative – zig-zag patterns and beakhead designs that look almost cartoonish and pagan. On the rim of the arch are the signs of the zodiac and the symbols of the evangelists.

It's on the cusp of being over-restored. One thing naturally-accrued dirt does for carving is accentuate the lines. The zig-zag patterns make it look as if the doors and arches are pulsing, but it's the south door that really fires up the sense of being in the presence of a different kind of human consciousness. Here it's fantastic beasts, dragons and centaurs and serpents, a sphinx and a Green Man, motifs from Celtic and Saxon carving. It feels like something from a video game, some holographic portal I'd pass through on the way to another world. A threshold in the city of thresholds.

Up the road I go. To the next threshold – the barrier, like the one on Tree Lane, stopping cars from crossing between Rose Hill and Iffley Village. The walkers in front of me reach it and turn back. They've done their circuit. They have wellies and Barbours and are definitely more interested in the pearl than the oyster. Coming from the other direction is a teenager making plans to meet friends in town. This is the short cut.

I cross into Rose Hill, onto Nowell Road and Lenthall Road, where many of the houses are prefabs dating from the inter-war and immediate post-war period. By the end of World War II, Oxford council's housing waiting-list was over 5000 names long. Pre-fabrication was an easy solution and hundreds were built here, usually on the edges of the city and within reach of the car plant – Barton, Wood Farm, Littlemore, Rose Hill. Many were only demolished and replaced in the last ten or fifteen years, but what's striking is how many still stand, and how differently they've fared. Some are lovingly painted and restored, some are decrepit and mouldy, their porches sagging, their pre-cast shells dirty and discoloured. This is one of the most deprived wards in Oxford, and like much of Rose Hill (the same is true of Barton), the people feel forgotten, peripheral to the city's sense of itself. One of the running themes in the *Oxford Mail*'s local reporting is the way Rose Hill gets bypassed – a loaded word here on the edge of an actual Bypass.

I imagine these houses being pieced together – bases, shells, interior walls, insulation – a few minutes' walk from Iffley Lock and the Norman church, the manor house and the Tudor cottage. They were just a few winters old when Mais wrote his article, when the

Iffley village postmaster, Mr Gibbs (unlikely to be any relation of Olive Gibbs), told him: 'We haven't got a bus, and we don't want one. We haven't got a through road, and we don't want one.'

Further up I find a Howard Prefab house with a leather three-piece suite poaching in the drizzle. There's an Oxford United scarf nailed over the door like a coat of arms, the tassels hanging down over the entrance. Beneath a first-floor window is the blue and yellow Oxford United Ox, coated in plastic and stuck to the wall. It makes me think of the winged ox of Luke the Evangelist carved onto a different entrance a few yards away – the door of St Mary the Virgin – more than 800 years ago.

I get to Rivermead Nature Park, an unexpected edgeland-oasis between the noisy Bypass and Rose Hill estate, but it's too dark to go much further. I head back via Lenthall Road, up to The Oval and on to Rose Hill shops. I turn and see the barrier I crossed an hour ago, which looks frail and ghostly in the late afternoon.

'We haven't got a through road, and we don't want one,' said the pearl to the oyster.

NATURE RESERVES AND RUBBISH DUMPS

Iffley Road goes to Iffley, just like Cowley Road goes to Cowley. But Cowley and Iffley are very different places, and those differences are visible in both roads from the moment they begin at The Plain, a few metres from each other. The roundabout is where they pull away from each other – gently at first – an extra half-pedal on the bike, three or four steps – and then with increasing starkness until they're barely on speaking terms.

The first differences are architectural, which is another way of saying that the first differences are social. The houses on Iffley Road are not only taller and broader, like well-fed bourgeois, but the façades are redder, the effects more decorative, also like well-fed bourgeois. A Victorian architect, James Castle, built two splendid Italianate villas here in the 1860s in an attempt to lure North Oxford types east. It never became the North Oxford style suburb he wanted, but it's well on the way now. Iffley Road was always going to have advantages: it's close to the river, which means it can't be developed southwards. Green and leafy, it lets Cowley Road deal with the urban hassle of feeding and watering two universities-worth of students. Oxford university's sports ground is here – swimming pool, athletics track, tennis courts and rugby ground. Roger Bannister ran the 4-Minute Mile here on 6 May 1954. For many students, the sports ground defines Oxford's eastern frontier.

At the edge of the rugby field is Jackdaw Lane, where Iffley Fields, East Oxford's North Oxford, begins. A grid of streets backed by two nature reserves, the houses themselves aren't particularly special, though most of them have been extended and loft- or basement-converted beyond recognition.

I moved here in 2014. I bought the house from the Whittakers, Windrush arrivals from the 1960s. Mr Whittaker came to Oxford as a young man, and his twin went to America. He was a carpenter, and bought this house before I was born. The day I moved in, he and his wife were there to give me the keys. It was symbolic, because I already had them. They wished me as much happiness as they had had. A tall order because they seemed very happy indeed, their children driving them away – in a Mini – to their new home. At the end of my day, I go to my study at the bottom of the garden, which Mr Whittaker built as his workshop, and write *Real Oxford*, or mark student essays, or scan my Wilko notebook for any lines or observations that might serve a poem. In the mornings, I look out over the garden and see the cranes from the salvage yard cranking up for the day. The clang of metal, the scrape of scrap. In the evenings, it's the rugby or the football on the sportsground, the klaxons of boat races, the loudhailers of rowing coaches on the riverbank, the cheers and the roars. Iffley Fields was not always so *bourge*, as my students say. It still has pockets of drug dealing around Meadow Lane, and the occasional illegal rave. Down Iffley Road, a rare book dealer I had a nodding acquaintance with was killed for a first edition of *Wind in the Willows*. A murder straight out of the great detective novel, Edmund Crispin's *The Moving Toyshop*, and a case for his amateur sleuth, Gervase Fen, an Oxford don who professes to enjoy 'a splendidly complicated crime'. Except it wasn't. It was a basic, grotty, greed-killing, the culprit found and charged a few days later.

Facing the University Sports Ground is a flat whose small balcony has been transformed into a state-of-the-art pigeon loft. It provides me with an avian study in the old clichés about Town and Gown:

Toffs and Toughs

There's a dovecote, tidy as a dollhouse,
on the third-floor balcony of our street's last slice
of flats: perspex side-walls and little porches

where thoroughbred pigeons air their plumes
and live their showhome lives. Dieted and groomed,
they take supplements, wear ankle rings, have names.

On the railing opposite the city pigeons eye them up.
They eat shavings of kebab and kerbside macerations
of burger baps and rain. Their feathers are greasy,

lubed with binjuice and exhaust-fume slick,
and their necks when they turn and catch the light
are the rainbows of petrol-station puddles.

Their bubble-gum claws are ringless, stumped
at the knuckle; leprous, cropped and nobbled.
Some have punctured eyes and threadbare tails

from scrapes with cats. They have a ragged
irony about them, a streetside-swagger
as they lounge and watch their overbred cousins

gentrify the air. They're on opposite ends
of what it to be the same, like the famous photo
of posh schoolboys outside Lord's, with their top hats,

carnations, canes; while the local kids, mitching
from school, more curious than envious,
peer at them across the species gulf that isn't one,

from the other side of nature that's all nurture.

The places I know as nature reserves – Aston's Eyot and The
Kidneys – were once Oxford's rubbish tips – so dense-packed with
detritus that they rose metres above ground-level. Today it's birds
and badgers, muntjacs and foxes, rare plants and fruit trees, dogs
running free, joggers inhaling wholesome riverside air, and young
people smoking weed in what poets call dappled glades. There are
still signs prohibiting digging, metal-detecting and 'bottling', the
practice of scouring Victorian and Edwardian rubbish dumps. The
scrap metal dealership is a living link to the area's rubbish pedigree.
What antique landfill am I walking over? What sort of underfoot
Oxford is this?

In Dorothy L. Sayers's *Gaudy Night*, Peter Wimsey and Harriet
Vane have a romantic moment ruined here. They are courting in a
punt (spoiler: in the next book, they marry):

'Good God!' said Peter, suddenly.

He peered with an air of alarm into the dark green water. A
string of oily bubbles floated slowly to the surface, showing where
the pole had struck a patch of mud; and at the same moment their
nostrils were assaulted by a loathsome stench of decay.

'What's the matter?'

'I've struck something horrible. Can't you smell it? It's
scandalous

the way corpses pursue me about. Honestly, Harriet ...'

'My dear idiot, it's only the corporation garbage dump.'

His eyes followed her pointing hand to the farther bank, where
a cloud of flies circled about a horrid mound of putrefaction.

'The Isis for me – there is no romance left on this river.'[12]

I stand at the edge of the bank behind my house. There's a dead
campfire with half-consumed logs: one end intact, the other
powdery ash. Empty beer cans, conscientiously crushed flat and
packed into a neatly tied plastic bag, yet the bag left here – littering
and tidying in one. Perhaps it's some offering to the old garbage
dump, a rite of municipal memory.

For years there's been a rope tied to the sturdy bough of the tree
that leans into the water opposite the boathouse. It's not the same
rope as in my day. The point of the game was to swing out while our
friends stopped us from landing by pushing us back or blocking the
bank as we slid down, the rope burning our hands, and fell in.
Today's rope is blue nylon twine. It's thinner and shorter, which
speeds up the game. This summer, I was walking here with my
daughter and we stumbled on a folk band rehearsing in a circle of
fallen tree trunks. They asked if we had a request. 'Calon Lân' was
all I could think of. One of the singers addressed us in Welsh and we
continued talking while they played. It was all real – Mari is my
witness – but somehow it's easier to file the whole thing under
'Dream'.

Come back, Peter Wimsey – the romance has returned.

Notes

1. https://library.oxfordarchaeology.com/176/1/OXTHPL07.pdf
2. See Kerem Öktem's excellent article: https://www.opendemocracy.net/en/two-ends-of-cowley-road-diversity-and-its-challenges/
   Also James Attlee's *Isolarion: A Different Oxford Journey.*
3. http://www.headington.org.uk/history/listed_buildings/warneford.htm
4. http://www.friendsoflyevalley.org.uk/
5. Richard Bedwin's 1978 history of the choir is now available online at the Oxford Welsh Male Voice Choir website: https://www.oxfordwelshmvc.org.uk/history.html
6. http://www.bbc.co.uk/oxford/content/articles/2007/10/01/joy_feature.shtml
7. D.H. Lawrence, *The Letters of D.H. Lawrence, vol 2*, eds Zytaruk and Boulton (Cambridge: Cambridge University Press, 1981), p. 431.
8 http://web.prm.ox.ac.uk/england/englishness-Percy-Manning.html
9. Bill Heine, who died in 2019, was an Oxford institution. He arrived here from the US as a student and stayed. As a columnist, he wrote about Oxford with an insider's knowledge and an outsider's ability to find the unexpected perspective. A great lover of Oxford city's character and heritage, it's thanks to him that we still have the Ultimate Picture Palace on Jeune Street. In Heine's day it was the Penultimate Picture Palace.
10. http://www.headington.org.uk/art/x_subway.html
11. 'Iffley, A Village – but in the City',
    http://www.iffleyhistory.org.uk/Iffley%201955%20Article/1955Article.htm
12. The Friends of Aston's Eyot website has a full history of the area, along with a 'Literary Eyot' page: https://friendsofastonseyot.org/

NORTH

ST GILES

If I'd been writing 400 years ago, this book would have been a lot shorter. *Reale Oxenforde* would have begun 'North' pretty much in the middle of today's city. Now there's a vast ongoing building project on Cornmarket, the new Jesus College quadrangle, and a row of hi-tech businesses, called 'Northgate'. It jars to think of this epicentral development as marking one of Oxford's edges, and that the old city's perimeter is now only evoked in the names of shopping precincts. But then again that's what 'Cornmarket' was – a shopping precinct. Who's honouring it more? The business-people, developers and shoppers perpetuating its mercantile rhythms across the centuries? Or the middle-aged nostalgist who wants today to stop?

Actually, the new/old Northgate is convenient because it gives me an excuse to begin 'north' Oxford on St Giles. I've over-run my word-quota for Central, so any historical alibi for heading northward as soon as possible is welcome.

I'm amazed by how quickly the centre of Oxford ends, if by 'centre' we mean not just a circle on a map but something created by and through the magnetism of crowds. A few metres past Martyrs' Memorial, The Randolph and The Ashmolean, the tourist zone stops. There's no sign turning people away, though some Oxford residents suggest a zoning system that would have the same effect. 'Oxford's Tourist Hell' is a regular headline in the *Oxford Mail* and the national press. Today's pedestrians observe the old city's parameters. Tour groups and day-trip-clusters seem to know it instinctively, the way robotic lawnmowers sense the boundary-wire of the grass and turn back.

On the first Monday and Tuesday of September, Oxford gets an anarchic temporary skyline: the St Giles Fair. From Cornmarket to Banbury Road, roads close and colleges, libraries, museums and departments lock up. On the Sunday, the great beasts arrive, Meccano monsters ready to be assembled: The Claw, Vortex, The King, Storm, the waltzers and the wheels, the dodgems, helter-skelters and carousels. Elizabeth I watched their ancestors from a window in St John's College. This fair has only ever been cancelled for war or Covid.

It's not recorded whether Matthew Arnold's Scholar Gypsy worked here, but it's one of the great annual meeting-places of the travelling fairground community. The first mention of St Giles Fair dates from 1120, which makes it almost as old as the university. Over the years I've seen children who helped their parents collect tickets graduate to running the rides themselves as their own children collect tickets. The fair is run by the Guild of Showmen, and despite the bright, crowded apparent chaos of the place, it's a matter of precision-planning and precision-timing. To run something like this you need to be an accountant, a businessperson, an acrobat, an engineer and a mechanic.

There are amazing photographs of the fair through the ages – the hallowed, stately streets crowded with people of all ages and all classes, menageries, freak shows, trapeze artists, ghost trains, flea circuses.... I'd have loved to see the flea circus, a poster for which is in the Pitt Rivers's 'Other Within' collection: 'Dare-Devil Pete – a flea that rides and controls a cycle', and my personal favourite: 'Flea Dancing Girls'. That dates from 1954, and as if anticipating the age of Fake News, there's a guarantee: '£100 if not true'.

The university has always looked down its nose at the fair, not just because of the marauding gangs of ... *checks notes* ... ordinary people who come and take possession of St Giles for 48 hours and have noisy, colourful fun, but because of the association between travelling fairs and lawbreaking. Here, verbatim, is the text of an email those of us with departments or colleges around St Giles received from the University Security Services: 'Those further away should also not be complacent; the ne'er-do-wells are known to roam far and wide in their search for ill-gotten gains.' Though couched in the language of the Victorian bobby, the message is clear: watch out for the Other Within.

NOT ANOTHER F***ING ELF

Standing on the traffic island where St Giles forks into Banbury Road and Woodstock Road, I contemplate with relief the sudden thinning-out of things. With that comes – equal relief – the thinning-out of things to write about. I'm not taking the S3 bus to Woodstock via Peartree Park and Ride. Still less am I taking the 2A to Kidlington via Summertown. No, I'm moving laterally today, and my choice is Jericho or Mesopotamia. It has a rather Old Testament timbre to it.

I take the two St Giles pubs as markers. From The Eagle and

Child I can turn down Pusey Street and I'm in Jericho. From Lamb and Flag Passage I can turn down into South Parks Road, the museums and science faculties, into the University Parks and the piece of land called Mesopotamia. The Eagle and Child, known by people who want you to think they're in the know as The Bird and Baby, is a long narrow pub on St Giles. It's famous for being the place where the Inklings met – Tolkien, C.S. Lewis, Charles Williams and Hugo Dyson. There were other Inklings, but these are the ones we remember. Tolkien and Lewis everyone has heard of – creators of fantasy worlds that for all their unreality have an internal coherence that makes them not just persuasive but also truthful. Charles Williams is less known: poet and novelist, theologian and editor, he was admired by Auden and Eliot and is still admired by me in the face of universal indifference. Williams had a sense of the mystical and the magical, but unlike Lewis and Tolkien he didn't invent new worlds: his fantasies are set in the here and now, and the otherworldly infuses the ordinary. The fourth Inkling, Hugo Dyson, was an Oxford legend. He published little, existing mostly in memories and, in my case, memories of memories.

Dyson it was who, when Tolkien began reading another chunk of the *The Hobbit*, said 'Oh no, not another f***ing elf'. The line is often attributed to C.S. Lewis, and so poor Dyson, when not forgotten, is usurped.

Dyson was a great talker. I know this because he was my father's tutor. My father was also a great talker, but also complex-ridden, unhappy and alcoholic. He died young, though not quite as young as his own father, who had worked in the Newcastle shipyards. My dad was brought up in Wallsend-on-Tyne in the days when grammar schools ripped clever people out of their worlds and propelled them into places like Oxford. He was dazzled by it, and all the advantages he might have gained were wasted in social shame about class, accent, Irish name, home town, and family. His dream was to be a part of the English middle-classes, so he joined the civil service, which made him angry and miserable. He was ambitious for his children while at the same time resenting every step we climbed. I mention this not from self-pity but because it's a trait I've noticed among thwarted and controlling men: that they both want and fear their children having what they didn't.

But my father lit up when he got the chance to talk about Hugo Dyson. It was all golden stone, quads and *bon mots*. 'Not another f***ing Hugo Dyson story', my sister and I would say, as Kevin

McGuinness fired up another cigarette, expertly rolled by our silent Belgian mother, and started a Dysonian reminiscence. My father lived just long enough to see me get a fellowship at Oxford. I was a 'don', he kept saying, a word I can't stand, and which gives me the same feeling as fingernails dragged along a blackboard. The one and only time I brought my parents to High Table I expected my father to get stuck into the repartee. He'd evoked all this often enough. Now here it was: silver service waiters, good claret decanted in advance, shiny candelabra and the company of 'dons'. 'Get on with it', I thought, and maybe even said. Instead, he looked cowed and timid and dumbfounded; self-conscious and too scared even to drink.

So here's to Hugo Dyson, a man I never knew but with whom I feel a complicated connection. When I pass Holywell cemetery I'll go in and put a flower or a pinecone on his spartan grave, and text a picture to my sister who'll reply 'WTF?' The most rhetorical of rhetorical questions.

The Inklings went to the pub across the road when The Eagle and Child did a revamp and ruined their little meeting-room. They might have been the leading intellectuals of their time, ensconced in a bastion of privilege and spending half their time in imaginary worlds, but like all regulars, across the professions and the classes, the nations and the cultures, they didn't like it when their local was done up. So they moved to The Lamb and Flag. It's a similar sort of place – long and deep, low ceilings, wood panels, snug little tables, partitions and off-rooms, a pub where it's as possible to bump into someone immediately as it is to drink beside them for two hours and not notice them. The two pubs face each other across the two lanes of traffic as if reflected in a mirror that hasn't quite got the hang of reflecting things.

DINOSAURS AND DODOS

I'm going down the cobbled Lamb and Flag Passage where the smokers and the phoners huddle outside the pub. On the way to the Natural History Museum and the Pitt Rivers is a little street behind Keble College with graffiti that's an Oxford institution: REMEMBER WHAT HAPPENED TO THE DINOSAUR!

It's been there as long as I have. I read it as a warning to the university, a *memento mori* by a disgruntled student or academic.

But dinosaurs lived for 160 million years, making their epoch a remarkably stable and successful one. They're a pretty chastening example to our planet-roasting, resource-gobbling, lethally-squabbling species. As well as museums, the science departments are clustered around here: zoology, physics, chemistry, biology, earth sciences, botany, mineralogy, etc. This is an area with probably the densest *per capita* concentration in the world of people who genuinely know about dinosaurs. None of them would have written that, because they'd be too dinosaur-literate. So my hunch is that it was either written by an arts student or academic, or by a passing street-philosopher, fresh from a visit to where we're going now.

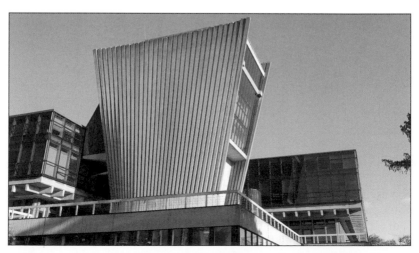

The Natural History Museum was built in 1860. It brought the sciences, then scattered among individual colleges, along with the disparately-housed collections of stones and bones that accompanied them, under one roof. They're separate again today, but now with multimillion-pound labs and departments, and international research-groups. The museum was designed by the Irish architect Benjamin Woodward, working in consultation with John Ruskin, then at the peak of his influence, and his friend Henry Acland. It has the pragmatism of a railway station and the spirituality of a cathedral. The galleries are held up by thirty columns, each made of a different British rock, while the capitals (the top bits, in layperson's terms) are floral patterns, carved after live specimens brought from the botanical gardens. The stone is from all parts of what was then Britain, which includes Cork and Galway. Imperial stones, imperial geology. The sculptors were the O'Shea brothers, paid by public subscriptions which ran out and led to a dispute with the university – which is why they added, in revenge, the faces of certain academics to the animals they carved.

Things I never much think about – God, intelligent design, science generally, nature and industry – are all here in this splendid actualization of the Victorian world view at its richest and most dazzling, but also its most open and curious. What I admire most about the Victorians is how well they dealt with the total reshaping of their world-view. The ground – often literally – was being pulled from under their feet. Excavations had revealed fossils and bones, travel had revealed new species, evolution was threatening their religion, while astronomy had shown them new planets, new contexts in which to place the world they lived in and thought they knew. They had a crash course in science and lived through a time when the old certainties seemed to melt away before them. Henry Acland wrote of how this building would extend our knowledge 'of the great material design of which the Supreme Master-Worker has made us a constituent part'. That's very Victorian – the hunger to understand and the need for mystery coexisted happily in the Victorian mind. They were understanding the world faster than it could be expressed, that's all.

I've read and loved Ruskin for years, and I come here for the sense of him in the view from the galleries. Forget the dinosaurs for a moment – look at the fine, gilded iron leaf on the top of the iron pillar. It doesn't look like a tree but it does what a tree does. The gothic, or at any rate Ruskin's idea of it, is organic. It never tries to hide its materials, to belong to any moment but its own. Ruskin would have deplored a lot of Baudelaire, not least the man himself, but he'd have understood Baudelaire's image of trees as living pillars.

Down below I can see children marvelling at objects labelled 'Please Touch'. They're experiencing how wonder and understanding come from the same place, and may well finish up there too. The Victorians who built this place thought they did. If the term doesn't already exist, let me offer it here: Wonderstanding.

PITT RIVERS AND UNCOMFORTABLE OXFORD

Past the huge slabs of amber with million-year-old insects trying to find their way out, there's a little archway marked Pitt Rivers Collection. It looks like another office. It's easy to imagine a door like this inspiring C.S. Lewis or Lewis Carroll, two writers who loved, and know children love, the disproportion between the door and the room it leads to. In I go. After the bold bright lights of the Natural History Museum, this feels velvety and dark. But only for a moment, because when my eyes have adjusted it opens: a huge hangar with another vaulted roof like a Victorian railway station, with two levels of galleries looking down, wrought iron pillars and golden-lit cases and display boxes. This is an industrial carapace, much less ornate than the Natural History Museum, and has the feel of a station, even a terminus: it's where objects have ended up.

The objects here are arranged typologically, according to use or purpose rather than age or origin. It's a refreshing way of thinking about things – lateral rather than linear – and it's where an adult can discover how to be a child again. The shortest short-cut to a child's sense of unexpected connectivity. But maybe the child can also sense something of the adult world here too: the imperial habit of invading people's countries and stealing their things, sacred and profane. It was once famous for the shrunken heads and the Maori masks, both of which have been returned to their original nations – places where they mean something more than glass-case imperialism.

The real value of this museum is in the labels attached to the artefacts. They are exhibits too. Exhibits of how we look, where we look from, what goes into our looking: the prejudices, the assumptions, the entitlement. The museum knows this, which is why they've kept many of the original labels – so we can think not just about how the world looked when we thought we owned it, but how we thought we understood it. It's a cultural out-of-body experience to see how we described American Indians or Maoris, and how we labelled them by labelling their objects. I take my students here sometimes, and we discuss how seeing is always something conditioned, and it's nice to discuss taxonomy – the process by which we label things as a culture – by showing them real, literal, labels. The labels are actually mirrors, and they need labels too. There's no end to it, but I defy anyone to come here and not emerge educated – not just 'knowing more' (an easy confusion in a university city) but *educated*.

For earthier concerns, I recommend the dentistry section, which curates various drills and hammers and spikes and pliers from the very earliest days of dentistry to the present. After we've done the labels stuff, I show my students this section and watch them grimace. They're thinking: 'well, actually Prof, this looks like progress to me'.... There's no better illustration of the difference between moral progress (no such thing) and technical progress (yes please) than the Pitt Rivers.

What does it most remind me of? Silvester's hardware store. The arrangement is the same, the sense of discovery, of things grouped by use, that serve the same functions though they might look very different: Apollinaire defined surrealism as inventing the wheel, which does the same thing as a leg but doesn't look at all like one. Surrealism is often invoked as shorthand for chaos or disjunction; it's not really, it's a search for different layers and different levels of order and connectedness. The oar or the spade that do what the arm and the hand did; the bowl that does what the hand does, cupped. Surrealism in this respect is a poetic anthropology, and in the Pitt Rivers I can see why the Surrealists spent so much time in museums.

Which brings me to something else, and the Pitt Rivers is a good place to start it from, though the whole of Oxford is implicated: imperialism, colonialism, looting, racism, slavery, pith-helmeted piracy and blood. All the rapacious pillaging hiding behind that genteel and rather languid word 'collecting'. The buildings we admire, the objects we study, the statues and decorations, the paintings, the gold and the silver, the endowed chairs and the professorships – so much of what shines is steeped in a darker history. It's a history that until recently Oxford didn't care to tell, and rarely to acknowledge.

In 2018, a group of students set up 'Uncomfortable Oxford',

tours, lectures, online resources and events to counteract the various dreaming spires narratives: the glories of Oxford, Oxford's finest buildings, Great Men of Oxford, Harry Potter's Oxford, etc.[1] The idea behind Uncomfortable Oxford isn't just to make us reflect on where things came from and at what cost to whom, but simply to 'track and trace' histories that haven't been told. They remind us that we live in a compromised state, but also that history is what we're living now, in the twenty-first century. History doesn't stop at the moment we decide to read about it. We are it: a building funded by an arms dealer here, oil money there, a chair endowed by a repressive state or a Mafia-friendly régime. The colleges and university thrive – and have for centuries – on bequests and donations, and today's alumni offices have the difficult task of making sure those donations keep coming. People remember their time in Oxford – they remember it more the further they are from it. Nostalgia is marketable, and however soft it might be at the edges, the cash it generates in the form of donations and bequests is hard. Many of those donations, then as now, come from human inhumanity in its many forms.

The statues of racists and slave traders, arms dealers and colonialists remind us that our university and our city are mired in history – they don't stand outside or above it. The 'Rhodes Must Fall' movement here in Oxford, like the toppling of statues of slave-traders, colonialists and racists, isn't an abolition of history but its reinvigoration, and is, in its way, a dynamic way of studying once again those parts of our history that had become censored by apathy, ossified and deadened by being ignored.[2] In 2020 Britain, many statues and memorials only registered on our consciousness when they were taken down, not when they were standing up.

If all Uncomfortable Oxford did was make us uncomfortable, that would already be something – there's not enough discomfort here. But in just two years they've opened up so much history and so many new perspectives that they're almost a faculty in themselves.

STREET SHRINE

For the last twenty-one years there's been a bouquet of flowers tied around a tree opposite the museum on Parks Road. They're in memory of Emma Johnson, who died when the car she rode in crashed into the tree in November 1999. Her parents put a new bouquet there every Saturday. Sometimes they got removed, but Melvin and Alison Johnson always replaced them. Melvin died in 2014. The flowers keep coming, for him now as well as for his daughter. There are debates in the *Oxford Mail* about whether this and other roadside memorials distract drivers or trigger passers-by with private sorrows of their own. People write in suggesting cut-off points after which bouquets and teddies and roadside shrines should be removed or dismantled – one year? five? ten? And who decides? I don't have much sympathy for the armchair-legislators because grief bends time into a circle around us, and I'm always moved by small personal memorials like this one. As I see this one most days, it has a meaning for me too, which means it's doing what it's meant to do: a few flowers in a tinfoil vase roped to a tree, fragile but defiant in a city of statues, monuments and plaques.

UNIVERSITY PARKS, MESOPOTAMIA, PARSON'S PLEASURE

Through the parks and over the little bridges, dodging the cyclists who should dismount but don't. Cattle-grids and lifebuoys on poles. The bridges: flat or arched, wooden or made of concrete and iron, they seem to change with the vegetation around them as much as Monet's bridges at Giverney. Come now, as I have, in the spring, it's bright and unseasonally hot – 27 degrees. The grass is high, the bushes bulging. It's full of birds, crowding the eye and ear. It's full of people too, doing the same, and trying to get out of each other's way. There are little side-tracks leading to more little bridges, fishing spots, bathing-places or shelters to smoke and drink in. In the winter the bridges are stark, the greenery either gone or stripped back to its browns and greys. In winter the dominant feeling is of stark lines, not today's soft rounded edges.

On my right is Mesopotamia, the thin strip of land between two waters with a path that connects North to East Oxford and emerges behind the Islamic Centre on Marston Road. On my left is Parson's Pleasure, a legendary bathing-place for university men – women punters had to take a detour. Parson's Pleasure also figures in Oxford's queer history as a place of male display. Researching it, I find a trove of articles about Queer Oxford, and about the photographs, paintings and cartoons of the place. There's a famous painting by

William Roberts from 1930 of men naked, their intellectualism conveyed by one smoking a pipe. Another is about to take a dive. Because Roberts was associated with the Vorticists, an English take on Futurism, the men's buffness is cubist rather than organic. Skinny-dipping Playmobil. Seven years earlier, and ninety-nine years before my visit today, C.S. Lewis bussed in from Headington, borrowed a copy of Benedetto Croce's *Essence of Aesthetic*, and came here for a swim. That's what passes for beach reading around here. 23 May – the water, he says, was 63 degrees. Five years earlier, Lewis had been wounded in the trenches at the Somme. Here at Parson's Pleasure, he wrote: 'Amid so much nudity I was interested to note the passing of my own generation: two years ago every second man had a wound mark, but I did not see one today.'[3]

S.L.O.A.P.

My favourite acronym: Space Left Over After Planning. Sloap. Sloapy. To Sloap. I sloap, you sloap, he she or it sloaps. It's an urban planning term, but it works for time as well as space. There are sloapy parts of the day, sloapy phases of life. A walk can be sloapy, an hour can be sloapy. Like the sloapy hour I've got this morning. A student didn't turn up, so I walk to Marston via the University Parks intending to be back in time for the next class. The hour that had looked so rigidly planned in its little square of timetable has suddenly become *SLOAP*.

There are two kinds of SLOAP. The first is energetic, unpredictable: oddments of space which throw up surprising views, or little locations where energies meet. Every edge different, every vista unexpected. SLOAP can be minutes or hours too. We have square miles and square metres – why not square minutes and square hours?

Then there's dead-zone SLOAP, rigid blocks of nowhere-special with bits in between no-one asked about or thought were important at the time. Grey stuff, filler, universal spores of urban void, ripe for roadcones and doubleyellowlining. There's none of that where I'm going.

Today's SLOAP walk takes me down the side of the University Parks, over a couple of footbridges, down a busy cyclepath through the grass, to the start of Marston. Rows of lucky houses – Edgeway Road and Ferry Road – back onto the meadows. I can see climbing frames and sheds and people sitting outdoors drinking tea in that way many of us who live in Oxford exist in our own homes or colleges: half-private, half-public. My first room was eye-level with the open-top buses on Longwall Street, so close to my desk I could see where the tourists had bought their sandwiches from the napkins; my first teaching-room overlooked the Burger King on Cornmarket; and my first shared rental was on the river in Cowley Place. I'd pop into the garden for a pee because the bathroom was occupied, and find, when I turned, boatloads of tourists waving at me from the riverbank.

Some Marston gardens are so stylishly overgrown that the brambles arch over the fences and join private to public grounds. It's a sudden transition: brief countryside, then brief suburbia. If I lived here I'd be able to walk or cycle almost directly to my teaching room on Banbury Road in half the time it takes me today, though I'd be at the mercy of the flooding. Up the road is a small Russian Orthodox church – St Nicholas the Wonderworker (echoing Acland's 'Supreme Master-Worker' of the museum across the river) – consecrated ten years ago in an old Mission Hall. The new porch is carved like a traditional Russian country church. Newly-renovated, the frescoes are barely dry, and a new iconostasis glows with reds and golds. There's still a skip outside. We're never very far from a skip. Apart from that, Ferry Road is a normal suburban street. On one side of the church is a house for rent, on the other, an old-school car mechanic. There's a special aroma here: incense from the church, exhaust fume, motor oil and cigarettes. You could blindfold me and drop me here and I'd know where I was.

There are no smells today. I have very little time, even if it is SLOAP. Facing each other across William Street are a Londis that, according to the big letters on its awnings, specialises in FRESH GERMAN SAUSAGE, and the Scout Hall. The Scout Hall houses the tenth troop and has been here since 1913. Their slogan is more transcendent: ENGLAND EXPECTS EVERY MAN TO DO HIS DUTY. The Londis seems to be asking rather less of me. I go in and ask about the FRESH GERMAN SAUSAGE. There's no German sausage here, I'm told, in a voice that suggests I've misjudged the purpose of a Londis: this is a general store not a specific one.

Apologetically, I point out that they have FRESH GERMAN SAUSAGE in two-foot letters on the front of their shop. I don't walk around the city asking for FRESH GERMAN SAUSAGE by name. 'Ah,' he says, wearily, as if remembering a very old controversy, 'that came with the shop fittings'. I should have popped to the Scout Hall and offered to do my duty. It would have been easier.

I check my watch. My SLOAP is running out – I have another class in 16 minutes.

SLOAP II

It must be my lucky day: a second cancellation. I check my emails on my smartphone and – yes! – the next tutorial is another no-show. SLOAP on a roll. At this rate, I'm going to buy a boat and call it

SLOAP, and just spend my days sidling along the riverbank near Woodstock Road, ready to pop into college on the rare occasions a student decides to turn up. That's an exaggeration: my students turn up, and they're clever, engaged people I admire and am privileged to teach. But still – an extra hour? That can only mean one thing: New Marston.

Marston Road stretches from the edge of St Clement's to Headley Way, where Oxford's biggest hospital, the John Radcliffe, hulks over the city from Headington Hill. Like most residents, I've spent my share of time at the JR: at the eye-clinic after putting a biro in my eye (essay-marking accident), the hand-clinic (gardening accident), and in casualty when I fell on a glass-topped table and had to have the shard extracted from my jawbone (traditional domestic accident). I've waited here for friends, fetched and dropped people off, and my sister was born there the year it opened, 1972. I remember driving there with my father, then a mature student studying for a diploma, in our Morris Marina in the depths of December, unsure, even aged 4, whether it would get us there without breaking down. When I'm asked why I've only ever bought Volkswagens, I reply: Morris Marina.

Some of my earliest memories are centred around here: we had a flat in Norham Road, in what colleges call 'married accommodation'. The walks I took with my pregnant mother were always SLOAPY ones. My room in college is a few yards from where we lived. I remember the gates into the University Parks, the walk down the path to the lake, then across into Marston, to where I am now. Our frontier was the gardens of Ferry Road, the cattle grid and bike-gate I've just passed.

Before Google Maps gave us drone's-eye views, we made do with roofs and, if we were lucky, towers. From the top of Magdalen Tower in the 90s I'd look west over the protected skyline of classic Oxford. It was a tradition to take guests up there on summer evenings, or students after their post-exams 'Schools Dinner'. Also visible, to the north and north-east, were the JR, the chimney of its clinical waste incinerator, and the towers of Northway, Wood Farm and Blackbird Leys. But looking over Marston and towards North Oxford, what I saw was fields and woods, river-meanders, brooks and pools, all with evocative names like Angel and Greyhound Meadow, Bat Willow Meadow, Water Meadow, Music Meadow.... The green stretched all the way up to the Marston Ferry Road, past Summertown, over and beyond the Northern Bypass.

NEW MARSTON

On the maps, New Marston looks outskirty: long busy roads bending into North Oxford (Cherwell Drive and Marston Ferry Road), Headington (Headley Way) or St Clement's and Cowley (Marston Road). The traffic tells me the same. The JR has its own force field, making this one part of Oxford where the university isn't the master of all it surveys. But the maps are not the territory, because the people of New Marston can get to Oxford quicker than the rest of us. And with pleasanter commutes.

Down Marston Road, past the wittily-named 'Up in Arms' pub (a reference to the community activism that saved it from developers) and a quick stop at St Michael and All Angels church. I pause here not just to admire its modernist/renaissance campanile and its vaguely cubist reliefs and Tympanum, but because it was designed by Lawrence Dale, author of an eloquent and visionary book, *Towards a Plan for Oxford City*. Dale had extraordinary plans for Oxford, but his built legacy is in churches. Three of my favourites are in Oxford. Dale was building during the boom years of council housebuilding – the 30s and the 50s – and his churches were responding to Oxford's new populations. Apart from this one, on the corner of Marston Road and Jack Straw's Lane, there's St Alban's on Charles Street, a genuine backstreet revelation off Cowley Road, and St Francis of Assisi on Hollow Way.

On and around Croft Road, beside New Marston recreation ground, are corporation houses. Like the ones in Rose Hill and Cutteslowe, they're sizeable, light, with front and back gardens and communal lawned spaces between road and pavement. The streets curve or come full-circle in cul-de-sacs. Rectangular plaques above the doors mark their date – here, 1935.[4] I have colleagues who live here: high, square rooms, proper-sized gardens, thoughtful planning and the parade with proper shops. The damp walls, wormy floorboards and windowframes that crumble like pie-crust that have followed me around all my Oxford dwellings aren't a problem here.

At the bottom of Croft Road, before the recreation ground, a shed roof is decorated with Henry the Hoovers. A castellation of smiling vacuum-cleaner drums, the top halves removed and filled with dead or dying plants. There may have been a moment when

it was cheerful, but it started to look scary some time ago, and now resembles something from horror films with haunted puppets. The garden looks onto the recreation ground, so perhaps the feature is intended to warn people off, like Vlad's impaled heads or Mr Kurtz's rows of skulls in *Heart of Darkness*. After the trepanned Henrys, the recreation ground suddenly opens out. It hits first of all with its spread: it stretches in front of me, but also back eastwards, where I can see more greenery, playing fields, a couple of pavilions on mounds. I can't cross over because there's Peasmoor Brook cutting me off – I could follow it down to Parson's Pleasure. The sky is suddenly huge. I can't be more than fifteen minutes' walk from the science area, Parks Road, even St Giles.

I cross, passing groups of parents and children at play. New rides are being built, because small squares are fenced off with warning signs. 'DANGER: BUILDING SITE', around a two-metre square plot with four posts in it. They inhabit that interzone where playground fixtures resemble torture instruments. Nearby, another fence protects four rectangular holes in the ground that look like they're just waiting for coffins. It's all a bit medieval around here today – graves, gallows, heads on walls.

LOST THEN FOUND

Over Peasmoor Brook on the footbridge, past a row of lock-ups, it's secret suburbia again. Is this still Marston? I've never been here. I don't know this yet, but if I walk north along the dramatically-named Rippington Drive, I get back to the join of Old Marston Road and Oxford Road, whose names are reminders that this used to be a between-place rather than a place. For now, I walk down Fairfax Avenue, where the houses are painted in different pastel colours, and come to The Link, which does exactly what it says: links the two halves of this estate within an estate. I do a circuit, and at Salford Road shops I find a locksmith whose name sounds familiar, but which I can't place. I wander on to Arlington Drive and come to Marston Brook. I can't find a crossing and ask the way back to Marston. I'm told I am in Marston (there's the answer to my earlier question, then), and am pointed up the drive. Off Raymund Road, I take a little path to the right, and I'm facing Old Marston.

I know exactly where I am. I was just disorientated by the approach. The reassurance of knowing where I am quickly gives way to the disappointment. It all settles back into the known. I've walked these streets from the Old Marston end and barely noticed them. But because this time I approached from the green fields, the backs of houses and the ominous garden, and because I did so with half a mind in my childhood, hand in hand with my mum, I had this little expedition off the map.

It's like a mist evaporating. Things suddenly reassume their outlines. No more SLOAP. It was good while it lasted. I even remember the locksmith now: he opened my car when I'd locked myself out of it at the Abingdon Road Tesco.

NORTHWAY

I know most of Oxford by now. Sure, there are little corners here and there, new places, new non-places, popping up all the time. But I had the measure of it, or so I thought, until I discovered Northway.

All these years I'd skirted it, or stopped at its edges and turned back, attributing it to somewhere else – Headington or Marston, or the hospital conurbation of the JR. It's part of all of these and none. I'd seen, but without properly placing, its one tower block, Plowman

Tower, and always assumed it was Wood Farm that I was looking at.
While I've always had a good sense of direction, it's never been a
sense of *which* direction.

I'm not sure what prompts me to go there today, but I'm at
Cherwell Drive shops and instead of going the usual route into
Headington, up Headley Way and on to London Road, I decide to
hit Old Headington without hitting the traffic. I turn down Copse
Lane – multi-occupancy houses and maisonettes, with bikes and
cars filling the front gardens. Foothills of the John Radcliffe, so the
people walking by are hospital staff. Like all Britain's hospital zones,
it's multi-cultural, multi-racial and multi-lingual. Despite that it's a
pretty unpromising street, I think to myself as I watch the X13 bus
grinding uphill to the JR. It's even more unpromising when I see a
primary school tucked away behind some houses, advertising its
spaces for events.

Then suddenly – I should be used to this by now, Oxford's
counterpoint of concrete and grass, grey and green – another nature
reserve, wooded and wild-looking, with a disappearing path fringed
with beer cans and marked by an engorged bin. Then a flat field in
a hollow with a townscape that looks like it's come out of urban
Holland. It's the Greensquare development of flats and houses: to
my mind Oxford's most attractive. As if someone has cleared a space
among the 1950s houses, in the shadow of the 1965 Tower Block,
and plonked down a colourful segment of modern Rotterdam, using
the edge of Marston Brook as the Rotte. This is proper design –
low-intensity, eco-friendly, plenty of glass and light, and houses

facing each other across shared spaces rather than turning away and surrounding themselves with barriers. There's a Community Centre with a bar, table-football, vending machines and people eating packed lunches while their children play. *Welkom bij Northway.*

As if that wasn't European enough, Northway Community Field opposite isn't just a football pitch with a playground attached, but part of a flood alleviation system, which catches the water running down from Headington Hill before it flash-floods the houses and shops. I trudge across to see where the water goes – the kind of tunnel with bars across it that marks the start of a child's adventure.

Plowman Tower looms above me and, like all Oxford's tower blocks, has recently been cleaned up and reclad. A parade of neglected shops that nonetheless have an atmosphere about them: the pickled 1950s. There's a closed police station, a shuttered takeaway, an off-licence and a shop with Oxford's most eclectic window-display: cleaning products, royal wedding crockery, a toilet plunger, envelopes, toy cars, a catflap, jigsaw puzzle conserver. Many of the objects have faded behind the glass, and the spaces between them are unnervingly large, as if each thing is the last of its kind. Pitt Rivers minus labels.

SAXON WAY, DUNSTAN ROAD, HEADINGTON CEMETERY

I walk up Saxon Way, my eye caught by a 1930s ferro-concrete community centre. It's now a boxing gym. I've no idea where this road leads. Headington? Classic 50s terraces on a slope, then suddenly the outskirts of a village. On my right is Headington cemetery – one of Oxford's most majestic, if macabre, vistas. Perched on a hill and with views across the city that resemble the opening credits of a dark Scandinavian thriller. Old graves, new graves, a hospital like the Death Star in *StarWars*, and its incinerator chimney. 'What do they burn there?' I asked a consultant friend. I wish I hadn't.

Leaving the cemetery, I spot the tops of a short row of modernist houses. Their architecture fits with the Scandinavian tracking-shot I've just filled up on at the cemetery. They're hidden from the street, but if I climb onto the cemetery gate I can peer over and catch their roofs. There's something brutalist about them, with their grey concrete and windows almost as big as their walls, but they look sleek and inviting. I cross the road and lift myself up to look over. Someone emerges from one of the houses and challenges me.

Things could go either way. 'What are you looking at?' she asks. I tell her I'm trying to look at her house but that it's very difficult. 'Well, you're not coming in,' she says, but tells me about the houses in sparkling detail. I ask her if they're as amazing to live in as they appear. She says yes, despite a few small issues to do with ageing materials. You don't just pop down to B&Q when things go wrong here. The houses were built in 1968 by Ahrends, Burton and Koralek – famous, she tells me, for a building Prince Charles labelled a 'monstrous carbuncle'. Their firm was badly damaged by his comments. She expresses some views about Prince Charles, and they match mine. What can she see from her house, I ask: she can see down to Beckley and the surrounding countryside, but the roar of the ring road is surprisingly loud. As she says that, I realise I too can hear it. There's no escape.

I pass the parish church. I'm not sure where I'm going now – there's a warren of little streets, all pretty unremarkable. Tidy lawns, hanging baskets, *faux*-old houses made with local stone but by Wimpey homes, ornamental wheelbarrows that cost more than real ones. This is more Prince Charles's scene. A man in his late 60s, gardening pedantically with clean gloves and a kneeling-stool, asks me if I can read. He has well-groomed white hair, a pink pastel V-neck – the kind of person they use to advertise cruises or funeral plans, which amount to more or less the same thing, on daytime TV. Because I'm still on a high from the conversation with the woman on Dunstan Road, I assume he's after a chat. I've known more random opening lines in my time. Yes, I can, I reply brightly. 'Then why are you here?' he asks. Oh, it's going to be like this. He gets agitated, jerks his secateurs towards the top of the road, and tells me it says 'Private Road'. I hadn't seen the sign. Maybe there was a hanging basket in the way.

I only mention this low-grade episode of suburban psychopathology because it's the only occasion in my years of walking around Oxford and striking up conversations that I've ever encountered it.

OLD MARSTON

After New Marston, Old Marston feels like a model village. Past the traffic lights off Marston Ferry Road, it's old houses, thatched roofs, stone walls and young parents with pristine outdoor gear: clean wellies, chunky knitwear and children whose traditional names have a hipster twist. The Northern Bypass Road came in 1932, the Marston Ferry Road in 1971, but Old Marston is as intact today as it was when it had its own dialect and its own boat-crossing.

My first stop is the allotments – quite the most untidy allotments in Oxford. Maybe this is where I'll hear the old dialect. A vegetable favela of shanty-town doors and windows, carpets and transplanted indoor furniture. Moth-eaten brassica, leeks, the last of some potatoes. A metal heron on the top of a pile of scrap, ogling a rusty barrow and some sticks.

I see a strange gate with a sign on it. I always read signs, especially signs like this. And I always pay attention to gates and doors – especially ones that don't lead anywhere. This one is made of wood, and has been placed at the edge of the allotments. It blocks nothing, and it opens onto nothing. I can walk past it, over it, around it, and, at a pinch, under it. It's entirely without any gate-value. It's more a statement in gate-form than a gate. Someone

THIS GATE IS NOT AUTHORISED IN THIS
POSITION BY ANY OF
COURT PLACE FARM ALLOTMENT
ASSOCIATION
OXFORDSHIRE COUNTY COUNCIL
(responsible for rights of way)
OXFORD CITY COUNCIL (landowner)
IF WHOEVER INSTALLED IT DOES NOT
REMOVE IT WITHIN SEVEN DAYS from the
date below, COURT PLACE FARM
ALLOTMENT ASSOCIATION WILL REMOVE
IT
18.11.20

is triggered, because there's a laminated notice from the allotment committee threatening that if this gate isn't removed by a certain date it will be – and this is where the *Fawlty Towers* vibe comes in to overlay the Kafka base-note – removed. The theme today has been passive-aggression, tidy borders and property-rights.

Further down, by Marston Rugby Club, I finally see proper gardeners, sharing bulbs and laying them out on their plots. Their boots are dirty and their jumpers have holes in. That's more like it

I push on through the village, past the Red Lion pub and St Nicholas's Church, to the house where Cromwell negotiated the Royalist surrender that ended the English Civil War. Oxford was the Royalist capital. Cambridge was solidly on the side of Cromwell. Having studied at both, I can believe one was Cavalier and the other Roundhead. Oxford paid a price both ways: first because the King confiscated college wealth and melted down its silver for coins, and then because Cromwell's forces besieged Oxford three times. The last siege ended here behind this plaque on the wall of a house that happens to belong to my colleague, the philosophy don at my college.

It gets dark quickly here – the streetlights thin out and I follow a road that gets less and less like a road. The houses are spaced out,

then disappear. There's a path across the fields which takes me to
North Oxford, but I'm aiming for the ring road because I want the
Old Marston/Cutteslowe pairing. It's part of my aim to cram in as
much contrast into as short a walk as possible.

It's a very long walk, as it happens, but I wasn't to know. I hit the
ringroad path. Cyclists, runners with headlamps, walkers with lights
attached to their dogs. I turn left. In about twenty minutes, I'll reach
the footbridge that leads over the Bypass from Cutteslowe.

THE CUTTESLOWE WALLS

Sounds nice doesn't it? Close your eyes: *Cutteslowe...* there's a
pleasant *olde worlde* ring to it. The kind of place Miss Marple might
live. Maybe the walls are cosy little decorative features, ancient
markers of a simpler world, garnished with a little rustic lichen,
clumps of lobelia making their homes in the cracks. Or, to go full
dreaming spires, wisteria languidly climbing honeyed stone.

Open your eyes again: the Cutteslowe walls were nine-foot brick
partitions topped with turning spikes. They were erected by a
developer in 1934 to separate the council tenants of pre-ring road
north Oxford from the inhabitants of his newly-built private estate.
He feared the 'slums' next door would put off potential buyers. The
walls lasted twenty-five years, coming down on 9 March, 1959, after
years of campaigning that united town and gown, socialists, liberals
and tories, against a new kind of enemy: the modern developer.[5]

The Cutteslowe Walls were a *cause célèbre*, and play a role in Oxford's under-exposed radical history. The communist politician, Abe Lazarus, led strikes at the Pressed Steel Factory in 1934 and organised residents against unfit living conditions in Florence Park. He mobilised two thousand people to demonstrate at the walls before being turned away by police and making a fiery speech from a tree. Lazarus had a pickaxe, but when the walls finally came down, it was Olive Gibbs, Labour Lord Mayor of Oxford, who wielded the hammer. There's something to that symbolism: the pickaxe of rhetoric giving way to the hammer of sheer determination. Olive Gibbs and Abe Lazarus: the Bonnie and Clyde of Oxford socialism. But it's Olive Gibbs's mark that I keep encountering in Oxford, and I'll encounter it once more when I get to Jericho.

TARMAC SCAR

I'm standing by the blue plaque where Aldrich Road becomes Wentworth Road. One of the Cutteslowe walls came to the very edge of this ex-council house on the Aldrich Road side. Next door is the double-bay-fronted white house of Wentworth Road. The contrast is still there, and it's stark – even without the puzzling fact of the same road having two names.

A woman comes out and greets me. I ask her how long she's lived here, expecting her to be a recent arrival. But I'm in luck – the house belonged to her grandmother, who was here the day the walls came down. This house is in the iconic photos of Olive Gibbs and her husband, Edmund, breaching the walls, the bricks strewn around where I'm standing now. Her grandmother was one of the crowd. Ann Spokes Symonds, former mayor of Oxford and alumna of my college was one of the first to cross over. She kept one of the bricks, which can be seen in the Museum of Oxford, along with some of the iron spikes.

Oxford Council recently resurfaced the road and stopped on the exact dividing line where the walls stood. The posh end of the road got resurfaced, the council end didn't. That was in 2018, and someone scrawled CLASS WAR on the bit where the brand new tarmac ended and the old frayed plebeian surface began.[6] The border-theme of my walk continues.

Somewhere in the Kafkaesque coils of its municipal memory, the council still observes the partition. I can still see where one surface ends and the other starts, a badly-healed scar, a little class-suture between Oxfords. The tarmacs join in the middle of a white centre-line: on the Wentworth Road side, tarmac and white paint are fresh and distinct; on the Aldrich Road, the tarmac is old and the paint faded. Even the council road-marking machine stopped painting at the frontier.

CHARITY SHOP DOUBLE

In his gloriously nasty novel, *Dirty Tricks*, Michael Dibdin calls the people of Summertown the 'lumpenbourgeoisie'. It's a play on Marx's Lumpenproletariat, but you don't need to know German political theory to realise it's not a compliment. The whole novel is a *tour de force* of misanthropy, but the denizens of Summertown get it especially badly. It's set in the 1980s, and relates the story of a snobby, ageing bohemian Oxford graduate teaching EFL (English as a Foreign Language) for crappy pay. At a dull North Oxford dinner party, he meets the intimacy-starved wife of an accountant who thinks that wine clubs, golf clubs, a BMW and a new conservatory will give him the status he aspires to. A homage to Zola's *Thérèse Raquin*, it's set here, in the fleshpots of Summertown.

I can see why: a shopping parade with M&S, Co-Op, Tesco, a shop specialising in school uniforms (there are several eye-wateringly expensive private schools, 'prep' schools and upper-crust nurseries here), a gourmet ready-made meal company, a Farrow and Ball paint shop, estate agents, French bakeries. A disturbing lack of pubs – just one, the Dewdrop Inn – attests to a suburb where pleasure is taken in private, often behind high gates and probably in conservatories. A big draw in Summertown is the quality of the charity shops. It's the Sotheby's of charity shopping. I wrote earlier that hardware shops were the canary in the coalmine of a community. In the same vein, charity shops are the pulse of its demographic. Its stopped pulse maybe, but still its pulse. In Summertown, I know I'm in a university city, because the books are doggedly annotated for the first twenty or so pages, then unread. The furniture is outstanding – I have a marble-topped console table, some kitchen chairs, and a bookshelf from Helen and Douglas House. I've always found clothes here that fitted me uncannily well – many of them bespoke-tailored, like the ones my grandmother, Bouillon's *couturière*, made for me when I was sent to school in England. I possess a wardrobe of tailored jackets, a suit, and several shirts that fit me so perfectly that I feel she's there, on the other side, using the charity shop, that portal between worlds, to attire me for my adult life.

I'm always looking out for her latest confections, which reach me through the vestimentary ouija-boards of Oxford's charity shops. I'm wearing my favourite jacket right now: hand-made for someone exactly my size, with embroidered cuffs and a silk lining, it fits me perfectly while having been designed for someone else. It strikes me as I write that this is how I feel about my life in Oxford.

SUMMERTOWN

People in North Oxford are, by and large, wealthy, healthy and educated. The postcode, OX2, is shorthand for a certain lifestyle and social class. It's prime academic and retired-academic territory, but also, as Dibdin's novel observed, home to commuters and *nouveau riche*, actors and games-show hosts. A BMW garage completes the look. I know Summertown thanks to the friends who live there, and who don't in any way resemble Dibdin's *dramatis personae*. I visit a friend on Capel Close, who gives me a tour. Because she knows my inclinations, she shows me three things. The first is a new restaurant-café called Pompette (the French for tipsy) on South Parade, where I make immediate plans to dine. The second is a suburban house just off the parade that's been revamped with high gates and new walls, painted to resemble a high-security Florida mansion, with showroom cars parked at rakish angles on the freshly-laid drive. Its garden has been laid with astroturf and has a silver ball water-feature in a white marble pond. Maybe Donald Trump wants to retire here. The third is a narrow path from the edge of Kings Cross Road that takes me behind the houses, behind the playing fields, under Marston Ferry Road, and winds down to the old North Oxford. That's Summertown in three locations.

I remember that Dibdin's narrator disdains the people of Summertown because they have what he wants, and what he spends the whole novel trying to get for himself. Much as I disdained the gentrification of OX4 while being a symptom of it. Years ago I knew Summertown well because I taught at several of the language schools and tutorial colleges (we called them 'crammers') that are based here. I've seen the other side of the EFL and 'crammer' tapestry: over-qualified teachers underpaid to teach overcharged students, while the owners of the school reap staggering fees. The language-school owner in *Dirty Tricks* comes in for a lot of grief, all of it deserved.

I'm outside Costa Coffee on the corner of Oakthorpe Road and Banbury Road, where the language-school students smoke and wait for the espressos that will help them look enigmatic. I had an interview nearby in 1992 with a man with a Russian name and the poshest English drawl I'd ever heard. 'White Russian,' he told me. I was sufficiently well-versed in history to know he wasn't offering me a cocktail, because Oxford has a history of White Russians, notably Cyril Arapov, the photographer who captured the naked male society of Parson's Pleasure in the 1930s. The interview was in a house full of antiques, and consisted of questions about Magdalen High Table, how I would run a college tour, and Oxford landmarks. I was being primed to take students around Oxford, to 'be' Oxford, not just to teach. And wow, did I teach. When the Italian tutor conked out, I took over Italian GCSE literature, and when the Spanish tutor conked out, I took over Spanish. I even taught German literature GCSE. It's what made me the comparatist I am.

Things are changing here in Summertown: there's a new KFC on its way, and a controversial easyHotel is being built as I write – due to open in 2021. I think they're just what the area needs.

LIFE EXPECTANCY: OX2 TO OX4

Oxford has one of the highest life expectancies in the UK, but not all of it. The difference between OX2 and OX4 is almost nine years for men. Six for women. The distance between Summertown and Blackbird Leys, the two poles from which these stats are taken, is just under six miles. That's 1.6 years drop per mile. Oxford's other statistics include the highest rates of intentional self-harm in the country and homelessness rates significantly higher than the national average.[7]

North Oxford is one of the richest parts of the country. Really rich, not just hipster-pub and sourdough bread well-off, or even Summertown golf club and conservatory comfortable, but Mayfair or Park Lane rich, to use terms from Monopoly. Some of the houses on North Parade, Bardwell Road, and Polstead Road come in at three million. And they are magnificent. Blue plaques everywhere: T.E. Lawrence, Tolkien, Walter and Clara Pater. I won't list them – they're on the Oxford Blue Plaque website. The lower parts of North Oxford, between Norham Road, North Parade, Linton Road, the Dragon School and the University Parks, were built for patrician academics and were expensive even when they were built.

Much of the North Oxford/Summertown we know is a direct result of the university allowing academics to marry and leave their colleges in 1877. My own room in St Anne's is the ground-floor dining-room of a Banbury Road house, and when the college was founded, several of these cavernous Victorian homes were incorporated. The house next door belonged to T.H. Green, philosopher and advocate of women's education, whose wife was secretary to the 'Association of Home Students', the college's first incarnation.

These academics and their families required trades and services and shops. North Oxford, formerly fields, cottages and a few farms, adapted. Not all of North Oxford was easeful or moneyed. Sunnymead, between Cutteslowe and Summertown, was 'Soapsud Island', where Oxford's dirty washing came to be cleaned. The proximity of the river meant that commercial laundries and private washerwomen set up businesses here. One laundry was still going into the early 2000s. It was on Islip Road, where I often visit a retired colleague and chat to her neighbour, whose family are Sunnymead going back generations. There are tales of soapsuds overflowing the drains and women carrying baskets of dons' laundry from Banbury Road to the tin tubs of Sunnymead. To think of Walter Pater's smalls and Clara Pater's petticoats, carried up from Bradmore Road (where a house recently sold for £10,000,000), washboarded, scrubbed and dolly-sticked in Sunnymead, before being dried and ironed and returned, is also to think of the social changes that made North Oxford what it is today.

IRIS MURDOCH AND JOHN BAYLEY: A NORTH OXFORD STORY

Think of this as the OX2 counterpart to Doris and Olive's OX4 in 'East'.

In the old days these houses would have been grand; then they'd have been shabby-grand, as the salaries failed to keep pace with the costs of running them. As their inhabitants aged and their active circumferences shrank, it didn't matter if half the rooms were mothballed, a few chimneys blocked, windows painted shut. I knew a few old academics here, fellows *emerita/us* of the colleges, for whom I'd do odd jobs – remove rigor-mortised squirrels from fireplaces, chase pigeons out of drawing-rooms, and, once, remove a wasps' nest from beneath an octogenarian's bedroom window using a broomstick and wearing an antique riding helmet. They were open-minded, cultured, leftish, and, despite the opulence of their homes, frugal. Many were Europeans who escaped Nazism or Communism. One had escaped the Prague Spring. Another had known Evelyn Waugh – she was a founding fellow of my college and one of its English tutors. Then in her 90s, she shared a house in North Parade with her companion, Britain's first woman lecturer in Arabic. They were remarkable people, tough and without anger or resentment, despite having endured plenty of hardship and discrimination.

When I lived on Linton Road I was a neighbour of John Bayley and Iris Murdoch. I was a guest, in the early 1990s, at a party in the countryside they gave me a lift to. Iris's mind was starting to go. They both talked like thesauruses, but hers had missing pages. Iris asked me for my address – the scaffolding of conversation was there, and she wanted to write it down. She took a napkin, and leaned across and took someone's breadstick for a pen. And wrote. John was beside her, waited until she had finished writing, and returned the breadstick to the puzzled party guest and thanked him kindly. Bayley's instinct was to give Iris the sense of being in normality, to build the normality around her. It was very moving to see. On the drive back, a white-knuckle ride as terrifying as anything the St Giles Fair offered, John expressed his disappointment in today's students. He thought they weren't having enough sex, taking enough drugs, smoking properly and drinking enough. Out of politeness, and with no great confidence, I tried to reassure him that they were, that it was all as debauched as before. 'Oh good!' he declared, taking his hands off the driving wheel and clapping with delight, 'Oh I am relieved!', and jumped another red light.

All around them, as the businesspeople moved into the grand north Oxford houses, gravelled and paved their front gardens for their 4x4s, put up security gates and installed alarms, breakfast bars and wet-rooms, the Murdoch-Bayleys held the fort for upper-crust bohemia: their front garden spread over the pavement, taking parts of the fence with it; it looked like a Hokusai wave of brambly greenery. Their front path was hard to make out, but they were there, and continued entertaining with their legendary meals, notably baked beans with anchovies and Birdseye 'Captain's Coins', a now-discontinued range of frozen mini-fishcakes. One of their desserts was Wall's Vienetta, an ice cream meringue they treated as a cake and served gloopy and at room temperature, having been stored in the larder.

WOLVERCOTE VIA PORT MEADOW

Or, as it's called in the Domesday Book, 'Ulfgarcote'. For years I only saw it from a distance, across a parched summer Port Meadow or across a flooded winter Port Meadow, its cattle and horses huddled on shrinking islands, while the Thames held its mirror to the sky. I knew Wolvercote from the Jericho side, on my way to the Perch in Binsey or the Trout in Godstow, or to the bathing-place at the edge of Port Meadow where Castle Mill Stream and the Thames meet.

Today, I've walked down from St Anne's with a towel borrowed from a college bathroom. I wasn't planning this, but it's so ferociously hot that it's impossible to concentrate. I need a swim, but have come at the wrong time – the afternoon free-for-all.

Post-work crowds in suits, students, early-doors pub-goers, stoners. It smells of barbecued meat, weed and burned grass. The pool by the bridge is so full it looks like a simmering stockpot. People are divebombing off the bridge. There's not even space to unfurl my towel by the bank.

I look towards Wolvercote, remembering a bathing-place up there that's bound to be calmer, when something catches my peripheral vision. My peripheral hearing too. Cries of panic and fear, but also spaced-out laughter; the thumping of hooves. It's four frightened horses galloping in terror through the meadow, barrelling through the crowds, over the blankets and smoking barbecues. People scatter, or fetch their children to safety, while a couple of boys on bikes cycle alongside the horses geeing them up like cowboys. It's a good time to be leaving, so on I push, northwards to where Oxford starts to end.

Wolvercote is its own place. I think that's because it's only accessible by way of a couple of roads, First Turn (there isn't a second) and Godstow Road just after the Jury's Inn on the roundabout. But it's not as small as it looks, or as confined – Wolvercote stretches out towards Oxford Parkway, the new station that connects Oxford to Marylebone via Bicester Village Retail Park. On the other side of the ring road, it stretches into Lakeside and Linkside, and its cemetery almost borders on Cutteslowe.

I'm almost alone at the bathing-place. I've worked up a hell of a sweat, and am so desperate to get that hit of cold water that it's only when I've dunked my head in and let myself float on my back that I realise I left my socks on.

Refreshed, and with my 'smalls' rolled in the towel, I explore. By 'explore', I mean I stop for a drink at The Plough for the first time in ten years. It's a resolutely local pub, and all the better for it – the tourists and day-trippers are after The Perch and The Trout, where Morse and Lewis often have their post-case drink. Morse checks the head of his pint, takes a sip, evaluates it, licks the froth off his lips, and takes another, longer, deeper sip. Lewis has orange juice, because he's driving. A bittersweet *bon mot* ensues, because there's always something ambivalent about solving a case: maybe we liked the murderer; maybe we disliked the innocent party; maybe only one kind of guilt was punished; maybe Morse has yet again failed to get his leg over. Lewis (Welsh in the novels, before being turned into a Geordie for Kevin Whately) has a wife and a home to go to, and being a plebeian of good heart, looks at Morse sympathetically from the dull flatlands of contentment. He has to go home to OX4 for his egg and chips. Morse looks into his glass. Has he drunk his pint that quickly? Time for another. The camera pans out, we see the tables outside The Perch, the water foaming under the stone bridge towards Port Meadow, which by my reckoning must be like a rave by now, and the credits kick in. Morse's last case is always himself.

JERICHO

> How long was the peril, how breathless the day,
> In topaz and beryl, the sun dies away,
> His rays lying static at quarter to six
> On polychromatical lacing of bricks...[8]

is what goes through my mind as I come into Oxford from Birmingham New Street and catch sight of the campanile of St Barnabas's Church. Betjeman's middlebrow muse is on peak form, and it helps that the poem's metre is perfectly suited to the rhythms of a slow-moving train.

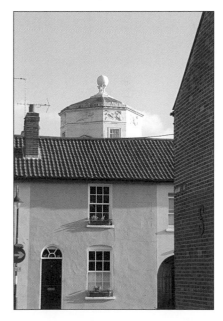

Jericho is the suburb of Oxford called Beersheba in *Jude the Obscure*. It also features in Philip Pullman's *Northern Lights* and one of Colin Dexter's earliest and best Inspector Morses, *The Dead of*

Jericho. Jericho is an Oxford legend, a hidden gem, a place that has lost none of its charm despite losing all of its affordability. When I was a student, it was full of pubs, all of them historic, and catering to the residents of the small, red-brick terrace houses, who worked in Oxford colleges or in local industries, notably the Eagle Ironworks, known as the Lucy Factory. By the mid-1990s, the pubs were closing, which is why so many of the houses are pub-shaped and still have the old brewery tiles at their doors. Houses started being bought by people who wanted to live in North Oxford but couldn't afford it, or by London commuters wanting somewhere close to the station. The Lucy Factory, among whose products are the drain-grilles and manhole-covers in underfoot Oxford, the railings outside the big houses of North Oxford, and library-shelves for the university, closed in 2005 and was demolished for flats in 2007. The Eagle Ironworks were Oxford's last foundry, then became an electrical switchgear company, and finally became the property developer that developed itself.

I leave the station and take the first turning on the right – past the bollards beside the Thatcher Business Centre. Oxford housing is now so densely-crammed into every bit of what was once SLOAP that hundreds of flats are lined up on the west side of the railway track, and a whole housing estate spreads over the east side. I cross a cul-de-sac of new-builds and come to the river. The walk into Jericho from the back is still my favourite approach because of the little bridges and the tangle of waterways. The first bridge takes me out of the estate and onto a messy stretch of stagnant canal. There's

a weir to my left, and houses whose gardens come out to the river's edge. There are a few barges, and it's hard to tell if they're inhabited or not. Not like the spruce ones further upstream. I cross a stone bridge, and I'm on the towpath.

Hang on. This isn't right. The familiar backs of Jericho stretch up ahead – church, houses, boatyard – but something else is there too: long sheets of printed plastic with developer's plans for the area I'm actually looking at. It's uncanny: the real scene is there in the pictures, but interspersed with a square (sorry – 'piazza'), dozens of flats and houses, and some kind of New York-style loft-warehouse occupying the riverbank that is, at present, just space. SLOAP. I'm seeing double: Jericho present and Jericho future. All along the towpath, it's the same, because the developers have crammed the riverbank with huge drawings and slabs of marketing prose: 'retail units', 'community centre', 'vibrant public space'. The obligatory 'hub'.

This backwater (in the best sense of the word), with its little terraces and quiet houseboats, is destined to be jazzed up and hubbed over into a developer's cash cow. It's been going on for years – Jericho has resisted several attempts to turn the canalside into flats, notably in 2008 when Philip Pullman was a big-name supporter of the residents' objections. These plans are better, therefore likelier to get through – though they too have hung over the area for a decade. This is where, in Pullman's novels, the 'Gyptians' live – the boat-dwelling folk who make up the city's travelling sub-culture. So much of Pullman's Oxford, especially here in Jericho, is a kind of re-making of what was there before and still exists. The greatest things about his imagination is the way he creates a universe that's a double of the real – as if he has only pushed it one or two degrees to the side and waited for a new world to coalesce. I'm sure I've seen a few Gyptians around here, notably at The Bookbinders or The Harcourt Arms around closing-time.

MOUNT PLACE, HARCOURT ARMS, ST SEPULCHRE'S

Past the social housing block with balconies overlooking the river at the end of Canal Street, I get to the bridge. Before crossing I check to see that the derelict boat I use as a landmark is still there – yes – and then make sure the man in the barge next door who collects stuff and stores it on a home-made raft of plastic barrels is also in place – yes. I'm still in the Jericho I know, not its developed double. For now. I can see the walkway of planks that leads into his boat, currently covered by a big green tarpaulin. I'm not sure how he and others like him will fare when the New Model Jericho gets built. He doesn't strike me as being 'piazza' material.

Over the bridge I'm in Mount Place. It's nowhere special – a bench on a square paved with concrete slabs, a few trees that look inconvenient but too old to move. There are occasional plans to turn it into something more like another bloody piazza. 'Contoured seating' (what even is that?), an 'arboretum', window boxes, 'crescentic gardens', etc. Thankfully, none of that has happened. The bench is the perfect spot from which to admire Oxford's most beautiful house: it's on the corner of Mount Place and Canal Street, and has distempered walls, green with algae and cracked so as to show the bricks behind it. If St Barnabas is based on the San Clemente basilica in Rome, this house is lifted from the Venetian backstreets. I half-expect to see colourfully-striped *Pali de Casada*, the Venetian poles, protruding form the Jericho tarmac; perhaps a gondola with a shaking oil-lamp; a carnival mask. The place is a bit of a cult in Oxford – everyone knows it, while also thinking they're the only people who know it. A bit like Jericho itself.

The lady who lives there is sharply aware of this, because one day, as I sat admiring it and taking photos, she leaned out of the first floor window and told me how much pleasure it gave people, how she would never change it. Standing in front of it, or running my hands along its walls, I could be in the 1890s. Jude Fawley probably came past this very house looking for Sue Bridehead as she knelt in St Barnabas and inhaled the incense.

I like to sit outside The Bookbinders Arms on Canal Street and watch the boatyard staff come in for after-work drinks, or their clients pop in while they get their barges fixed. Gyptians. I like watching the boatyard at work: half a barge under a scaffolding of tarpaulin, the sound of drills or saws, looking like a patient, conscious but anaesthetised, in an operating theatre. We're near Oxford University Press – hence the name. But today it's the Harcourt Arms I'm visiting – a pub I've been stopping at since I first came to Oxford and 'discovered' Jericho.

I first walked in here in autumn 1991, and found two open fires, a clientele made up entirely of regulars and their dogs, no music and no food. Unless you count pickled eggs, which I do not. All that and Fullers beer. John the landlord was an Oxford legend (he still comes in for a drink), and won awards for quality of his beers without ever being a beer-bore or a pedant of the pint. Today's landlord has similar values, though has transformed the garden, introduced limited but good music, and lets pop-up restaurants do occasional food. Thirty years on from the day I came, it's still the most local of Jericho's pubs. However far away I've lived – and it is increasingly far – it's still my local.

Oxford University Press occupies the eighteenth century Clarendon Building, mistaken by the few tourists who make it here for another college. But the press existed long before that time. Its history is full of political and social turmoil, and its global reach is in itself a tale of the British Empire's tentacular cultural spread – just look at the list of where it still has offices. It has its own museum, and houses the legendary Oxford English Dictionary 'Word Room', where words that have been rejected for use sit on index cards in a vault, waiting for a time they might be admitted to the OED. There's an admissions process for words, just as there is for students, but the words get a few more cracks of the whip.

Jericho plays a big part in my adult life, which is also my Oxford life. On both occasions my parents visited me here, my mother wanted to see Canal Street, the Canal Reach of Colin Dexter's *The Dead of Jericho*. We walked here trying to spot the house where the first murder took place, then the house where the pervert-voyeur lived, then the pub where Morse and Lewis drank (that was The Bookbinders). I then took them to The Grog Shop, an old-style off-licence where there was always some under-the-counter special to be had, often sherry and sometimes home-brew, which they'd pour for you in whatever receptacle you had to hand. You could also drink at the till, which my father liked. It's still there, inevitably under new ownership.

Jericho is where I took my partner for our first meal together, soon after we began 'stepping out' (in John Bayley's phrase). Where else but The Standard Tandoori, a 1970s Indian restaurant with no-fuss food and lapidary customer relations? The Standard is now run by the son of the owner I knew, and he has removed the old seats, the flock wallpaper and the menu board with the missing letters and the flickering bulb behind it. His clientele is different, and so are his prices – that's the new Jericho. As Angharad sat in the Standard in June 1996 and I was upstairs at the gents', the waiter saw his chance to sweet-talk her: 'You're the most beautiful lady I've seen here in...', he gave the calculation some thought: 'at least two weeks'. The place was usually deserted, and often half-lit, unlike today, when you have to book. Try that compliment in today's Standard and you might get somewhere.

Round the back of OUP, opposite Ali's Jericho Store on the corner of Albert Street and Wellington Street, someone has sculpted a quizzical gargoyle out of leftover cement, and stuck it to the wall under a security camera. Like everything else in Jericho, it's a double of something – a *doppelgargoyle* of the ones around the colleges and university buildings.

My favourite micro-SLOAP walk is to St Sepulchre's, a disused cemetery behind a minimarket on Walton Street. The Lucy Factory enclosed the cemetery on three sides, and the factory site stretched back to the riverbank. Red-brick with huge windows and iron pillars supporting station-platform-like glass canopies, it lit up the graveyard at night and filled it with the sound of machines and conveyor belts.

There were little balconies, footways between the factory blocks, Z-shaped fire escapes with gooseneck ladders. In the right light, with the air-conditioning units outside, I could imagine myself in New Orleans. The graves are still there – professors buried alongside porters, knights and dames of the realm lying near college

servants and factory-hands – but now the factory is flats. Just the
names survive – Furnace House, Foundry House – and the old
eagle-topped iron gates on Walton Well Road. The graveyard feels
more haunted by the age of manufacturing than by any of its
underground residents.

Oxford's last examples of socially-mixed accommodation might
be its cemeteries.

Jericho too was considered a slum, and plans were afoot to have
it 'St Ebbed' in the late 1960s. Some of the old dons I knew
considered it seedy and outright dangerous, and would warn me
against going there after dark. Olive Gibbs campaigned against its
destruction, lobbying in London to have the area saved by a local
improvement plan. The trauma and ill-feeling caused by the
clearance of Oxford's working-class centre were still fresh in
people's minds. So while we still have Jericho, it's also a reminder of
what St Ebbe's once was and what it could have been.[9]

UNIVERSITY PARKS, NORHAM ROAD, TRAFFIC LIGHTS

Today, like most days during term, I'm teaching in a room whose
bay window faces the paths I walked with my mother in that strange
interregnum between being an only child and being a first child.
Forty-something years ago. The intersection of Norham Gardens,
Banbirdy Road (as I called it) and Parks Road. My pram's eye view

of the world is now my desk's eye view of the world. When I had chicken pox, broiling in my sheets and encrusted with fiery blisters, our doctor was a gentle, witty man called Dr Livingstone. One of my clearest early memories is of his cool hand on my forehead as I watched black-and-white cartoons. These were the days of house-calls – younger readers may remember them from black-and-white films. The smell of a doctor's bag – leather and disinfectant, and faded cologne on his cuff. In 1998, when I started at St Anne's, I registered routinely with the college doctor, on Banbury Road. It was Dr Livingstone, still there twenty-five years later, and an occasional guest at High Table. Was I going around in circles? Was I trapped in Oxford amber, like the insects in the museum?

Of all the ways I could be in Oxford, this is how I am, now, in 'real time': facing where I lived and walked as a child. I could have ended up in so many other cities. In Oxford alone I could have worked at so many different colleges. Even here, in St Anne's, there are scores of rooms I could have been given. In an hour or so I'll stop writing, switch off my computer, lock my room and walk to that intersection. It's my strongest memory of Oxford as a child – even stronger than my school, the flat we lived in, or Boswells toy department. There's nothing like an intersection to make us feel temporary, to remind us that we're leaving.

Notes

1. https://www.uncomfortableoxford.co.uk/
2. For an account of the Rhodes Must Fall action in Oxford, see Simukai Chigudu: 'Rhodes Must Fall in Oxford: A Critical Testimony', Critical African Studies, vol 12, issue 3, pp. 302-312. https://www.tandfonline.com/doi/full/10.1080/21681392.2020.1788401
3. https://queeroxford.info/2017/09/24/parsons-pleasure/
4. For a useful history of Oxford's council housing, see https://www.oxford.gov.uk/news/article/1636/100_years_of_council_housing_in_oxford
5. For an exhaustive account of the dispute and its social ramifications, see Peter Collinson, The Cutteslowe Walls: A Study in Social Class, London: Faber and Faber, 1963. Also the BBC Oxford site http://www.bbc.co.uk/oxford/content/articles/2009/03/26/cutteslowe_feature.shtml
6. https://www.oxfordmail.co.uk/news/16692123.invisible-wall-old-wounds-reopened-class-war-re-emerges-oxford/#gallery5
7. https://www.oxford.gov.uk/info/20127/health/457/oxfords_health
8. The whole poem, along with a history of the church, can be found on the Jericho Living Heritage Trust page: http://www.jlht.org/st-barnabas-church/
9. For a fascinating and warm portrait of Olive Gibbs and Oxford, see (and hear) Liz Woolley's article and podcast: https://womenofoxford.wordpress.com/2018/02/28/series-2-olive-gibbs-1918-1995/

WEST

OFF THE MAP

The footbridge between Oxford station and the car park on Becket Street marks the beginning of Botley Road. The footbridge is recent. I only noticed it was there when I realised I'd crossed the road without navigating the traffic and the logjammed cars. It never looked new. Maybe there's a company that specialises in tired-looking municipal fittings that look pre-vandalised and pre-weathered and pre-neglected so that people omit to damage or deface them.

I have my 1895 edition of *Alden's Oxford Guide*, updated every year by the Oxford printer and publisher Edward Alden. Aimed at the well-to-do tourist, it's all about colleges, museums, churches and university buildings. No mention of the Gas Works a few hundred yards from Christ Church, or the breweries and the Jam Factory, whose emanations will have been part of the pedestrian's eyeline as well their noseline. No St Ebbe's, no St Thomas's, no Jericho – nothing industrial or working-class. Alden's Guide is the perfect companion because it says precisely nothing about where I'm going.

With this guidebook, I'm the one guiding it.

Alden's Oxford stops at the railway line. I cross the footbridge, lungs full of fumes and ears buzzing with car horns and the scrape/screech of rail-lines. I'm stepping off the map. It's a dizzying feeling, though on reflection that's probably the carbon dioxide hitting my brain. After this it's the Wild West – not a bad way to think of it, because in the eighteenth and early nineteenth centuries Botley Road, this hardened artery of static traffic, was a muddy track where highwaymen and robbers lay in wait. It wasn't even in the same county as Oxford, which meant neither city nor university had jurisdiction here.

A WRONG TURN: BOTLEY

C.S. Lewis obviously didn't have a guidebook when he first arrived in Oxford in 1916, or else he wouldn't have made this mistake:

> I sallied out of the railway station on foot to find either a lodging-house or a cheap hotel; all agog for 'dreaming spires' and 'last enchantments'. My first disappointment at what I saw could be

dealt with. Towns always show their worst face to the railway. But as I walked on and on I became more bewildered. Could this succession of mean shops really be Oxford?

Well, yes and no. No, because Botley was at the time part of Berkshire. And yes, because Lewis was just going the wrong way. Lewis has an attractive habit of taking life's disappointments and recuperating them into belated revelations. My favourite of these takes place further along this road:

> Only when it became obvious that there was very little town left ahead of me, that I was in fact getting to open country, did I turn round and look. There behind me, far away, never more beautiful since, was the fabled cluster of spires and towers. I had come out of the station on the wrong side and been all this time walking into what was even then the mean and sprawling suburb of Botley. I did not see to what extent this little adventure was an allegory of my whole life.[1]

Lewis was writing in the 1950s about the 1910s. A lot has changed. I can't promise anything allegorical, but I'm heading off to find the spot on Botley Road from which he saw 'the fabled cluster of spires and towers'.

The footbridge runs parallel to the railway bridge, so I'm watching the London train nosing into the station. On the west-facing side of Botley Railway Bridge was once written 'Welcome To Oxford – Home of Pressed Steel'. A little jibe from the car plant at the university. Botley Road starts in a dip just beneath the bridge, and until 1979, when it was rebuilt, only low double-deckers could pass. Some vehicles still get stuck there – skip lorries or trucks carrying diggers to one of Oxford's building-sites. I can see the lines and gouges in the concrete of its grimy underbelly.

The raised pavements on either side of the road burrow under the bridge through damp graffiti'd tunnels. I pause here to see the double-deckers pass – there's about six inches between their roofs and the tunnel, and each time they go under I think this is the day they'll have their tops peeled off.

Like much of West and South Oxford, the area around the station is vulnerable to flooding, even with recent improvements to Oxford's flood defences. In 2014, trains were cancelled and Becket

Street car park was a makeshift bus station for the euphemistically-named 'Rail Replacement Services'. Osney and Botley were cut off. That was nothing compared to the 2007 floods, which marked Oxford so deeply that the local papers celebrate the anniversary with pictures that underplay the grimness and the filth and overplay the feelgood dimension of crisis: people 'pulling together', 'community spirit', 'neighbourliness'. Photos of people pouring tea from two-handled teapots and channelling the Blitz spirit – a pastime the English need only a slender pretext for indulging.

The aesthetic side of Oxford's flooding history is seen in charming old prints of men with the 3 B's – blazers, beards and boaters – rowing along St Aldate's, or little sailing boats taking to the meadows. In one 1875 print, a GWR train, ancestor of the one I've just seen sliding into platform 1, threshes the waters of south Oxford as it approaches the station. It all looks adventure-story exciting. All it takes is a few days of rain to realise just how much water still defines Oxford. There are seven rivers and streams passing through a city that's built in a swamp and has spent over a thousand years trying to control the water.

But water gets its revenge after all the years of being blocked up, diverted and filled in; its banks concreted over, its quays knocked down, its working thoroughfares turned into pleasure lanes as the road took over from the river. A lot of river is also covered up, with whole stretches of the Thames and its tributaries underground. It's the Freudian theory of repression illustrated in water.

When we think of floods, we think of our streets becoming like Venice, gondolas and children splashing about in wellies. Most of us don't think of the sewage coming back up, our rinsed-down, flushed-away detritus resurfacing, slopping across our WELCOME mats and leaving tidemarks on our skirting boards. But here in South-West Oxford it's high on the list of everyday concerns. We can even consult the Thames Water water-level internet site, updated every day. It's sandbags at the ready. Osney has been flooded so many times that it was nicknamed Frog Island.

Human beings have an innate sense of borders, and the first border of all was water. At its most basic, it's a border not just because it separates two places, but because crossing it requires doing something different with our bodies. There comes a time in every moment of human development when people decide they need to swim or to climb, dig or fly. Or stay where they are – the decision that thinks it isn't one. The products of the former are the bridge or the tunnel, the plane or the boat. The products of the latter include my spending thirty years here despite thinking I'd leave soon. The water-border came before the security gate or the barbed wire frontier, and water still defines, from some undercurrent in our cognitive mapping, the way we think about Oxford.

At the surface of my cognitive mapping today, however, and just as important as finding where C.S. Lewis stopped and turned, is a trip to Aldi on Botley Road. They do champagne for £11.99, and I'm buying it for a colleague who has just been awarded her doctorate. Aldi also do a £10.99 champagne, but I'm not interested in the cheapo stuff.

BOTLEY ROAD: THE APPROACH

As a result of the 1972 Local Government Act, most of what we think of as West and South Oxford was transferred to Oxfordshire as part of the newly-formed Vale of White Horse District. Hard as it is to imagine today, with the Park and Ride, the bus lanes and university shuttles, the cars and the cycle paths, links between Botley and Oxford were tenuous. History books tell me there was a footpath to Oxford here from 1210, and a causeway built in 1530. Medieval maps even show the floodplains, so today's developers and estate agents can't say they weren't warned. The path and causeway are the ancestors of this road, which was turnpiked in 1767. This made some difference, if only to help highwaymen decide which side of the toll booth to do their robbing. On the west side was open country, farms, and a lot of waterway – a range of escape routes. From the seventeenth to the nineteenth century, Botley had a reputation for lawlessness. Students and townspeople came here to drink, safely outside the city limits. A few pints in Botley and you could be back in your cloistered college in half an hour.

'All this was just fields' goes the saying. It's not hard to believe here, because beyond the built-up spine of Botley Road, it pretty much still is. Behind the retail park are meadows, pylons and water. On the other side of the road towards Wolvercote and North Oxford, some new-build cul-de-sacs, more meadows, more pylons, some allotments and more water. Thanks to its wide-open spaces, Botley was also where fairs and circuses were held, and there was a Butlin's funfair here during World War II. I always thought Oxford was missing a Butlin's, so I feel vindicated to discover it actually had one.

OSNEY 'TOWN': A SWYVER'S VIEW

In Chaucer's Miller's Tale, 'Oseneye' is where a possessive husband, a carpenter called John, goes to work while his young and comely wife Alisoun *swyves* (look it up if you think you need to) the naughty scholar, Nicholas. Nicholas has learned all the curriculum has to teach and is now branching out into astrology, claiming to be able to predict the weather – a useful skill here in West Oxford. Like many people who claim knowledge of astrology, his motives are erotic and pecuniary. He warns John of an imminent flood, larger than Noah's, and persuades him to sleep in a tub hanging from the roof of his house, the better to escape and float away.

While John sleeps in a tub in the air, Alisoun and Nicholas get on with earthier pleasures. It's a classic tale of lust and gullibility, the plot as complicated as it is bawdy. A second amorous scholar, Absalom, emerges to vye for Alisoun's swyvings. She promises him a kiss out of her window, out of which she instead sticks her arse, and Absalom kisses what the Miller calls her 'ncther eye'. Nicholas, wanting to humiliate his rival, wants a piece of this action. Out of the window he pokes his own arse, and for good measure 'let[s] fle a fart, as great as it had been a thonder-dent'. Absalom is pretty angry now. Armed with a burning poker ('his iron hoot') he smites 'Nicholas amydde de ers'. Nicholas cries out 'Water! Water!', John is woken and thinks the flood has begun. He falls from his hanging bathtub, breaks his arm and everyone laughs at him. And we wonder where *Carry On* films come from.

Chaucer loves the moral-shaped tale, but I'm not sure there's a moral in this one. As for the Miller himself, he doesn't seem bothered: 'The tale is doon and God save all the rowte'. I enjoy a bit of swyving and smiting as much as anyone, but I especially like how the story presents the worlds of 'town and gown' as connected by lust and appetite and ribaldry, and how flooding is presented as an Oxford anxiety as well as a Biblical terror. The threat of water defines today's Oxford, where the place I'm standing – East Street – is one of the first to be flooded when the rivers overrun. Rereading The Miller's Tale in 2020, as a prelude to my Aldi trip, I'm struck by how many of the 'natural' disasters that befall humanity as religious signs, understood symbolically, continue to befall us as environmental ones. But today we understand them literally, because understanding them literally is our last chance.

SEVEN BRIDGES ROAD AND OSNEY ELECTRICITY STATION

Under Botley Bridge there's a little weir where a heron eats calmly from a rolling buffet like a customer at a sushi conveyor-belt. The traffic thunders overhead at the rate of 25,000 vehicles per day.

A few steps along from the heron, across the river, is Osney Power Station. Its front is on Arthur Street, but the back is the best way to see it. A handsome, low-key, Victorian industrial building with a façade of polychrome brick and elegant arched windows. Built in 1892, this was Oxford's first electrical power plant. It closed in 1968, and the university bought it for the engineering department. This is probably what stopped the building – still unlisted – meeting the same fate as so many other relics of Oxford's industrial past. When the engineers relinquished it, it was used to store artefacts from the Pitt Rivers and the Museum of Science. It was bought in 2019 by the Saïd Business School, consolidating its grip on West Oxford. But the building will be preserved, and hulks comfortingly over this narrow stretch of river, where, with the right light, the right water, and the right drink, I see its reflection picked out in canal-water and fantasise myself in Bruges.

The first electric lightbulb was powered here in Osney, and the electricity station is the subject of a bumptious mock-heroic ode by the young Hilaire Belloc. In a rare instance of up-to-date thinking, Oxford university's Newdigate Prize poetry competition set as its theme for 1893 'The Benefits of The Electric Light'. Here are four lines:

> Descend, O Muse, from thy divine abode,
> To Osney, on the Seven Bridges Road;
> For under Osney's solitary shade
> The bulk of the Electric Light is made.[2]

LITTLE GIFS OF THE PAST

'Seven Bridges Road' is what Botley Road used to be called – the clue is in the name. My 1895 *Alden's Oxford Guide* is full of excitement about the advent of electricity. Electric light adds to the sightseeing day, and extends the convivial nights. All the adverts for the posh hotels now feature 'Lighted by Electricity' in bold letters, alongside the reassuring words 'Carefully Selected Wine Cellars' and – my favourite culinary compliment – 'Irreproachable Cuisine': defensive yet defiant. English cooking in a nutshell. Perusing the old adverts I also notice how many of the upper-crust hotels boast of having dark-rooms, which tells me how the mass-production of cameras changed the way tourism was experienced.

I enjoy the adverts in old guide books and magazines. 'Escape with Gertrude!' proclaims one, before specifying: 'the horse-drawn narrowboat'; there's also 'Willey's for willing service!' (newsagents) and the country's first Oxfam shop: 'the most interesting shop I've seen... you have everything from cameos to chessmen'. Those three are from the 1958 Alden's guide. They're little GIFs of the past: short, dynamic, self-contained animations of another *now*. Tellingly, neither of my Alden's guides mention the source of all the electricity that so suddenly transformed Oxford. It's as if electricity suddenly appeared, an Act of God, like the gas that came from the gasworks a short walk from Christ Church, unmentioned in guidebooks despite having been there from 1818 to 1960.

THE WATERMANS, THE PUNTER AND THE BARGEMANS

Three names, one pub: one old name, one new name, one fictional name. At the end of East Street is my favourite West Oxford pub, The Watermans Arms. It turns up as 'The Bargeman's Arms' in John Wain's novel, *Where the Rivers Meet*, an underrated novel by an underrated writer.

Wain was a poet, novelist and critic, and Professor of Poetry here between 1973 and 1978. The novel maps social change in the city from 1926 to 1933, and starts here in Osney, at The Bargeman's Arms, where the narrator is the son of the pub landlord and landlady. He is part of the 'other' Oxford: his father works in one of the breweries, and though one of his uncles is a college servant, the university is, to him, 'the region known vaguely as "the Colleges"'. The book opens with Peter Leonard, the narrator, rushing home from Iffley Lock before six. It's quite a distance. I make a similar journey from Iffley Fields to The Watermans Arms when I meet people off trains. He follows the river down past Christ Church Meadow, to Folly Bridge and Abingdon Road, reaching the towpath to Osney Lock just as the bells begin to toll six p.m. In Peter's 1920s Oxford, as in my 2020s Oxford, the bells toll loud and they toll long. It can take five or ten minutes for the various spires and towers and belfries to finish ringing in six pm. Peter makes it home in time because the bells are still pealing – 'it hasn't gone six yet, honest, Mum'.[3] Even after thirty years here I still get that Oxford sensation Wain describes: of lateral rather than linear time when the bells start up. They seem to be arguing about the time rather than telling it, and while they're at it we have a few extra minutes to put the kettle on and make tea, or walk from the station to the Watermans Arms and get a pint lined up.

Wain knows the costs as well as the advantages of social mobility, and I respond to his books because they tell me something about my father's world, and about his relationship with his family, his class and his people. Who are my people – or would be, if I'd been allowed to know them. There's a symbolic moment early in the book when Peter and his brother Brian, aged 14 and 16 respectively, make their life choices. Or do the choices make them, as so many things we call 'our' choices do? The latter, I think. Brian leaves school and goes to work in the Morris factory, then just a few years old, while Peter stays on at school and is picked out as scholarship material. Soon, Brian gets a second-hand Bullnose Morris and starts his adult life in the *milieu* he was born in. Peter gets a place at 'Episcopus College' (Wain himself went to St John's). The journey from The Bargeman's Arms to his college – a journey of half a mile – is described with poignant attention to the widening gap opening between himself and his parents.

Oxford is not a big place, but it contains many kinds of distance. City of tiny chasms.

BRIDGE STREET:
THE HANDS IN THE WINDOW

The Watermans Arms was one of my locals in the early 90s. I knew John Wain's poems back then, but not his fiction. I like to think he might have been there when I was. I was writing my doctorate and staying, in the usual *mise-en-abyme* of sub-sub-sub-letting that goes on among students during vacations, on Bridge Street. The pub was basic, had decent beer, food one never tried, and a pinball machine hogged all day by the local pinball wizard.

In 2010 it was taken over and renamed The Punter. The Waterman was founded in 1871 to cater for those who lived and worked on the river, and spent almost 130 years with a perfectly good and meaningful name. Names are, in their own way, environmental matters because they are the places in everyday language, rather than in reference books and archives, where the histories of where we live can still be imagined. I think they should be protected – listed in the same way as buildings or green spaces. But what am I complaining about? The food is excellent and the beer is good. Besides, an afternoon at The Punter/Watermans Arms, watching the barges changing level to the sound of sluicing water, is one of the best things Oxford has to offer.

Despite the floods and the traces of floods – sandbags, watermarks on front doors, cellars too damp to use – Osney is charming and central and therefore expensive. A few doors from where I was staying on Bridge Street was Woodwards Bakery. It shut in 1998 and had served Osney since 1882. If I got up early, or didn't go to bed at all, I'd be able to smell the bread baking from 4 am – idyllic all year round, but especially in the summer when the days can't wait to get started and don't want to end. Bridge Street was once Osney's commercial centre, and I can still tell from the size and height of the windows that many of the houses were shops.

One shop closed in front of my eyes. Well, that's how I remember it.

Usually I arrive too late. The corpse of the business, the café, the factory, the farm, the shop, is cold. Here I watched it expire. One day it was a local grocer's, next day it was a house with a curtain drawn across the empty display window. One of my most carefully-curated memories is of walking past very late and seeing a pair of hands empty the shop window. Magician's hands,

puppeteer's fingers, sweeping the stage clean. Things disappeared, but in this trick they never came back. That was the trick. But maybe I imagined it all. I was also, at the time, studying the avant-garde puppet theatre and shadow theatre of the 1890s. It could merely be an academic article I wrote that crossed into my dream life and grew there. I just know that at the beginning of the summer, it was a shop, and by the autumn it wasn't. The memory has a resinous quality – it's not sharp and hard like a fact, and nor is it soft and hazy like something imagined after a few pints at the Watermans. But it's there – a pair of hands against a black backdrop, sweeping the stage clean. It's a response to having been in Osney just as things were turning. Turning where? Turning to what?

The answer is a few hundred yards up the Botley Road, where the big shops we usually think of as 'out of town' line the road out of town.

DRIVE-BY SHOP GAME

Aldi, Waitrose,
Carpetright, Screwfix,
Carphone Warehouse,

Homebase, Wickes...
DUNELM!

One of the games I used to play with my children when they were small was the 'Dreary drive-by shop game'. It's very basic: as I drove past each of these big chainstore nowheres, they would call out the shop names and I would feign, nod by nod, blink by blink, to fall asleep at the wheel while the children, giggling, prodded me and shouted at me to wake up. The climax of the game was Dunelm, the killer blow, where my head would fall forward – out for the count, in the clutches of Hypnos, god of sleep, himself – and they would scream in terrified hilarity.

They're now 15 and 17. They don't like my music or my jokes any more, but this is the only one of the childhood Dad games they still enjoy. So obviously I play it as often as I can. When the day comes for them to drive me around, I will demand to play it with them and together we will bend Time.

OSNEY LOCK AND OSNEY MARINA

From The Watermans, I watch the barges coming in and out of Osney Lock. The boating folk sometimes wave, embarrassed to be on display. In the summer they have their whole living rooms on deck or on the roof. Tables and chairs, barbecues, children's toys, cats and dogs. On winter afternoons I see the glow of their lamps as they eat or read or watch TV. It's like walking down the street and peering into people's living rooms, except here it's the street that's moving. Their cabins have the same colours, and the same soft intimacy as Dutch interior paintings. But with packets of biscuits instead of lustrous fruit in bowls and cans of beer instead of bright milk in pails.

I'm still heading to Aldi, but I've taken the long way around. I cross the next weir and pass the lock-keeper's house with its neat little garden. There's been a weir in Osney since 1227, and a lock since 1790s. A new building houses Osney Lock Hydro, a community-owned electricity generating scheme that echoes, across a few metres of river and 140 years of technology that's changed less than we think, the original electricity plant. Behind Osney Lock Hydro I look into the back gardens of Bridge Street. The water laps at their lawns. I can see footballs, a trampoline, a basketball-hoop gibbet missing its net. Across the weir there's a miniature dock serving Osney Mead Industrial Estate.

A towpath follows the river south. The railway bridge and Osney Marina are nearby. Osney Marina is on the site of the old Abbey, some rubble of which remains. A derelict mill, abandoned since 1945, stood here until it was developed into flats in 2011. The flats look good and the mill's façade is preserved, though the area was shaken by a bizarre explosion nearby, on Gibbs Crescent, in February 2017. For reasons still unclear, a resident hoarder blew up himself and his collection of car parts on Valentine's Day. Deliberate or accidental, all we know is that relations with his neighbours were strained, and that he was the only fatality. Walking past a day or two after, I could still smell the fire that followed the blast. One side of the building was gone, the roof was about to collapse and I could see scorched wallpaper and curtains billowing out of blown-out windows. It was an odd sight in this picturesque bit of town, among the barges and the boats, and the joggers, walkers, cyclists enjoying the Thames Path. So Gibbs Crescent is not quite a crescent any more – three years on the damaged block has been removed and the broken edges painted over and tidied up, though I can still see the lines where the floors used to be.

Today, there's a couple canoeing precariously past the marina in a sturdy inflatable. A barge called Godot is moored on the near side of the river. There's also a small trailer nearby, a wooden pod the length and breadth of a king-size bed: no engine, no deck, just a room on the water which can be attached to a barge the way you'd hook a caravan to a car. I peer in and it is indeed a floating guest bedroom, but the craft it belongs to is nowhere to be seen.

The path is narrow and the other side of the river dense with trees. The air is humid and there's a late-summer straggliness to all the greenery. I almost forget that on the opposite bank is a huge shopping centre, an ice rink and a major road artery. Until the trains come: their far-off build-up, something rumbling, muscling in on the silence, getting louder and louder; thrumming underfoot; then the little metallic details I can only hear when they're near – screeching, scraping, clattering – and the Paddington train rattles across the bridge above my head.

OSNEY MEAD INDUSTRIAL ESTATE

There's another reason I brought Alden's *Oxford Guide*: Osney Mead Industrial Estate is where Alden's finished up before they went out of business in 2011. Their building here has been derelict since 2008, and is due to be bulldozed, like most of what's around me now, to make way for a huge university development.

The history of Aldens is a part of modern Oxford's history: founded in 1831 to publish anti-slavery pamphlets, the company began on the High Street, where my 1895 Alden's Guide was printed. By 1958, printing was done on Binsey Lane, off Botley Road. The company moved to this purpose-built office in 1965. Osney Mead Industrial Estate was created after a public enquiry in 1961. At the time it was a glimpse of the future: a business zone close to the station and the road out of town. Just don't mention the flooding. As well as Alden's, Blackwell Scientific Publications moved here, along with the *Oxford Mail* and *Oxford Times* and the local builders Knowles – a name, like Kingerlee, still seen on the building projects around the city today. Only the *Oxford Mail* and *Times* are still here. The Bodleian library has its digital offices here, and tried in 2007 to create new storage facilities on this estate. Planning was refused, and the facility was built – all 153 miles of shelving – on the outskirts of Swindon. The engineering department has its Thermofluids institute in a high-tech and very secure site abutting the river. It's where one of my friends works, and last time I went they were testing driverless cars and heat-resistant aeroplane engine components.

On the riverbank side of the estate, the Ruskin School of Art has a large hangar housing studios and used for degree shows. It's very bohemian, with tents and makeshift bars outside, and avant-garde artwork inside. A contrast with the Kings Centre next door, a purpose-built business and conference centre, whose lanyarded attendees smoke outside in all weathers. Behind the engineering lab there's a Chinese import/export company, a gym and a Booker Wholesalers. I've tried to go in to take a look around, but the security is even tighter than the Thermofluids lab.

The university, which owns the land, calls this 'a largely under-utilised, 44-acre site in an important area of Oxford'. It's true that it's haphazard and bitty. It's true too that it never took off. Businesses were drawn here with the promise of a new road. The new road never came – hence these husks of big companies interspersed with small quick-build offices and indentikit units. It's cheap yet central. There's only one distinguished building, the *Oxford Mail* HQ, whose low slung, Nordic-looking offices were spoiled when they added a yellowish-grey-brick wall and a car barrier across the front. That too is slated for demolition. We'll have to wait until it's gone before we can appreciate it.

The cheapness and scrappiness of the estate has advantages: it has, at the last count, over seventy small businesses, many of them operating from industrial units at the Botley end. There's a famous video game company, Rebellion, along with software companies and a company that makes beamlines and monochromators for international laboratories. Behind these unassuming units, tens of millions of pounds are being made. There's also an old engineering company which is now a coffee roastery, car hire firms, roofing contractors, a state of the art recording studio, a couple of charities, NGOs and a hairdressing school. Not to mention a gourmet fish market and restaurant, and Oxford's oldest butchers. Both used to sell in the Covered Market, but moved here. The 'under-utilised' claim is quite a bold one, because while it's true that it's never crowded – on the contrary, it's a good place to go and stroll and see nobody – hundreds of people work here and hundreds more use it every day.

All this makes for a lively and varied cross-section of people: arty types, suits, librarians and archivists, hipster coffee-roasters, international scientists, aeronautical engineers, builders, chefs, computer wunderkinds, hairdressers, journalists, charity workers, fishmongers and butchers, and a diaspora of small shop-owners replenishing their stock at Bookers. Musicians and radio presenters can occasionally be spotted heading to or from recordings. It's like the city centre's old self, a memory of the days before it was taken over by chain stores, food outlets and souvenir shops. I think of it as an exiled

High Street that has secretly regrouped and adapted to a new habitat.

The fishmonger is the best in Oxford. A mound of fresh fish and shellfish on top of dripping ice, and freezers full of marine exotica. Smoked fish, vegetables, French chickens, cheese, and a selection of wines. Upstairs, they cook a choice of two fish dishes a day, and fish and chips on Fridays. I order and pay downstairs in the shop, and take the receipt upstairs to a busy, gleaming, two-chef kitchen. Today it's mussels and chips, Belgian style. I choose a table. It's ex-office furniture, and the square, industrial unit windows overlook the smokers around the *Oxford Times* building.

Next door to the fishmonger is… Aldens. And it's bustling. But that's because this is Alden's the butcher, founded in Oxford in 1793 and run from Eastwyke Farm in South Oxford – a ten-minute kayak ride from here. They moved here from the Covered Market and their elegant old shop sign now adorns the top of their ultra-modern red-brick industrial unit. It looks both out of place and beautifully fitting. Their vans are parked outside the way the old carts would have been, ready to take their deliveries to the colleges and halls of the university.

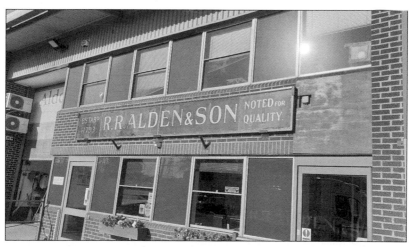

Behind the *Oxford Times*, in the shadow of a huge pylon, is a concrete enclosure marked out in spiked aluminium fencing where the tour buses go at night. After a day of ferrying tourists around the dreaming spires, the buses come to this anonymous edgeland and sleep.

THE FLIT OF A BUTTERFLY

Who knows when the new development will take place, or when all these businesses will have to move out? It's likely that several of the university's big building projects will be delayed or even cancelled. I hope so. The infopanels explaining the 'Osney Mead Masterplan' have a new kind of humanity I'm in no hurry to see: uniformly white, young, thin, sporty and hetero. Where there are same-sex couples, it's underscored that they've just been doing healthy exercise: two blonde women with tied-back hair holding water bottles; two men with bikes and sports bags. It's implied that the women are discussing fitness regimes, and the men international affairs, though not polemically.

The sketchy riverbank is, according to the masterplan, a gravel path with a glass barrier. The kind of trees favoured by committees are planted at mathematically precise intervals: fluffy, far too green, and of indistinct species. The buildings are sleek grey boxes laid out in a grid. There are no people of colour on the panels. No-one is partially-sighted or requires a wheelchair. In terms of lifestyle choices, no-one smokes, or eats on the hoof, sips from a can of lager or is overweight; no one is badly-dressed or scruffy, or has their shirt hanging out. Every 'Masterplan' has its master-race. It's a vision of the kind of society dreamed up by people who use the word 'hub' a lot.

If Osney Mead Industrial Estate is still there when you read this, go and eat some fish and have a coffee, walk around and breathe in the place's transient charm. Go and look at the old Alden's publishers building, and try to spot the sign on the front near the doorbells which gives you the company's phone number with Oxford's old dialling code, and – *memento mori* of what the future used to look like – the fax number. In a city like Oxford, so full of ancient pasts so carefully preserved, there's nothing quite so gone as the recently-gone. Look out for the mossy carcass of an old sofa by the bank between my friend Budimir's lab and Lung Wah Chong Wholesalers. It's been there for years and in the summer it's dry enough to sit on and listen to the pylons hum. If the new development is there, peopled with Aryans of the Algorithm, take some pictures for me and I'll update this section of my book.

I leave Osney Mead via Ferry Hinksey Road, having bought some smoked anchovies. They'll go well with the Aldi fizz. Oxford

isn't over yet, but it's starting to thin out. Pylons, more edgeland and empty sky. A few more minutes and I'll hear the ring road. Richard Mabey called this sort of landscape the 'unofficial countryside' and it's a good way to think about it: a place where town and country are in perpetual but friendly dispute. It's the inconclusiveness of the dispute that makes the place. East Oxford seems to go on endlessly, but West and South end abruptly. The pylons have their own itinerary, which goes at a 45 degree angle to Botley Road, up towards North Hinksey and beyond, to Raleigh Park, Harcourt Hill and Cumnor – places with the classic views of Oxford painted by Turner and evoked by Matthew Arnold and Thomas Hardy.

Ferry Hinksey Road is named after the old village of Ferry Hinksey, now split into South Hinksey and North Hinksey because there's no ferry any more. It survives, like Marston Ferry Road, in the name, and some of the streams still exist, albeit thinned and diverted and shallowed. In wet winters they overrun and in dry summers they poach algae and breed midges. 'Ferry': the word conjures up great white oceangoing vessels. Here it meant a small boat designed for people and livestock, rowed or pulled by a tow rope from one bank to the other. The contrast between Oxford on the one side of the Isis and Hinksey and Botley on the other has been a commonplace of literature and painting for hundreds of years. There are watercolours and etchings of the spires and towers seen from this side of the river, or from Bulstake Stream nearby. Laurence Binyon, of 'They shall not grow old' fame, has a very tired poem set right here. I'm not going to quote it – I'd fall asleep at the keyboard – it's a literary Dunelm.

If I could harness all the energy spent mourning the English countryside, I'd be able to power a city. These books and images emphasise the pastoral, and are peopled with the kind of human beings writers liked to call 'swains'. In 1872 the *Imperial Gazetteer of England and Wales* described 'tottering, time worn Hinksey':

> This most Arcadian village, as secluded as a wood pigeon's nest, as tranquil as the grotto of Silence, the home of none but simplest peasantry, is scarce the flit of a butterfly from Oxford, that great laboratory of mind […] Happy Hinksey!-the tree of knowledge is still fatal; and whoever tastes of its fruit his state of paradisiacal simplicity expires. Once more then happy Hinksey ! Up and down its stony lanes, and by its limpid, lightfooted stream, the only babbler to be heard in the place, along its grey, mossy bearded, mouldering walls, I wander for hours through a solitude as deep as that of a savannah.[4]

Breathy and purple as this passage is, there's still enough around here to see what the author meant. I especially like his way of measuring distance – the flit of a butterfly that covers, nonetheless, a huge social and cultural separation. It's the tug of tow-rope on a long-gone ferry between the banks of two worlds.

ELECTRIC AVENUE, OATLANDS, WILLOW WALK

Electric Avenue, Osney, is hardly Eddy Grant's, Brixton's landmark street, but I always sing it as I pass. A dormant earworm from my schooldays. 'Avenue' is a misnomer – it's a couple of car hire firms and a company that leases theatre equipment. The 'Electric' in the name comes from the small, fenced-off, electricity substation that abuts it. There are small pylons there too, in contrast to the giant ones that start on the industrial estate and push out across the fields. It looks like a nursery for pylon toddlers, a buzzing pylon crèche. The parents hulk skeletally nearby.

The path here is overgrown, with ditches on either side. I know I'm on the right track because it's barely a track. I cross a metal footbridge over a sludgy stream and in front of me is a majestic pylon. Its scale is breath-taking. This one isn't fenced off, so I can walk right up to it and see the iron sheeting, the rivets, the little

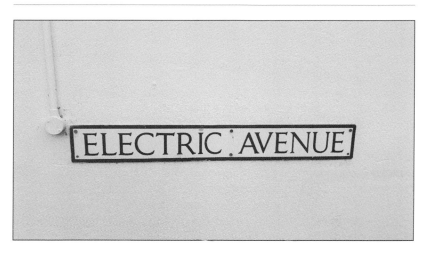

patches of lichen. A date painted in yellow: 24/9/93. In front of me is the wide-open space of Oatlands Recreation Ground; up ahead, Seacourt Nature Reserve. I've often seen it submerged in water. Under a hard winter sun and blue sky, it's beautiful: geese and ducks perched on the playground fittings, pylons threading their cables over the trees and houses towards North Hinksey and beyond.

This is pylon territory. The pleasure comes from the contrast between their geometries of metal and cable and the messy organics

of the bushes and trees. It's full of wildlife and vegetation. I could fill my rucksack with blackberries today. I'm in the city but the city is ending. The ring road sounds sharper, more distinct. To start with, it was like a waterfall, an almost soothing sound-blur. As I get closer, the noises separate out – cars, lorries, motorbikes, different speeds, different revs, tyre-suck on tarmac, tyre-slush in rain.... It stops being restful and instead becomes jagged and distracting. If you want to hear the difference between background noise and foreground noise, walk slowly to and from a ring road.

At the corner of Oatlands and Seacourt Nature Reserve, I stop and turn back for one of the most satisfying sights this part of town offers. It's a niche pleasure, but – trust me – a real one. Looking south east through the last pylon before the retail park I can see a line of pylons, one inside the other, perfectly framed – on and on, deeper and deeper until the eye gives up. Russian Pylon dolls. I always try to take a photo, but the only way of enjoying that dizzying fractal feeling is to be there.

'LITERARY GIANTS TRIED BUILDING A ROAD'

Give or take a few 'executive' family homes and private cul-de-sacs, North Hinksey is seventeenth- and eighteenth- century England. Pale stone houses, thatched roofs, wooden beams. A pretty little church and, last before the ring road, a graveyard designed for the wind to whistle through. It has the feel of deep countryside: no shops, a tiny school, a community noticeboard with notices on rusty drawing-pins. A pickled English village a few minutes' walk from a large McDonalds, the retail parks of Botley, the West Way development of shops and flats, and a Premier Inn that looms, at once threatening and bland, over the ring road. There's a shortcut from North Hinksey to the A34 at the Botley Interchange, so villagers can pass seamlessly from country idyll to convenient commute.

I've come for 'Ruskin Cottage', opposite The Fishes, a once-rural pub with a car park full of silver BMWs, Teslas and Range Rovers. A seventeenth-century cottage with a gabled thatched roof, Ruskin never lived here, though he commended it in his writings and in his lectures. There's a plaque, but also a notice pointing out wearily that it's not a museum. The owners have obviously had their fill of Ruskin groupies.

The plaque on the cottage refers to one of Oxford's most peculiar escapades. In 1874, Ruskin decided that North Hinksey needed a proper road linking it to Ferry Hinksey. He saw an opportunity to teach students what a proper country road should look like: sensitively built, useful and harmonious. It wasn't just about education and infrastructure, but about public health – he wanted to improve sanitation at a time when cholera was a big problem in Oxford's poorer areas. He picked a bunch of undergraduates he felt would benefit from the 'pleasure of *useful* muscular work'. The plaque which quotes him misses out the italics. They're important – Ruskin disliked sport, and called Oxford 'a mere cockney watering place for learning how to row'. He couldn't understand how, with so much still to be done in the world, people chose to expend their energy and strength in pointless competitions. Put like that, it's a pretty persuasive view.

So it was that near this cottage, a group of upper-class under-graduates (there being no other kind back then) set to work with pickaxes and hammers, spades and wheelbarrows – objects with which they were probably unfamiliar. It was hard, dirty, thankless work: breaking stones, levelling ground, draining soggy earth. It was also controversial – gentlemen didn't sully themselves with manual labour, especially with such a ready supply of *swains* around.

People came to watch and mock. The *Punch* cartoon satirising them shows people of all classes, including children, lolling around laughing at the students. It was accompanied by a little ditty:

Scholars of Ruskin, to him be true.
The truth he has writ in the *Stones of Venice*.
May be taught by the Stones of Hinksey too.[5]

Haha.... It's meant as an insult, but it inadvertently gets to the core of the greatness of Ruskin's vision: the connectedness of the social and the aesthetic. In *Stones of Venice*, he writes:

> We want one man to be always thinking, and another to be always working, and we call one a gentleman, and the other an operative; whereas the workman ought often to be thinking, and the thinker often to be working, and both should be gentlemen, in the best sense. As it is, we make both ungentle, the one envying, the other despising, his brother; and the mass of society is made up of morbid thinkers and miserable workers.

And it's in the 'Stones of Hinksey' that he puts the words into practice. The two sets of stones are not separated by a chasm of bathos – quite the opposite. The episode of 'Ruskin's Road Gang' has another bonus: one of the worker-students was Oscar Wilde, who, we forget, was a big man and no shirker. Wilde remembered:

> Ruskin worked with us in the mist and mud of an Oxford winter and our friends and enemies came out and mocked us from the banks, but we did not mind them much.

In *The Importance of Being Earnest*, Cecily tells Gwendolen 'When I see a spade I call it a spade', to which Gwendolen replies: 'I am glad to say that I have never seen a spade. It is obvious that our social spheres have been widely different'.

At least we know Wilde himself had seen a spade. Not only that, but he was 'entrusted with Mr Ruskin's especial wheelbarrow'. Among the other roadbuilders was Arnold Toynbee, economist, social reformer and historian of the industrial revolution. Toynbee died aged 30 less than a decade later – a short life that improved countless other lives to come. Another was Hardwick Rawnsley, founder of the National Trust and the Keswick School of Industrial Art.

In September 2011, the *Oxford Mail* ran an article with the headline 'Literary Giants tried building a Road'. It sounds like a variant on the 'How many academics does it take to change a lightbulb?' joke. The road they built didn't last long, but the values and the ideas that brought it into being are as necessary today as they were then.

Reading Ruskin as a student changed the weather in my head, and I see him all over Oxford. Outside this little cottage, the stones of Hinksey hold their own with the stones of Venice. That's the whole point of Ruskin, and I'm thrilled and moved to follow the tracks of the great man's 'especial wheelbarrow'.

BOTLEY INTERCHANGE

I take the little public footpath that looks like someone's drive. It threads its narrow way among some beautiful old houses – contemporaries, or near enough, of the cottage. The owners haven't built walls or fences to block off their private spaces from the track that goes between their houses. All they've done is lay out some plant pots to mark out where their gardens begin. I don't know these people and have never seen any of them on my walks, but I warm to them for that.

The path takes me to the church and graveyard. I turn up to the ring road. My legs are starting to notice that I'm going uphill. Until the early twentieth century I could have seen most of the Oxford skyline from Ferry Hinksey and North Hinksey. Now it's too overbuilt and overgrown. If I want to see the views that Turner painted – J.M.W. Turner not 'the Oxford Turner', though he did a few as well – I need to go higher.

I crest the ring road and the southbound traffic until I reach the underpass to Westminster Way. I'm aiming for Raleigh Park and Harcourt Hill, from which I intend to gaze romantically down at the city. The underpass orders 'cyclists and equestrians' to dismount. There's a 'Police Operation in Progress' sign tied to the railings. The tunnel looks clean and freshly-painted; no-one has pissed there or strewn litter, and it's brightly lit and the little graffiti there is timorous stuff. We're on a hill. The houses and even the churches are modern. I walk up Raleigh Park Road. It's getting quite steep now, which is why I'm puzzled when a jaunty Irishman cycles effortlessly past me. We exchange pleasantries. I can tell he's from Dublin. A few minutes later, his small son does the same, and calls out to him to wait. He's from Oxford.

At the top, I take a left onto the path that leads to Raleigh Park. That's it, I think, that's Turner's view. I take a bunch of photos – panoramic landscape shots with different levels of zoom or wide-angle. Pointless. First, because the photos are rubbish – it's impossible to get a good image of the spires and towers from here. I can't even convey a sense of distance. Second, it's not the buildings that are interfering with the view, it's the trees. So much of what was flat meadow is now wooded greenbelt. Oxford's skyline is protected, and this is one of the 'viewing cones' that have afforded views more or less unchanged over the centuries. What I see are cranes: red cranes, white cranes, yellow cranes; erect cranes, drooping cranes, moving cranes and still cranes. Increasingly, the best way to see Oxford is from the cabin of a crane. I wonder if there are 'Crane Tours'.

Turner painted both his first (1787) and last (1839) paintings of Oxford from here. The second is the famous one: a farmer on horseback with women gathering crops where I'm standing. Their picnic and messy hay bale are here in front of me. The light is red-gold and the river bends around Osney in the distance. The spires and towers are picked out in a clever mix of bright sunlight, pale sunlight and shadow. Turner wants to distinguish them, not submit them to the same conditions – that way we can see the sun at different stages of setting. Many of Turner's suns exist for the spectacle, but this one is charting the *now* of an afternoon dying across a city. Two dons in black gowns and mortar boards are in conversation on a path to the side of the picture, a little behind the women. I suppose they're my professional ancestors. I wonder what they're talking about. What would have been suitable topic in 1839? The Chartist riots up the road in Birmingham? The Newport Rising? The Opium Wars? Fox Talbot's first photographic exhibition? And so on. Maybe they're discussing Turner himself, whose 'Fighting Temeraire' had just been shown at the Royal Academy.

If you want a Turner sunset, pounding with symbolism and emotion, that's where you need to look. This is just the ordinary one – come up here any day and you'll see: it's still here.

WESTMINSTER COLLEGE

A man with a dog tells me the views are better if I push on south. He recommends looking at the millionaires' homes on Vernon Avenue, then crossing to the meadow where there's another Oxford view. I do that, passing a handsome, well-spoken young couple. They're smoking but look so good and are so beautifully surrounded that I feel I've walked into an interactive cigarette advert.

Vernon Avenue is a private road and is indeed the land of the super-rich – modern architect-designed houses and cheesy new-build *faux*-country homes, complete with driveways lit by *faux*-Victorian street lamps and statues that are millionaire's versions of garden gnomes. A gated community so gated it doesn't even need the gate. There's only a small patch between the trees where I can see Oxford, so I make my way down to it. I catch a glimpse of the back gardens. These are the people with the views now. They all have balconies and terraces overlooking the city, high enough to be untroubled by trees and buildings. A man wearing red trousers and a pink jumper sits in a recliner on his lawn, reading something on a tablet. Beside him a little trolley has two cordless phones. Millionaire, obviously, but 80s style – think *Minder*'s Arthur Daley crossed with *The Long Good Friday*'s Harold Shand. The plastic cover of the heated pool has been peeled back but no-one swims.

Behind the gardens and back downhill is Conduit House, which piped clean water down to the city at the ornate Carfax Conduit. Built in 1610 – and with the graffiti to prove it – this squat, practical building gathered water from the fresh streams of Hinksey and sent them down to Oxford through 1.5 miles of lead piping. It's the modest counterpart to the superfancy Conduit itself, with its coats of arms and ornate statues, which became a gaudy obstacle to traffic and is now a folly in Nuneham Courtney, a short drive from here.

The Conduit's successor was the Harcourt Hill Water Tower, demolished in 1993. I'm heading that way now, to Westminster College, to find out where the buses to Oxford Brookes University's 'Harcourt Hill Campus' go. Westminster College was founded in 1851 in London, but moved here in 1959. Originally a Wesleyan teacher training college, the Methodist Church leased it to Oxford Brookes in 2000. Brookes kept the name and now run it as one of its four campuses. A university up here is about the last thing you'd expect to see.

I've always thought Brookes was stretching itself a bit thin, with campuses here, Headington, Wheatley and Swindon. It's not alone. University expansion is everywhere: new campuses, student accommodation, privately-owned halls of residence and whole suburbs of towns and cities given over to student lets. Something's got to give. Up here it looks like it already has. It's deserted, apart from me and two dog-walkers swinging turd-bags in time to their steps. Dogshit metronomes. Someone zips past on a cargo bike with a child in the pod. In the distance I hear, rather than see, a couple entering an accommodation block. They're far away but it's so bare up here that the *beep* of their keyfob carries.

Because of the distance from Oxford, Westminster College was conceived as a self-contained campus. Despite modern additions, it still has that feel: a quadrangle built around a Chapel, with a dining hall, theatre, lecture rooms, science laboratories, workshops and art studios. The outer buildings housed a hospital and flats for tutors. When I get to the main gate, I find it closed, so I head for the brick tower with its white wood-clad spire tower and green copper tip. I'd say it was out of place, but there isn't anything up here for it to look out of place in relation to. Now I'm in front of it, I'm taken aback by the modesty of its scale. A concrete imperial staircase with iron rails curves on both sides onto a terrace which leads to the chapel. This is where they have the graduation ceremonies, and it's a very satisfying piece of architecture. I look it up in Sherwood and Pevsner's *Oxfordshire* (that's why I have the rucksack), but it's not mentioned, perhaps because it was in Berkshire at the time.

I like Westminster College because it looks elegant and democratic and unashamed of its materials – concrete and brick and wood – and true to its own time while trying, albeit realistically, to reach back to another. It announces what it's modelled on, but it doesn't pretend to be it. The style is New England American, and this is the only example of it in Oxford. It's as if someone had said: 'Build me an Ivy League university, but only using materials from Botley Road B&Q'.

A Brookes security van arrives. The driver asks me if I'm lost. I say I'm looking for 'the campus'. I've learned that this is always a useful answer when caught wandering off-limits in Oxford. I'm pleasantly escorted off the premises. 'You're miles away', he tells me. Even the people who work here don't think it's the right place.

Random ingredients often make the best walks, if rarely the best dishes: a trip to Aldi I decided to prolong with a visit to Osney Mead, a fish lunch and a Ruskin homage, a decision finally to see the strange old campus whose name I'd only seen on buses, and a search for a Turner view.

On my way back down I come across the couple I saw earlier. He's on his knees and holding her hand; she has her back to me so I can't see her face. He's proposing. It's idyllic: lush green grass just dry enough to kneel on without staining his Chinos, Turner's Oxford spread before them, a bright blue sky and a hot September sun on the skin. He's lined things up nicely. They greet me again, as pleasantly as before, then get back to the matter in hand. I won't say what she replied.

'BOTLEY TWINNED WITH FUKUSHIMA!'

North Oxford is rich, East Oxford is bohemian, Central Oxford is a world-heritage dreamland and South Oxford is charming, residential and more or less intact. West Oxford has been the poor relation from the beginning: a provider of views rather than a view in itself. But as my long, looping walk shows, there's plenty here.

Michael Dibdin's narrator in *Dirty Tricks* describes Botley as "a suburb of Oxford which sounds like a form of food poisoning and looks like its effects, gobs of half-digested architectural matter sprayed across the countryside with desperate abandon."

Ouch. Also, yes: as my daughter says, 'No offence, but prepare for the offence'. I can see what Dibdin means as I walk down Westminster Road, following the slope of the Southern Bypass Road's sound-absorbing barriers. I reach 'West Way Village', a huge shopping-cum-residential complex. It's opposed by many locals as well as by environmental and heritage groups for its size and – especially – height. Remember the 'Viewing Cones'. The old 1960s West Way was decrepit, with an increasing number of empty units. Perhaps the new one will, as promised, 'regenerate' the area. But it will also add hundreds of high-rise (for Oxford) flats and draw in thousands more cars. Far from being a magnet for the sort of flashy gentrifying businesses claimed in the development plan, the only shops committed to coming so far are the usual suspects: Tesco, Iceland, Co-Op.

Tomorrow's yesterday, today.

In front of this mammoth shopping village, where Botley Road becomes Cumnor Hill, is Elms Parade, a row of shops dating from 1937 and still owned by the family who built it. It's more on the yesterday side of things, and a reminder of what shopping was like between the era of the individual shop and the era of the shopping centre. Oxford has a few of these, and they have a comforting, slightly dated charm. Elms Parade has a butcher, a barber, a dry cleaners, a grocery market, a funeral director and an estate agents. Developers have applied to knock it down, but it still stands, defiantly unfashionable, defiantly local, and defiantly holding its own. Which is more than can be said for the small shops and businesses that were booted out of the old shopping centre.

This is the prowling-ground of Oxford's most urbane vandal, 'Waldo Skipsey'. Graffiti began to appear attacking the developers, Mace, and the local politicians who backed them. When the much-loved family-run West Way Chippy closed down, the words 'So long and thanks for all the fish' appeared outside (a reference to Douglas Adams's *Hitch-hiker's Guide to the Galaxy*). In a letter to the *Oxford Mail*, 'Skipsey' declared that it was the 'amateurish and callous eviction' of the old shopping centre's small businesses that drove them to aerosol action. I look into it, still on my smartphone, to see more examples of their work. 'BOTLEY TWINNED WITH FUKUSHIMA' is my favourite. Other Skipsey classics include 'OH, THE IRONY!', written on the paving slabs below a developer's panel claiming to care for the 'local community', 'Welcome to Dystopia', and the mildly threatening 'Enjoy your new car Mr Barber'. The last is a reference to the conservative councillor who led the development plans, to whom 'Skipsey' cleverly imputes an element of personal gain without it being possible to construe defamation. 'Skipsey' is not exactly Banksy, but they have a point. Even their detractors were at pains to point out how 'well-behaved' they were – even sending money to the owners of the Elms Park shop to repaint the wall on they'd written 'MACE HANDS OFF BOTLEY'.

Planning decisions in Botley are made not in Oxford by Oxford people (which by and large the residents feel themselves to be), but by Vale of White Horse District Council, and councillors in Wantage and Abingdon. 'Waldo Skipsey' speaks for Botley's forgotten constituency, which is another way of saying Botley itself.

CUMNOR HILL AND THE SCHOLAR-GIPSY

My usual West Oxford excursion is Farmoor Reservoir, a futurist-brutalist oasis outside the city limits, where wild birds and their binocular-toting watchers, fishermen and windsurfers, share two huge concrete water-basins beside the sewage treatment works.

But today I leave Skipsey and the battle of West Way behind and catch the 4B from Elms Parade. It's a spontaneous decision – the bus is right in front of me and it's only a few minutes to another of Oxford's totemic vistas: Cumnor Hill. This detour fits nicely into the narrative – as well as the cartographical – arc of my walk.

Cumnor turns up in poems and novels, paintings and photographs, and provides some of the best views of the city. It's Matthew Arnold territory – or rather, that of his most famous character, the Scholar Gipsy. Arnold versifies the legend of an Oxford student who, unable to pay his fees, left and joined the gypsies. The poem's speaker imagines seeing him – the original university drop-out –

taking a journey much like mine, albeit in a different season and without the help of the 4B bus:

> Have I not pass'd thee on the wooden bridge,
> Wrapt in thy cloak and battling with the snow,
> Thy face tow'rd Hinksey and its wintry ridge?
> And thou has climb'd the hill,
> And gain'd the white brow of the Cumner range;
> Turn'd once to watch, while thick the snowflakes fall,
> The line of festal light in Christ-Church hall—[6]

That 'line of festal light' stands for the allure of Oxford as a place of desire and aspiration that lay out of the reach of so many. Inside are the scholars, warm at Oxford's bosom; outside, the shivering, excluded world. Not much change there then.

I alight at the bus stop nearest to Arnold's Way. I run my favourite lines from the poem, which I don't much like as a whole, in my head – 'this strange disease of modern life/With its sick hurry, its divided aims'. Suddenly it occurs to me that 'Skipsey' might be a contraction of *scholar* and *gypsy*. It's the kind of allusive reference an erudite Oxford malcontent would enjoy.

Off Arnold's Way are streets named after his poems. There's Dover Close and Scholar Place, pleasant modern developments with big houses and tall hedges. I don't see a Gypsy Road – they've obviously decided to play up the academic over the traveller life. Mustn't frighten the buyers. Besides, genuine travelling people setting up camp in Oxford are more likely to get served with a writ than with a poem.

I have another reason for coming up here. It's so I can follow the footsteps of the scholar gypsy's tragic descendant, Jude Fawley in Thomas Hardy's *Jude the Obscure*. In Hardy's North Wessex, Cumnor is Lumsdon, and in his day anyone walking down from here to Oxford would have had this view. It gives Jude his first 'near view' of Oxford. Tellingly, he wants to walk it, 'rather from choice than from necessity, having always fancied himself arriving thus'. Since the 4B bus covers the same route, I get back in and return to Botley, mindful of my errands. Jude Fawley will be joining me later.

BOTLEY CEMETERY

At the Park and Ride under Seacourt Tower I cross into Old Botley. I want the contrast between the tower, the retail parks, the Bypass with the buses and cars, and the little seventeenth- and eighteen-century houses that survived all the demolitions and replannings. Round the back of McDonalds I could be in an Edward Thomas poem: a quarter of a street, three hundred and fifty years old – walled-off gardens with climbing pear trees, orchards, and a little stream. Jude Fawley and the scholar gypsy would have seen these very buildings. I'm back on North Hinksey Lane, but looking east into the city.

Botley cemetery isn't Oxford's oldest or most atmospheric – that would be Holywell or St Sepulchre – but it is the most diverse. It contains Oxfordshire's largest War Graves Cemetery, with 740 graves from both World Wars and a variety of nations, not just Commonwealth countries and allied nations, but enemy combatants. The Remembrance Stone was designed by Lutyens, and there's a round pale stone shelter with a dome and a bench I often see people sitting alone on. The closest group of graves on the right as I enter are the dead of the First War – soldiers who were treated at the Examination Schools on the High Street when it was a hospital, and who died there from their wounds. Four Germans and ten Italians face them on the other side like outnumbered chess pieces. Buried with respect, but buried as enemies.[7]

There's a section of Belgian graves I always stop at, thinking of my small Belgian town, of my great-grandmother who saw the Germans march in in 1914 and again in 1939, who lost a brother in the first war and a son in the second. Remembrance of war itself in Belgium is divisive: in World War I, eighty per cent of the army was made up of Flemish soldiers, while the officer-class as well as the doctors and administrators were French speakers. Many Flemish soldiers were punished, some executed, for misunderstanding orders given in a language they didn't understand. The mistreatment of Flemish troops still overshadows Belgian remembrance events. I see this here, in its small way: of the five Belgian soldiers, one is francophone (he's from Lille, France), the others Flemish. The language on their tombstones is Dutch. Two of them died on the same day, and they all died in November and December 1914 – little more than three months after the Germans invaded our country and marched down the Grand'Rue in Bouillon, the first Belgian town after the French border, past my great-grandmother Julia's window. It's where I sit and read when I'm back there, where I sat and kept her company when I was a child.

Around the war graves is the working cemetery – on the western edge there's a Muslim section, and further north a children's section, which I can make out even on this darkening afternoon thanks to the birthday balloons rising from one of the graves. The ring road traffic is constant, and visible in flashes of colour through the breaks in the hedging. This is the last of Oxford Council's cemeteries to have grave-space, but not for long. The city will run out of cemetery space by 2021, and last year the council voted to allow 'grave reclamation', which permits new graves to be dug six inches above existing human remains. This cemetery and Wolvercote will be the first to do so.

For now, however, it's still 'open for new burials' (like the B&B 'Vacancies' sign), though today there's no sign of the black road cone with the word 'FUNERAL' on it. The section closest to Hinksey Lane has new graves, many not yet with headstones. As I walk leave, a young mother arrives with flowers and heads to a plot nearby. Her children are small and rush around laughing and trying to climb the big tree – for them it's a taste of freedom, it's all green and unfamiliar, a chance to breathe and play. I wonder who she's taking the flowers to, and if her children ever knew them. And if they did, if they'll ever remember them.

I've been there myself, in that chasm between generations, the everyday oblivion that runs between us. There's nothing more gone than the recently-gone, I wrote earlier. That goes for people too.

CURTIS INDUSTRIAL ESTATE AND THE TAP SOCIAL

Curtis Industrial Estate is smaller and more concentrated than Osney Mead. Less sleepy too, more buzzing, but no less interesting. Annual rents for a unit here start at £8,500 a year – that's around £9 per square foot per annum. I know this because when I looked the place up to get its co-ordinates, I got sidetracked by the rental prices on estate agency websites. One agency was advertising retail premises on North Parade, the heart of North Oxford's richest suburb, for £240,000, or £556.84 per square foot per annum. We wonder why Oxford is so expensive – the £7 sandwich, the £6 pint, the gravity-defying mark-ups on everything from a new bike to a pair of shoes – but it's worth remembering the rents these businesses have to pay.

Perhaps that's why the industrial estates on the edges of official Oxford have the most interesting businesses. I need a lift after my trip to the cemetery, so I go to the Tap Social, a small business set up in 2016 with two aims: rehabilitating ex-prisoners and brewing excellent beer. I think of the place as inheriting Oxford's tradition of local breweries, while also providing a hopeful epilogue to its history as a prison city. The buzz I mentioned comes from here, and from the 'criminally good beer' of Tap Social's strapline. Ex- and serving prisoners are taught to brew and offered training in the hospitality industry, while the colourful labels on the beers are designed by serving prisoners. The industrial unit I'm now in has carpets arranged with a bohemian haphazardness, and old, comfortable, mismatched furniture. But the real reason to come is to drink the beer and enjoy the space, which is still a proudly industrial unit with a concrete floor, skylights in the roof, and a great rollershutter door winched three-quarters of the way up. There's a terrace outside with overspilling outdoor drinkers, and high-quality food shacks.

Behind the bar are the gleaming stills of a working taproom, but Tap Social have expanded to a new brewing space in Kennington.

They've also taken over the White House pub on Abingdon Road. These days I find their beers all over the city, from my local Co-Op to the TOAD gin distillery beside the Warneford. When I meet Tess Taylor, one of the co-founders, I've ordered a pint of their lager. It's called False Economy, but it isn't. Even for a Belgian like me, the tastiness and individuality of these beers is impressive. I've chosen the lager because it's hot outside, and I don't want anything too rich – just cold, smooth, and European. Last time I was here, drinking at the terrace at a trestle table back in the summer of 2019, the Premier Inn in front of me was just a fretwork of scaffolding; now it blocks the sun. I hope its customers come here. I know the Scholar Gypsy would have. Tess is about to start her evening shift and tells me the history of the company she founded with her sister, a criminology PhD student and former Ministry of Justice Advisor, and her sister's partner, Paul, a barrister.

I mention that the Oxford Foodbank is right opposite – there's a little wooden bower with a bench so its volunteers can take shelter in the rain. Oxford Foodbank doesn't just distribute donations, but makes use of surplus food and distributes it to charities. A few doors from the foodbank is The Natural Bread Company – another business that thrives away from city centre rents. Tess tells me that Tap Social and Oxford Foodbank have collaborated with them on a beer, made from leftover bread, sold to benefit the foodbank. I began this book with an elegy to Oxford's brewing heritage, but on reflection, it looks pretty safe these days, not just thanks to Tap Social but to other small brewers that have come in to revive our stunned palates: Shotover Brewery, Little Ox, Heavy Water Brewery...

Belgians, Beer, Bread, and... Beds: Minty Beds, the winningly-named Oxford bed company is a few units down at the entrance to the Curtis Estate. In the 1940s, Minty made cabinets and furniture, and employed 150 people. Its Varsity Chair and its Oxford Sectional Bookcase were bestsellers. Today, its showroom has a whiff of the lunchtime pint about it, whether from the staff or the customers I don't know, but whenever I go in, it's full of adults in states of disinhibition bouncing around on mattresses in front of strangers. Last time I bought a bed here, two years ago, the man who showed me around had his own nicknames for them. He reminded me of a farmer who knew his animals by name, while also knowing that one day he must part with them. The day Minty were due to deliver my mattress, I'd broken down on the motorway back to Oxford. Minty Beds, outside my house, rang to ask where I was.

I told them. Their first reaction was to check I was fine (I was at Knutsford motorway services, so: not really), then they said it was no problem. When they delivered a few days later, they asked if I'd got my car fixed with just the right mix of irony and concern. I'd inconvenienced them and made them come out for nothing, but they didn't mind. What can I say? Shop in places where people treat you like a person. You'll get a better deal and you'll feel like a human being among other human beings.

At the base of Seacourt Tower, beside an old boarded-up house that was once the home of someone wealthy in pre-ring road Botley, Minty Beds vans are parked with panels declaiming: 'Oxford's Very Own Bed Specialist'. It's arranged so that a commuter's first or last view of Oxford is a Minty Bed advert. It's clever product placement: after all, what are we all thinking about both at the beginning and end of every day?

SEACOURT TOWER AND GHOST BIKE

I know it's a cliché of place-writing to say this, but Botley is a palimpsest: Oxfordshire overlaying Berkshire, with the imaginary county of Thomas Hardy's Wessex overlaying them both. The way Hardy imagines places puts reality itself to shame. When I've visited his fictional landscapes, I've felt them pushing up out of the ground. It's surprisingly easy to feel this in Botley, because all the different calques of place are distinct. No-one could be bothered to preserve Botley, and no-one could be bothered to raze it all and start again. So here it hangs, having fallen through the cracks of our two biggest impulses.

I get snatches of Hardy's world in the thatched cottages of North Hinksey, Botley cemetery, or the old roads with their chipped stones from the metal rims of cart-wheels they occasionally dig up when they work on flood alleviation. In 2017, archaeologists found a 500 year-old road made of river pebbles, limestone and chalk rocks, complete with horseshoes and wheel-ruts. I get a flash of it when I look up at Seacourt Tower opposite the cemetery: an ugly needle-topped block of offices that sits on the edge of the ring road and the Park and Ride. It's on the site of an abandoned Saxon village, a place already long-emptied and long-ruined by the time Chaucer's Miller told his tale, let alone when Jude Fawley walked down here. Now there's a B&Q.

Opposite the tower, a white, flower-decked 'Ghost Bike' commemorates Claudia Comberti, killed here when she was hit by a 4B bus in 2017. The silent cycle-ride vigil through Oxford in her memory was one of the most moving events I've witnessed. A few yards from the memorial bike, Oxford begins with a big sign announcing 'Welcome to Oxford: A Cycling City'. It's as Hardyesque an irony as anyone could think up.

Ghost-villages, ghost-bikes, ghosts of all kinds, crowding our busiest intersections. Hardy's lost world is also itself haunted by lost worlds, and his people do what we all do: attach themselves to carved names on posts or graves, to memorials and milestones, towers and monuments. And still we forget and still we are forgotten.

RETAIL PARK REVERIE

These are heavy thoughts, and unlikely to make me the life and soul of this evening's celebration. I should probably change tack and perk up. If only Butlins was still here.

Time to knuckle down and do my shopping. But I'm waylaid by Aldi's famous 'middle aisle'. Or, as we call it, 'the aisle of unnecessity'. It sounds like something out of Dante. 'Condemned to toil eternally along the aisle of unnecessity…' etc. I linger over the gardening equipment because my garden in Iffley Fields is straggly and unkempt. Maybe the solution lies in some gizmo I can buy here. It's preferable to the hard work of proper weeding. There are plastic barrels painted to look like old wooden casks of the sort that Botley used to have plenty of in the old days. Hanging baskets. Knee pads for low pruning with stiff joints. In the end, I opt for a dressing gown – I've never owned one, but I have a classic consumer vision of myself by the fire in the autumn that lies just around the corner in an Aldi dressing gown. That's my trolley: two bottles of champagne and a dressing gown. The Noel Coward of budget shopping. The real Noel Coward would have done his shopping just across the road:

ICE-RINK, CINEMA, CHANNEL TUNNEL

The plot of land that's now Oxford's biggest Waitrose is the site of Oxford's first ice-rink. A vast art deco building, it opened in 1930 and was, until New York got its Madison Square rink, the biggest in the world. It was in this handsome but utilitarian building that Oxford University beat Germany, Canada, Russia and France at Ice Hockey in 1930, and where socialites like the Mitfords came to see and be seen. Within a few years, it was losing money, and became, in 1934, the Majestic Cinema – 'the largest picture theatre in the South Midlands'. Screenings stopped in 1940, when the building was used to house evacuees. After the war, Frank Cooper's son William bought it for a new marmalade factory, before moving production to Wantage in 1967. The website 'Cinema Treasures' tells me it was only demolished in 1987, four years before I came, having housed, in its final years, Carpetland and an MFI megastore. How are the mighty fallen.

The futile, short-lived industrial units that replaced it were themselves knocked down in 2014 for this Waitrose. It made the news recently by being the first supermarket in the country to trial bring-your-own-container refill stations for basic food and drink. Being Waitrose, they also offered a choice of four different wines on tap, as well as real ales and lagers. 'Waitrose Unpacked' was due to last a few weeks. A year on, it's a nationwide success. In the local news Vox Pops, the young people support it for environmental reasons, while the older generation like it because it resembles the shopping habits of their childhoods. One demographic approves because they're looking to the future, another because it reminds them of the past.

Beside Waitrose is Prestwich Place, a small nondescript modern estate named after Joseph Prestwich, Professor of Geology at the

university. The plaque set into the old wall notes that he was
instrumental in 'gaining improvement to the poor drainage of the
New Botley in the 1880s'. So many of these distinguished
Victorians were committed to improving the real world in practical
ways. Some – Ruskin, Acland, Prestwich – started right here, in
Oxford's sidelined neighbourhoods. Among Prestwich's other
distinctions was a prizewinning paper entitled 'On the Geological
Conditions affecting the Construction of a Tunnel between
England and France' in 1873. The Channel Tunnel and Botley's
drains? All in a day's work for a Victorian.

BINSEY

The Bulstake Stream, once an important Oxford waterway, winds
around the back of Waitrose, whose car park is fenced off from the
grassy edgelands behind it. The map shows me the green spaces
with evocative names – Binsey, Botley Park, Twenty Pound
Meadow, Tumbling Bay; and, further north, Fiddlers Island, Port
Meadow and Wolvercote. But much of the space around here
doesn't have a name. In the A to Z it's grey blocks of nowhere-land
irrigated by blue waterways – the kind of places SatNavs call
'Unnamed Road'. That's the most striking thing about the maps of
this part of town: there's water everywhere. Maybe the land doesn't
have a name because we've only borrowed it from the water.

Passing Waitrose I see a man pushing the handle of a knife into
the top of two wine bottles. There's a bench outside the allotments
down the road, popular with daytime drinkers. I wonder why he
hasn't bought a screwtop bottle, because Waitrose do a good
screwtop 'Bargaindy' (their joke) for £9. He must be new to the
area because he doesn't know about Aldi – he could have saved a
few quid. Later, as I walk back into town, I see him with his friends
outside the allotments. They've just arrived, they tell me, pointing to
their bags and towards the station. They're not impressed with
Oxford so far: 'Is this it?' The classic C.S. Lewis mistake.

Which reminds me – I still haven't worked out where Lewis
turned around and realised he'd gone the wrong way. My money is
on Osney Ditch Bridge just before Osney Mead. It's a solid stone
bridge with a noticeable camber, giving you just the right amount
of height to see the Oxford skyline. Any nearer the station and he'd
have been too close to see; any further and he'd have been hitting

the countryside, because this is roughly where the Victorian development would have ended – what Lewis called a 'suburb'. I wonder if he passed Warlands, the cycle shop on the corner of Botley Road and Alexandra Road. It would have been celebrating its first decade in business in 1916. Maybe he bought his first bike here. Bike shops are a good way of getting a feel for a neighbourhood's demographic, and Warlands is a classic old-school shop that moves with the times. What can I deduce from the bikes they're promoting? One, that Botley Road has a lot of families with enough money to buy big cargo bikes. Two, it has a lot of London commuters, judging by the variety of folding bikes on offer: the Breakfast, Briefcase, Brompton crew. Three, there's an overlap between One and Two.

I take a left into Binsey Lane, which starts as a normal-looking suburban street, then comes to an abrupt end in a wall of greenery. I pass OISE – Oxford Intensive School of English, where I used to teach English as a Foreign Language. I enjoyed the years I spent among Oxford's EFL community because I met so many different people: students like myself, but also professionals who had taught all over the world and spoke many languages, steadfastly refusing to become the lawyers and managers their contemporaries had become. They felt like a last bastion – of what or who, I'm not exactly sure, but they took time out from the rat-race to write novels or poems, or paint or compose. They introduced me to another Oxford, the one being a student had made me too incurious to notice.

A bridge the width of a car disappears into trees. It's so narrow that I have to let the cars pass, and there are many. There are only two places you can be going through here – if, that is, you have a destination, which I don't: the golf club or The Perch pub. It used to be a way to Tumbling Bay bathing place, one of Oxford's many swimming spots. The path from here is cut off at the moment because the Environment Agency is building a 'fish pass'.

When I've had enough of dodging the cars and the taxis coming to pick up drinkers, I try to find a spot to sit and eat my Waitrose samosa. I'm surprised at how much of this area is now fenced off. It used to be open ground, soggy and indeterminate and free to walk. Now there's lopped trees and barbed wire, pointless prohibition-signs laminated in plastic, and aluminium fencing with razorwire. Developers lick their lips. There's a concrete clearing with some metal storage containers, two of which have been turned into a house with windows and a staircase. Bikes outside advertise an eco-courier company.

I stop at the Golf Club/Driving Range, looking for a patch of grass. It's strange to see how crowded it is, here in this overgrown backwater of Oxford. The car park is full, but because golf is a slow, silent game, there's no noise. I settle down on some mown grass. An old supersize golf ball, big as a car, lies covered in moss and dirt in the undergrowth. It looks like a space-pod whose interplanetary travellers liked Oxford so much they stayed and left their craft to rot. Like the old decaying carriages on the station sidings across the river, or the pieces of old barge dredged up from the canal.

Even for me, resistant to the *Olde England* charms of thatched cottages and country pubs, Binsey is a special place. A tiny village with a church and a well, it has a legendary pub and until recently, contained two working farms. It's opposite Port Meadow and Jericho, and the little walk from my college, down Walton Well Road, past the back of the Lucy Factory whose machine noises I remember and keep on a mental soundtrack, and across the bridge to The Perch pub is idyllic at any time of year. I especially like it when the water is high, and I can see the sky reflected in the flooded grassland of Port Meadow. Everyone else likes that too, so our walks start out solitary and finish up as group outings.

St Margaret of Antioch's in Binsey dates from the twelfth century, and occupies the site of one of Frideswide's original monasteries. The village has two literary landmarks. One is a ghost-landmark – the Binsey Poplars of Gerard Manley Hopkins's elegiac poem. The other is St Margaret's Well, which is something of a misnomer because it's dedicated to St Frideswide, who fled to Binsey to escape a forced marriage. Her husband-(not)-to-be, Prince Algar of Mercia, came here looking for her and was struck by lightning and blinded. Frideswide prayed to God to restore his sight but not his desire for her, and healing water gushed up from what is now this well. The story is illustrated in a magnificent series of stained glass windows in St Frideswide's chapel in Christ Church Cathedral. The well was famed for its healing properties, and the church used the crutches of cured cripples to decorate its walls – an early version of the 'Satisfied Customer' testimonial.

But the well is perhaps more famous now as 'Alice's Well' – the 'Treacle Well' in Lewis Carroll's *Alice in Wonderland*. It's an addictive, infuriating book, manic and methodical as all true nonsense is. I won't quote it here, except to note that the 'treacle' which we image bubbling up, thick and gold from the well's mouth, was originally just a medieval French word – *triacle,* from the Greek *thēriakē* – meaning an antidote to poison. Carroll's madcap punning filled the well, and the heads of generations of fascinated children, with gloopy golden syrup.

BINSEY POPLARS

The 'Binsey Poplars' were on the road between here and Godstow, a village further north with the ruins of an abbey on the path to Wolvercote. Hopkins walked along here – the 'meadow and river and wind-wandering weed-winding bank' – in March 1879. He found the trees that had provided shade had been cut down. It's such a powerful poem not just because the trees are living creatures felled in their prime, but because Hopkins is so aware of time as a double loss – the thing itself, and then the knowledge of the thing:

> After-comers cannot guess the beauty been.
> Ten or twelve, only ten or twelve
> Strokes of havoc unselve
> The sweet especial scene…[8]

I find these lines painfully moving in their clarity: what are any of us but 'after-comers'? It's the bass-note to this book, and to most of what I've written.

When I look up the poem on my phone, I recall that, like many Hopkins poems, it was only published much later – in 1918. It wasn't a war poem, but it became one.

ALLOTMENTS

On the other side of the allotments, down Tumbling Bay Walk, is the bathing place – a concrete basin with a weir. It's still a good place to swim if you like neglected spartan brutalism. And I do. Botley Road allotments are my dream-garden. I enjoy gardening, and though I'm not very good at it, I've grown vegetables with pride and occasionally success: third prize in the North Wales Show for my 'Mixed Vegetable Platter'.

The best way to appreciate the allotments is by walking the footpath behind Abbey Road. It's a beautiful little walk that takes

me to Wolvercote via Fiddlers Island and Port Meadow. The
allotments abut the water and form a vegetable coastline. Little
sheds, greenhouses, raised beds, buckets, compost bins, stakes and
watering cans, manure piles, wheelbarrows and plant beds of every
shape and size. The allotments recently made the news when a new
development across the water on Abbey Road replaced the real
view in their brochures with a CGI of fake countryside. After all,
they had £1.3 million duplexes to sell. The name? Beaumont Gate
– another meaningless slab of nominative cleansing beloved of
developers. A tabloid ran a story about the developer 'misleading'
its 'premium buyers' by hiding the 'scruffy allotments'.

They're magnificent, and even a CGI-generated human being
would enjoy them. There are few more beautiful places to stand
than the little arching footbridge on the tip of Abbey Road. On my
right, the railway bridge on Roger Dudman Way has five busy
tracks whose comings and goings can be heard for miles around.
But here on this bridge, it's just water and greenery. I'm so close I
can discern the veg: leeks, courgette-flowers, beans climbing poles.

I've seen this bit of land in every season, in every light and every
weather. Of all the photos I have of it, my favourite is one I took
last winter. It had been a bright, cold sunny day, the kind where
things are so clear they seem to be vibrating. I wandered down here
after work to catch the early sunset and photographed the
allotments, so perfectly reflected in the unmoving water that it was
impossible to tell which was the real and which was the image. Not
unlike Oxford.

Notes

1. http://www.cslewis.org/resource/walkguide/
2. See the website 'Osney in Literature' – https://osneyisland.org.uk/osney-in-literature/
3. John Wain, *Where the Rivers Meet* (London: Hutchinson, 1988), p. 11.
4. JGB Historical GIS / University of Portsmouth, History of North Hinksey, in Vale of White Horse and Berkshire | Map and description, *A Vision of Britain through Time.*
   URL: http://www.visionofbritain.org.uk/place/5010
   Date accessed: 15th September 2020
5 https://www.oxfordmail.co.uk/news/9254637.literary-giants-tried-building-road/
6. https://www.poetryfoundation.org/poems/43606/the-scholar-gipsy
7. For a rich and elegantly-written history of Botley, see Malcolm Graham's *The Changing Faces of West Oxford*, Witney, Robert Boyd: 1998. See also his 'Botley Cemetery and the Great War': https://northhinksey-pc.gov.uk/wp-content/uploads/old_site/Files/Remembrance/Malcolm_Graham_address_Nov2014.pdf
8. https://www.poetryfoundation.org/poems/44390/binsey-poplars

SOUTH

OXFORD TOWN HALL

I'm not strictly in South Oxford yet, or not today's South Oxford. I'm at Oxford Town Hall, built in 1897 as a declaration of the city's status in the face of the university's historic dominance. The university had its own police force until 2003, its own MP until the constituency was abolished in 1950, and enforced its rules not just within the colleges and university but across the city as a whole. In my early days as an academic, some older members of college 'Governing Bodies' behaved as if police had no jurisdiction over college members. Once, a student at my college assaulted a student at another, leaving him with serious long-term damage. When criminal charges ensued, there was a sense among some senior 'dons' that the police had no business meddling, and that it was the college's job to mete out whatever sanctions it saw fit. This was 1997, not 1897. Perhaps these dons would have been among those who disrupted the opening of the Town Hall a hundred years before.

With Oxford Town Hall, the city authorities had a building of stature as well as size. The architect was Henry Hare, and his grand Jacobethan edifice stands on the site of two previous incarnations of Oxford's council: the Guildhall, built in 1292, and the first Town Hall, built in 1752. As well as a great hall and a council chamber, it housed a law court and a library, and some prison cells, several of which were put to use on the day of the building's opening in May 1897, when police officers from London baton-charged a group of demonstrating students.

A police station and more cells at the back of the building, on Blue Boar Street, came soon after, and saw plenty of action in the twentieth century too. In autumn 1968, when Enoch Powell spoke at the Town Hall a few months after his 'Rivers of Blood Speech', students tried to storm the premises and prevent him from speaking. An early instance of no-platforming. In the same vein, the building diagonally opposite, also designed by Hare, housed the Carfax Assembly Rooms, where Oswald Mosley gave a speech at which the British Union of Fascists attacked a group of protestors which included both students and car plant workers. The irony that William Morris had gifted Mosley £50,000 to found the BUF is one that slips through a lot of the city's rose-tinted histories. Most of Oxford's marches and protests begin outside the Town Hall or at

Carfax, and this square, where the four roads meet – St Aldate's/High Street/Queen Street/Cornmarket – has a noble history of protests, riots and demonstrations: from the St Scholastica's Day Riot of 1355, via the CND marches led by Councillor Olive Gibbs, to the Women Against Trump march of 2017.

The Town Hall also houses the Museum of Oxford, in the throes of a revamp as I write, which does a great job of reminding people that a real city exists, with its own traditions and its own histories. There's an online archive entitled *Oxford's Windrush Generations* where I can hear my friend Tim Daniel's cousin Irma James speaking about her arrival from St Vincent, about her husband Eli, and about the challenges of life in Britain for black workers. One of Blackbird Leys's great characters – charity fundraiser, living archive, and all-round life-force – I think of her now because I was going to speak to her for this book. But she has been ill recently.[1] Anyway, I can listen to her on the Museum of Oxford website, though it's not the same as being in her front room in Blackbird Leys drinking her tea and surrounded by her memorabilia.[2] Among the museum's artefacts are Cromwell's death mask, Captain Scott's Frank Cooper marmalade tin, and a slab of knucklebone pavement from the old city centre. It is what it sounds like: a paving slab made of hammered sheep knuckles. There are tours around the hall, the courts, the medieval crypt and the cells, and the Town Hall boasts of having hosted Nelson Mandela (when it presented him with the

Freedom of the City), and concerts by David Bowie and the Rolling Stones.

A little further down is 'Alice's Shop', a Lewis Carroll-themed tourist-magnet which sounds like a gimmick but isn't. Or not completely: it's been called Alice's Shop for 150 years, and was a local newsagents and sweetshop until recently. It also has a genuine claim on its material: this is the 'Old Sheep Shop' in *Through the Looking-Glass*, and Tenniel's famous illustration is this same building seen from the inside. Alice leaves here with the words: 'Well, this is the very queerest shop I ever saw'.

As well she might, because it's run by a sheep who insults her. Moreover, 'whenever she looked hard at any shelf, to make out exactly what it had on it, that particular shelf was always quite empty: though the others round it were crowded as full as they could hold'. Carroll's description fits the kind of high-intellectual hypothesising he and his fellow 'dons' specialised in, but it's also a pretty good description of being completely stoned. It's not hard to see why the *Alice* books inspired Jefferson Airplane's great psychedelic song, 'White Rabbit'. But you won't find any Jefferson Airplane in this wholesome emporium of £30 placemats and £50 trinket boxes. Note they don't call them *pill* boxes – 'one pill makes you larger, and one pill makes you small', sings Grace Slick – and I haven't been in to see if they sell replica 'Drink Me' bottles. I wonder if the sheep knuckle paving up the road gave Carroll the idea of a Sheep shop. As for Alice Liddell herself, her Red Cross medal for service in World War I, during which two of her sons were killed, is also on show at the Museum of Oxford.

The only businesses which have remained more or less unchanged in the three decades I've been here are the St Aldate's Tavern (which has undergone multiple refurbishments), The Old Tom pub (which has undergone none), and St Phillip's Rare Books. Entered through the gothic-arched door of a listed building beside Alice's Shop, via a cobbled passage, and with an imposingly-decorated ceiling, its books range from affordable paperbacks to specially-bound editions that belong in *The Name of the Rose*. It's such a perfect bookshop you'd think you were on a film set. Come to think of it, I'm sure it's been used in *Inspector Morse*. The Oxford I came to in 1991 had second-hand bookshops everywhere: the bottom of the High Street, the end of Broad Street, tucked away in Jericho (two on the same street for a while), down St Aldate's (also

two), on St Michael's Street near the station and in the Covered
Market. This is among the last ones standing.

THRESHOLDS: ST ALDATE'S

For one of Oxford's oldest thoroughfares, St Aldate's gives off the
city's most transient vibe. But this has probably been true since 800
AD. Even the Saxons, I suspect, probably allowed an extra few of
inches of their candle-clocks to get from one end to the other. Most
of its businesses today are snack bars, souvenir shops and
gadget-kiosks. How many shops selling the same thing can you fit
onto one street? Come to St Aldate's and find out.

It's a beautiful street – or would be if you could see it properly.
There are so many buses it's impossible to view it in one go unless
you come on Christmas Day. How many double-deckers can you
fit, by which I mean not fit at all but jostle, jam and randomly strew,
onto one road at the same time? St Aldate's has the answer to that
too. There are more bus-stops than this short road can take,
arranged at such staccato intervals that at peak times their queues
merge like fusing cells on a microscope slide. I remember
something else I heard on the Windrush recordings: Ermine
Rogers, who came here in 1956, mentions how dark and dirty
Oxford was, how the college buildings were ingrained with fumes
and soot, and how the clean, scrubbed facades we see today are
recent.[3] In St Aldate's you can see not just architecture of old and
ancient Oxford, but the layered grime that came with industrial and
modern Oxford. I remind myself that to my right, St Ebbe's was a
bustling, noisy suburb; of all the coal being burned, the petrol being
guzzled; of the working boatyard at the end of St Aldate's whose
cranes and winches are still there, ornamental, in the pub garden it
has become; of the St Ebbe's gasworks just to the south, which only
closed in 1960, and which Auden claimed provided his best views
of Oxford. The Oxford we see today is, or at any rate looks, cleaner
that it used to. Which is to say it's more ornamental than it was.

St Aldate's is full of history, which is perhaps what spared its
side-streets the same fate as St Ebbe's, a few minutes west. Having
Christ Church on one side and Pembroke College on the other, as
well as one of Oxford's finest secret colleges, Campion Hall, will
have helped preserve its eco-system of offshoots. Blue Boar Street
to the east, and, to the west, Pembroke Street, Rose Street, Brewer

Street, Beef Lane... they're picture-book Oxford, but not twee or spruce. They're dirty, greasy, exhaust-fume-slicked, the houses leaning in as they rise, floor by floor, until their attics look like they're gossiping in Shakespeare's English. More Falstaff's than Henry IV's too.

Turning off into these streets is a good way of getting a sense of the cheek-by-jowl relationship of the university to the old city: three hundred years ago I'd have passed through the huge oak doors of Christ Church's Tom Gate, begun by Cardinal Wolsey and finished with Christopher Wren's Tom Tower, and found myself in a bustling, noisy, smelly city. Like, but also not like, today. There would have been no long-drawn-out transition from higher thoughts to baser needs, from mind to body, in the old Oxford. But maybe there isn't now, either. I think that's partly where Lewis Carroll's (and C.S. Lewis's) fascination with doors and gates comes from – whether you live here or are just visiting, Oxford is a city of thresholds, of views suddenly given and then suddenly taken away. Take the view into Christ Church through the oak doors: a huge quadrangle with crisp green squares of lawn, a fountain, honey-coloured stone walls with, in late afternoon, warm lights at the leaded windows. Organ music from the cathedral – the city's cathedral, secreted away in a college. There's a pool around a fountain with waterlilies, from which Mercury, naked except for a winged helmet, floats off his pedestal. On the cobbles in the archway, the silhouettes of bowler-hatted porters – men and women – guard the entrance. You catch this view in between passing buses, to the honking of horns, the clatter of wheelie-cases clipping the uneven joins between the flagstones, then it's all gone again. The oak doors have closed, or you've moved on, or the Abingdon bus is in the way. Maybe you're on it. It's not so hard to see where Oxford's threshold-fetish comes from.

St Aldate's was once known as Fish Street, and the area between here and St Ebbe's was a warren of shops and businesses. This was one of the main thoroughfares into Oxford, and for the smell of burned diesel and the squeak of bus brakes we just need to substitute the smell of horseshit and the clatter of cart-wheels. There would have been taverns and brothels, butchers and bakers, boarding-houses, inns, stables, and all those professions we only see now in poems or history books: tanners, farriers, cutlers, curriers, pewterers, hosiers, mercers.... They're the ancestors of the phone-unlocking counters, the *bureaux de change*, the money-wiring newsagents, the luggage-shops and the souvenir-merchants. And what is this kebab-van in Pembroke Square but the descendant of the pie-cart?

THAMES VALLEY POLICE AND THE LAW COURTS

There are other signs that this area belongs to a modern city and not a pickled fantasy or a 3-D postcard, and that there's another Oxford in the shadow of these spires. The police station vacated Blue Boar Street in 1937 and moved to a purpose-built Neo-Georgian building at the bottom of St Aldate's. This is where Inspector Morse worked, and there's a plaque to him on the front. When Colin Dexter unveiled it, he boasted of his fictional universe: 'There have been 89 body bags. All of the murders were solved and this is a wonderful tribute to the force'. But judging from the comings and goings in the Crown Court and County Court, Thames Valley Police have less glamorous crimes to solve. The custody cells closed in 2014 to save money, and there's talk of them selling the building. I can already see it as a four star hotel: *Morse Towers by Holiday Inn*. Thames Valley Police were the first force in the country to get a Drugs Squad, in 1967, the year of 'White Rabbit', so perhaps a plaque to the Drugs Squad would also be fitting.

The courts themselves were originally the Morris car showroom, and their eight huge ground-floor *vitrines* are now blocked-in offices with small windows. The showroom was built in 1932, a symbol of Oxford's prosperity in the midst of economic depression. The cars were made far away in east Oxford, but they were sold here, in the prestigious surroundings of Christ Church Meadow. Test-driving my new car, I'd have swept through the vast entrance and turned left, into the bustling but not, as yet, overly-congested city; or right, down the Abingdon Road, into the open countryside towards the Hinkseys and Kennington. One of the last photos of the showroom displays three models of the car that was the UK's answer to the luxury executive saloon: the Leyland Wolseley, which became the Austin Princess.

When I was a child it was both a gangster car and a police car. The stuff of dreams, and built in Cowley, depicted on the mosaic mural in Templars Square Shopping Centre. Today, the showroom

entrance is fortified with impregnable metal doors, reinforced glass and security channels with metal detectors. This is a threshold where people smoke and worry and check their phones. It's catching, because as I pass, I check my smartphone for messages, then the *Oxford Mail* court reports to see what's going on inside. It's the sad daily filler of domestic violence, sexual assault, drink, drugs and racism. No-one's been stealing Etruscan artefacts or murdering Sanskrit professors over negative book reviews. The weapons aren't medieval daggers or Saxon brooches, but blunt, drab, available things: a hammer, a baseball bat, fists.

West towards Oxpens, it's blocks of sad modern streets – not even streets really, more like rows of not-quite-offices and not-quite-flats built around roads designed just to keep traffic moving. Even when we're trying to get rid of cars, cars define what we do. The best way to get a sense of the truncation of this historic area is to seek out the building that used to be The Wharf House pub, marooned on an overbuilt island between the heavy traffic of Speedwell Street and Thames Street. It still has the enamel Halls Brewery tile with the trademark hare by the door, and was once part of a living network of streets and homes. When I went in the 90s, the customers were a dwindling band of male regulars. As for passing trade, it was more passing than trade. The façade is still there, but it's now apartments whose inhabitants need to keep their windows closed all year round. It's one of those places my memory plays back to me in black and white, it feels so long ago. I check when it finally closed and I'm surprised to find it was as recently as 2006.

The Wharf House is surrounded by places with evocative names but no identity: Speedwell Street (a well-chosen spot for the council traffic offices), Butterwyke Place, Cromwell Street, Luther Street. Luther Street Medical Centre is a GP surgery for homeless people, and began as a Portakabin before raising money for a proper building. While the colleges tout for millions in donations for flagship building projects, the facilities for vulnerable people are financially starved and cleansed from the city's spaces. Around Luther Street Medical Centre, there's construction work going on – more and more privatised student flats, separated from the streets of St Ebbe's and St Aldate's by green mesh fencing and private security.

BROAD WALK AND CHRIST CHURCH MEADOW REPLANNED

If I turn left down Broad Walk, I'm in *Brideshead Revisited* – it's as iconic a view of this city as the view of Cambridge from the back of Kings College. I can walk home this way if I want to avoid the High Street: along the back of Christ Church, Merton College, Corpus Christi, all the way to the Botanic Gardens (I like their old name –

'physick gardens') and Magdalen. I could walk south to the riverbank through a meadow with grazing cows, steaming ground in the autumn and winter, through a very localised and very photogenic mist, to the river and the boathouses. This is Oxford at its best, or at any rate its most. Spires and towers, but also walls – this is a city of walls and gates and heavy doors, mostly closed. And the colleges, like today's media channels, have become pay-per-view.

In Thomas Sharp's *Oxford Replanned*, a lot of Christ Church Meadow, including the dreamy riverbank I've just evoked, would be the road to Magdalen Bridge and Cowley: 'Merton Mall'. I'd be standing on the hard shoulder, or trying to make my way to 'Christ Church Square', a modern transport 'hub' just south of here. Maybe I'd be driving my new Morris straight from the showroom to Iffley Fields, or watching the cars being delivered from Cowley. Maybe I'd have walked from the city centre through 'New Carfax', or perhaps done some shopping in 'The Friary', and 'New St Ebbe's Street' (roughly the Westgate area). Knock it all down, keep the old names, stick a 'new' in front of them – that should do it.

Sharp's plans are pretty alarming – great fat lines of red overwriting the maps with scant regard for the existing place. His new road drives a mental bulldozer through Oxpens and St Ebbe's, past the station, up through Jericho, and just a little north of the Radcliffe Observatory and St Anne's. A ring road, but inside rather than outside the city. If Sharp's road had come into being (leaving most of rich Victorian North Oxford intact), I'd be able to hear the rumble from my college room. It's the kind of plan we call 'bold' because we don't want to use the word 'terrifying'. At least Sharp understood the car problem, and predicted its ongoing damage to Oxford's buildings and air quality. He wasn't the first, but it was a minority view – especially in the city that had given the world Morris Motors. His plans also involved an early version of the Park and Ride: designated 'Car Stands' beyond which the city was for pedestrians and public transport.

In *An Oxford University Chest*, John Betjeman had divided Oxford into three: Christminster, The University, and Motopolis. The first was the old city, so-named after *Jude the Obscure*; the second, the colleges, departments and halls, the Vice-Chancellors, Proctors and Heads of House; and the third, Cowley, the car plant, and East Oxford. *An Oxford University Chest* remains, despite its avowed nostalgia and anti-modernity, a sympathetic and clever book. It pays serious (if not exactly profound) attention to the positive social changes brought by modern industry and large-scale employment, and describes, in ways that are still useful, the relations between the three Oxfords. Motopolis, he claimed, had won – it dominated the city. That's no longer true – it's a vestige. The problem with nostalgia is that it stretches the past and foreshortens the future, but at least Betjeman was conscious of his own blind spots:

> To escapists, to arty people like the author of these pages, the internal combustion engine is, next to the wireless, the most sinister modern invention. It booms overhead with its cargo of bombs, it roars down the lanes with its cargo of cads, it poisons the air, endangers the streets, deafens the ears and deadens the senses.[4]

It's not hard to see, standing here at the bottom of St Aldate's, that something needed to be done. It still does. Betjeman was writing in 1938, Sharp twenty years later. Today, we need to find our own way forward, because neither Betjeman's past nor Sharp's future is the solution.

'CHRIST CHURCH MALL'

A lesser-known Oxford planner, the architect Lawrence Dale, had equally draconian ideas for this part of town. Unlike Sharp's, his were not debated beyond the letters pages of newspapers. Dale was a poet in planning. His beautifully-written *Towards a Plan for Oxford City* (1944) is less of a planning proposal than a manifesto for a realist and very local utopianism. He includes watercolours of his future Oxford, as well as rather occult-looking diagrams of traffic-flow and of the relationship between 'The Gown' and 'The Town'. One diagram illustrates the different understandings of Beauty and Truth, Art and Virtue, and shows how they can be made to join together across the mind-body gulf, in other words, the university (mind) and the city (body). It's an amazing, exhilarating read. Long out of print, I got my copy on AbeBooks and am trying to persuade someone to republish it.

Dale's plan includes suburbs dedicated to 'light industry', academic precincts, a sports stadium and a 'soccer ground'. There's a new School of Design in St Clement's, where the university and Cowley come together in 'A centre of culture, The Arts and the arts. A meeting-ground of theory and practice, a burial-place of the

ancient hatchet'. St Clement's is a symbolic place for Dale: a join
between Central and East Oxford, the end of the university and the
beginning of Cowley, a place where the work of the mind and the
work of the body meet. Dale's vision is of civic responsibility, of
sharing the otherwise segregated spaces Oxford kept – and keeps
– creating. The vision strikes me as Ruskinian, though for some
reason Dale dislikes Ruskin and says so. Also, before we get too
carried away with admiration, here's a reminder that he, like many
others, thought St Ebbe's needed to be pulled down: 'a stagnant
backwater [...] to many a *terra incognita*'.

The centrepiece of Dale's plan is 'Christ Church Mall'. Long and
curving – 'luring one to see what is round the bend with ever fresh
rewards' – it takes more or less the same route as Sharp's. It has
balustrades and viewing-points for parking cars or cycles, and gives
Oxford what he calls a 'back'. Dale was probably thinking of the
Cambridge 'Backs', and notes, rightly, that it's impossible to get a
really good view of the back of the Oxford colleges – Christ Church,
Corpus, Merton, Magdalen Tower, and between them the Radcliffe
Camera, the University Church, All Souls. A new view of an old place:
'not so much a horizon regained as a horizon discovered'. In practical
terms too the 'mall' would have been a way of unifying the 'severed
city' between St Ebbe's and Cowley, light and heavy industry.

Dale often uses verbs of sundering and unification. His plan will
reconnect the people and the places of Oxford. The city, he says, is
riven – split, severed, broken – at the level of planning as well as
social and intellectual life. His book is a *tour de force* of whatever
genre you want to use to describe it, and I'm still not sure what
genre that would be.

Suddenly Lawrence Dale and his views disappear. They exist
nowhere but in his little book, long out of print, in his bright little
watercolours and strange poetic-polemical prose with its *New Age*
flourishes and precise yet visionary plans. His book came out when
Eliot was poetry editor at Faber – it would not have been out of
place on a poetry list that included Auden, Lawrence Durrell and
Lynette Roberts. One section, entitled 'Towards', ends with these
rousingly mystical lines:

> Not forwards nor backwards, not downwards nor upwards, not
> inwards nor outwards, but, like a flower, opening in the sun.
> Towards – self realization.[5]

Stick that in your Local Development Plan and take it to the Council Sub-Committee.

HEAD OF THE RIVER AND SALTER'S BOATYARD

I could head to the river, or to The Head *of* the River. It's one of Oxford's legendary pubs, but was once St Aldate's Yard – warehouses and stables for the dock that is now the pub's garden. It belonged to Salter's, the boatmakers who are still here – right here in front of me – six generations on. Old photos show boats being assembled or launched, and a crane, used to load and unload cargo, still hangs over today's drinkers. On the other side of Folly Bridge, another crane is half-hidden behind the bankside trees, and the wire basket on a pulley overhangs the river.

Salter's changed in order to stay the same: they started as boatmakers, then branched out into pleasure-cruises and tourism. Oxford's first station was a few hundred yards south, and they teamed up with GWR to run river and rail package tours. Their boatyards made prestigious racing boats and their fleet moved goods. 'Salter's Navy' employed hundreds of workers. I had a friend who lived in a Salter's flat under the arches of Folly Bridge, and when the Salter's offices had closed, she had the quayside to herself. More and more I find the parts of Oxford that give me the most pleasure and satisfaction, that light up the days, are these in-between moments and in-between sights: today as I pass, it's a woman on a deckchair at the edge of Salter's island, drinking something hot (I can see the steam) and facing eastwards where the river widens towards London, Kingston, Henley-on-Thames...

This was a bustling waterway – still is, but now it's university boats and tourist steamers, the occasional kayak expedition. Tourists might stray here, or stop at the edge of The Head of the River, but that's about it. At some point here, they turn back. Crossed or uncrossed, it's another Oxford threshold.

FOLLY BRIDGE ISLAND

Like East and West, South Oxford is reached by bridge. This is where historians believe the city got its name: where the original oxen originally forded. This was the principal approach: a great causeway that roughly corresponded to today's Abingdon Road, ending at today's Redbridge Park and Ride, the last stop before the recycling centre. The causeway was built by Robert D'Oyly, who also built Oxford Castle and the Norman Tower, in the eleventh century. Before that there was a Saxon causeway. The renaissance maps show an extraordinary edifice, forty arches long, some of which are still visible on the south side of Folly Bridge. Road resurfacing and council digging often reveal the old blocks. When the river is low you can make out old stones and debris which I think must be part of this road's centuries of rebuilding and remodelling as it too changes so it can stay the same.

This is an island, just large enough for a few buildings, and it sometimes even feels like one. A narrow, lozenge-shaped piece of land in the middle of the Thames, joined by one bridge you notice and one you generally don't. The one you notice is overlooked by an eccentric castellated house with statues and cast-iron balconies – it's the folly that gives the bridge its name. The bridge you don't notice comes a few yards later, and is six strides and two bike-wheel-revolutions long. On the old maps of Oxford, the main building on the island is a hexagonal tower with a portcullis and drawbridge. Built in the thirteenth century, it was used by the philosopher Roger Bacon as an observatory. 'Friar Bacon's Study' was its old name. Bacon is one of philosophy's maverick all-rounders: friar, alchemist, astronomer, his official title was *Doctor Mirabilis*. I'm not sure what sort of exams you have to do for that, but it's not a degree that's still on offer.

The lane named after him in St Ebbe's is Oxford's most depressing street: a dead passage made of liver-coloured brick along the outer wall of the Westgate Sainsbury's, it also serves as a late-night *pissoir*, whose gradient sends tributaries of post-pub urine down to the residential *plateau* of flats and houses. St Ebbe's: still getting pissed on after all these years. Roger Bacon Lane is a comedown from the fortified bridge that was an Oxford landmark for 500 years. Knocked down in 1779 to widen the road, it was the predecessor of the building I'm now in front of: 5 Folly Bridge.

Built of patterned brick, with a crenellated roof and little alcoves on the outer walls inset with white classical statues, it's the setting for a gothic costume drama; or, in certain lights, a Hammer House of Horror film. I keep expecting Vincent Price's face at the window. It was built in 1849 for the mathematician Joseph Caudwell, and was originally known as North Hinksey House and then 'Caudwell's Castle'. It's an unusual example of the building being designed to match the name of the address, rather than vice versa. There are cast-iron balconies and the top floor has a roof garden. On the roof overlooking the road, a not very big Atlas holds his arms aloft in an imploring pose. He's dropped his globe – maybe it's in the water with the old boat-timber and the slabs of causeway. On the ground floor, level with the water, is a jetty that serves as a terrace and bobs around when the current is strong. Sometimes there's a boat moored, a table and chairs, often a sofa, but today, all there is is half a bathtub. Are they planning to enact a nursery rhyme, I wonder? One part Lewis Carroll to three parts Edward Lear?

Another threshold is Folly Bridge Toll House, built in 1844 to catch the travellers using Grandpont Station. It used to be a sweet shop and newsagent that sold postcards and guide books and little souvenirs. Ice cream in the summer. It was the last outpost of tourist Oxford. It's been recently gutted and is now being transformed – probably into the same thing. Oxford is full of places that are stripped out and renovated with much fanfare, only to become exactly what they were before. It's the service industry version of reincarnation: endlessly reborn, but into the same body. The rush of change, its waste and its debris (and skips of course), but without the actual change. The little alley behind the booth takes me along the river to the houses and flats on the Oxpens side.

It's the best way to see Folly Bridge House, or No 4 Folly Island, whose garden stretches to the tip of the island. Folly Bridge House is not No 5 Folly Island, 'Caudwell's Castle', but a Victorian crenellated tower built twenty-five years later, with a house stuck to the back of it. It's hidden behind huge gates now, and the Victorian tower is studio flats and Airbnb, while the owners live in the attached house. A Union Jack flies from the back of their garden, which is where the land ends. What is it with people sticking flags into the soil?

In the old days, this would have been the way to the Oxpens cattle market and back into St Ebbe's, as well as the first Oxford gasworks, built in 1818 on the St Ebbe's side of the river. The new flats and houses are attractive and look Scandinavian in their openness: none of the 'Private – Keep Out' aura that a lot of new buildings have. Little balconies and terraces go right up to the public footpath and no-one seems afraid of having their garden furniture or their shrouded barbecues nicked. Their French doors are open – it's that time of the afternoon – the French call it *entre chien et loup*, between dog and wolf – when the pans come out and the lights on the cooker-hoods come on. I'd love to come back from work, turn off past the toll-booth that became a newsagent that became another newsagent that became another newsagent (etc.), walk down a little riverside path like this, and suddenly duck into my kitchen-dining room. I'd slide open the glass doors and leave them open so I could smell the river, which always smells stronger and deeper in the darkness.

Show me the spires and towers, the vistas and the views, but it's the lamplit windows of other people's houses that set me dreaming. Not out of voyeurism, I like to think, but out of curiosity about other people's everyday. I backtrack and cross the bridge, and head into Grandpont proper. Today it's quiet and serene, but this must have been a noisy place – a working waterway with a working dock, workshops and moorings. On the other side of Folly Bridge the river widens and the boats get bigger. I track the origin of the suspended cargo-basket, stopped in time, Ruskin's rust on it, winched half-across the water, to the blue crane that overhangs the path, and then to its base in the courtyard of a block of flats. It's still solidly riveted into the ground. This was still a boatyard when I was here, part of Salter's. The wheelie bins are arranged around it now like bodyguards. In the bushes a man is fishing furtively. I am not sure it's legal; nor, by the looks of it, is he.

THE UNDERSIDES OF MANY BRIDGES

Visiting Oxford by water is a special experience, and once I've passed the postcard-views – Botanic Gardens, Magdalen Deer Park, University Parks – I'm sliding along the banks of a totally different city. Some of it is picturesque water-suburbia – houseboats with literary names, burglar alarms and nice bikes; little postboxes, TV aerials, vegetable patches and sheds. Lavender and sage in containers on deck. Cats and dogs with collars and phone numbers of landlines. Some of it is more *louche* and transitional: riverbank-raves and parties, strange gatherings and activities at the river's edge. Some of it is feral, as frightened of me as I am of it, and I catch the silver moonlit rims of cans and bottles as I pass. I row by in my little boat, see the campfires or smell the weed, and because it's dark and there's no-one else it seems absurd and artificial not to say 'hello'. So I do: hello, hello, I call out. Small conversations ensue – oddments of politeness, the weather, the current, how warm it is. Or they don't ensue, the silence hardens up, and I sail on feeling watched. *Wind in the Willows* it isn't.

I start South Oxford at the gasworks bridge. It's an artificial division, but Oxford is the home of artificial divisions. It's especially artificial here because Osney, St Ebbe's, Oxpens and Folly Bridge would have been connected by river traffic, towpaths, backstreets and bridges.

The area around Folly Bridge would have been busy, noisy, happening – a water-St. Aldate's. Boats and barges in traffic jams, river-raging drivers, honking horns. A river-thoroughfare, shared between tourists and workers, heavy and light industry, commuters and boat-dwellers. The best way of getting a sense of this is by taking a boat – my inflatable kayak does the job – on the short journey from one island to the other: Folly Bridge to Osney. I've seen the underside of many Oxford bridges, from the industrial bridges like the one over the sheepwash channel behind the station where the pigeons line up on mounds of guano against a backdrop of graffiti tags, to the cool shade of the stone arches of Magdalen Bridge. My local bridge, the Donnington Bridge, is a relative newcomer – built in 1961, this major road-link must have radically changed the relationship between South and East Oxford. Suddenly the edges of Oxford, like Weirs Lane, New Hinksey, Old Abingdon Road, were ten minutes from Cowley Road or St Clement's. The waterways are a whole Oxford network, an entire set of bearings of their own: the river-city, the under-city, the inter-city.

Long before I thought of writing this book, we used to make the journey by paddle and punt from Cowley Place, where the garden of our rented house sloped down to the river, to Folly Bridge. We'd moor somewhere off Christ Church Meadow or by the little steps beside Salters, and head to St Aldate's to do our shopping. In those days there was a Co-Op on Cornmarket as well as the Westgate Sainsbury's. Where the St Aldate's Tesco now is, there was a lighting shop. One day we decided to add two bargain-basement floor-lamps to our shopping haul, and carried it all back to the punt. The weather had changed to heavy rain, or perhaps the weather had changed to heavy rain much earlier and the results were only coming downriver now, but suddenly the current was so powerful that, ballasted with shopping and the weight of our floor-lamp bases, we were propelled into the open water towards the huge and widening throat of the Thames. The water moved so fast we were unable to hit our turning for Cowley place (always a precarious operation anyway), and instead went on past Donnington Bridge. We watched seasoned rowers calling it a day, dragging their nimble sculls and canoes back to safety. The big houseboats battened down, literally, the hatches, while we were flushed downriver like something from a Joseph Conrad novel.

Luck brought us to a soggy bankside about two miles down from where we lived, and we drank our screwtop wine (a novelty back then) and lamented, our boat wedged between tree stumps. Several hours later we dragged ourselves home, fistful by fistful of bankside grass, to the turning where, at last, we could paddle our way back to the house. These were the days before Health and Safety.

OXPENS AND THE FRIAR'S QUARTER FROM THE SOUTH

Most people would say that Oxpens was Central Oxford, not South. They'd be right. After all, it's a quick walk to the station, it's on a main arterial road, and it's overlooked by the Westgate. Hence the traffic jams, the council parking by the ice rink, and the cheaper £5 all-day parking at City of Oxford College. But because I walk the bridges and the towpaths, I've ended up thinking of Oxpens and St Ebbe's as connected to South Oxford. That's what bridges do. But it's also what the people who once lived here did, because in terms of Oxford's industrial past, they are joined: the first Oxford gas works were built in the Friar's District of St Ebbe's in 1818. Later gas works were built on the other side, the space now occupied by Grandpont and Grandpont Nature Reserve, and were only closed in 1960. I'll get to them.

I've come with an old engraving of the St Ebbe's works. I'm going to hold it up in a *then and now* exercise and try to find the spot it was viewed from. Drawn by Frederick Mackenzie, a painter and draughtsman who specialised in church architecture and antiquities, it was engraved by Le Keux and published in 1835. Last time I checked, which was about two weeks ago, there was a print available in Sanders Antique Prints and Maps on Oxford High Street. It's mounted but unframed and costs £65 – the equivalent of two *Harry Potter* sweatshirts. It's a cut above the usual Oxford merchandise.

I'm on the south side of the river looking north, holding the past up to the present. Mackenzie's engraving makes it look as if an early industrial revolution has been dropped beside Oxford's river-idyll. In the foreground there's a 'swain', a few horses, three of whom are 'gambolling' (I think that's the first time I've ever written that word), and a cow lying heavily on its side. The turquoise water is foamy and ruffled. The artist has crammed together, in ways not at all exact to scale or topography, Oxford's most beautiful buildings: they're pale and finely detailed in the light. It's the middle ground that's dark, shadowed, like something hidden away – early industrial Oxford, hunched and cowering, a chimney pumping smoke eastwards, sandwiched between a slice of idealised countryside and a slice of idealised cityscape. The un-ideal filling in an idealization sandwich, an Id between two Superegos. Mackenzie had practiced

his shadowing on all those Pugin vaulted ceilings and gothic crannies, and he lets it loose on the gas works. I wonder if he hasn't composed the picture to reveal something about the relationship of the three Oxfords, or any city, at the start of the nineteenth century, and if he hasn't deliberately presented them like this: in layers or strata.

I take a picture of the engraving in front of what stands there now: trees overhanging the bank and blocking any view. What do I expect, two hundred years later? So instead I go to the gasworks bridge and ask a passer-by to hold it up. This shot provides dramatic, if anachronistic scenery, because the gas works bridge only arrived in 1886. The sky is very blue and the river is high, fast and toffee-brown. It's bright and cold. I was here two nights ago, walking the towpath on the other side, at the north end of this bridge, on my way to a newish Osney pub on Mill Street, behind the Electricity Station, The Porterhouse Grill. It used to be The Kite – it's where you ate if you were in the Watermans Arms and hungry.

This is one of my favourite walks: from Iffley Fields, down Meadow Lane, over Donnington Bridge and Weirs Lane, down Abingdon Road, off Folly Bridge, along the Oxpens towpath, past Gibbs Crescent with the blown-off west end and now shaped like a croissant with a bitten-off claw, along Osney cemetery railings and down to Botley. It's towpaths, footbridges, people's back gardens and straggly lines of squashed urban countryside scraping along the fenced-off railway line. I walk from Iffley to Wolvercote like this, and I suggest you do too.

Anyway, what I am about to relate (as they say in literature), is true.

It was about 8 pm when I crossed the gas works bridge and turned west. A woman was feeding pieces of pizza to geese and talking to them soothingly – so soothingly I thought she was telling me not to worry. I was a captive audience because I was at the time quite worried about various things, so I lingered to hear her out. She had a shopping bag on wheels from which she drew, once the pizza was finished, fistfuls of grain from a bag of specialist *Swan, Goose and Duck Feed.* The geese were honking grouchily at me, but they were used to her. She had names for them. Queenie was one. Delia another. As the geese milled about, the ground seemed to be moving beneath me. I felt a slight dizziness, a warm brushing at my ankles where my trousers met my shoes. Things eddying around me. But the ground wasn't moving, it was hundreds of rats. I measure rats by shoe-size, and these were size tens – that's a 44 for my European readers. The geese shared their food happily enough, but after a while the rats started darting around, crashing into each other and fighting, squeaking and jumping on their hind legs the way bears do in nature programmes. The avian food she was feeding them was high energy, and it showed. Rat metabolism is basically real time, give or take a very brief lag of the sort you get on Skype or Teams or Zoom: the human equivalent of shitting out your starters while tucking into your main course. The woman knew the rats too, though not by name. She only had names for the geese. We all draw the line somewhere.

The woman was defensive and afraid, but also angry when she saw me – she was attacked a few days ago for doing this, and was obviously someone who had been much harmed by others. She has received death threats. We were, after all, a few yards from hundreds of houses and flats. I'd have been queasy seeing this so close to my dining room. She told me about her eleven years in Oxford, how she fed these geese every day, knew them, tracked them and their families, and how the rats were part of the way we had to take nature, how we couldn't pick and choose the bits we wanted, or make judgments on the food chain from the top of the food chain. She talked about human cruelty, which she knew, and was coherent in every respect – not just in the abstract things she said about nature and the environment, but about what she had seen of humanity here, on this path, night after night, standing with her trolley and her leftovers and enduring abuse and malignity and violence. I realised, as I walked back, that the reason I knew she was mad was that everything she'd said had been true.

I went home and cleaned my shoes, put my rat-rubbed socks and trousers into the wash and settled down to watch David Attenborough. He merely said the same things she had, albeit in front of some whales. I thought of the David Attenborough mural off the Cowley Road between Chapel Street and East Avenue. It's also a dumping ground for drive-by tippers. Upturned sofas, abandoned supermarket trolleys, student fridges, binbags of sludgy stuff that someone forgot to put in the food bins and decided to get rid of here. Beneath the portrait is a reverent line from the man himself: 'The future of humanity and of all life on earth now depends on us'.

The next morning, I thought I'd dreamed it – that this mysterious woman and the geese with their grand names, the rats squeaking and leaping in the air, were the cast of some dark nursery rhyme that my unconscious had filmed with the help of David Lynch. So I had some tea and breakfast and came straight back – as if the place could confirm or deny what had happened. That's why I'm here now with my Mackenzie print. Today there's a mother and toddler feeding bread to the same geese. A different, happier nursery rhyme.

I put the engraving away and retrace my steps to the gas works pipe bridge. Built in 1927, it's now a narrow footbridge linking South Oxford to the little pocket of flats and houses of Dale Close,

Blackfriars Road, Trinity Street and Friar's Wharf. It's hidden, residential, mixed Oxford, with little pedestrian alleys and river walks, a playground and some gardens. There are sudden turnings that offer views, amid bollards or recycling bins, of the river and its barges, or of the double-deckers on Thames Street. Preachers Lane is where the first gas works were built, and the evocatively-named Gas Street, the entrance, no longer exists. I've already written about St Ebbe's, but this way of approaching it – from a once-working river, or from St Aldate's – is the best way to grasp not just its size but the way it once occupied a central place in Oxford's economic and social life. I enjoy the riverbank views with the geese, the kayaks, the barges, the runners and cyclists, the trains and their sirens, the red or yellow of the buses glimpsed through canopies of leaves; or, in winter, the bare black branches that leave the whole place exposed, though still somehow secret, from riverbank to shopping centre.

There's a children's playground in front of the Friar's Wharf flats, whose blocks are linked by little first-floor walkways, open-air corridors. People cross from one block to the other to see their friends and neighbours, just like their predecessors would have crossed the footbridges to work or socialise. I take a picture of the walkway, and of the view through to the Westgate. More cranes are scratching about somewhere north of Gloucester Green. All the bollards here are different, they've been knocked over and replaced so often. The one I'm sitting on has been broken and re-cemented like a crowned tooth. It's not exactly the Bridge of Sighs – there's one of those on New College Lane if you want the real thing – but it's a satisfying little view through to a place's daily life.

GRANDPONT STATION

This part of Oxford is unostentatiously full of history, and crucial to the development of the modern city. You wouldn't know it just to walk or cycle, let alone drive, from Folly Bridge to Redbridge Park and Ride. Opened just in time for Christmas 1973, it was the UK's first Park and Ride. Abingdon Road has three pubs, a few cafés, a couple of takeaways, a classic launderette, of the kind that's disappearing, a pharmacy, a barbers shop, some local supermarkets, and, at the south end, garages and MOT centres. It also has Akiport, a Portuguese café and supermarket. I'm having my coffee there in a minute. All these businesses are on, or just a few buildings off, the Abingdon Road spine.

Only the west side of Abingdon Road is built up, and even then the streets aren't very deep. They end in railway line, meadows or water. The east side of Abingdon Road is playing fields and allotments and, facing The White House pub (designed by Henry Hare of Oxford Town Hall and now being refurbished by Tap Social), one of the world's earliest purpose-built squash courts. It belongs to one of the colleges and is clearly used as a random storeroom, because the windows are crammed with stuff that looks like it's trying to get out. It's a shame because it would make a great squash court. A recent arrival, also on the east side, is the Spires Hotel which occupies the site and some of the buildings of the old Eastwyke Farm, still slaughtering animals and supplying Alden's butchers in the 1970s. Think of it: a working farm with its own abattoir ten minutes' walk from the city centre.

I turn right after the White House pub, currently serving drinks from a horse-box while the renovation works continue, to where Whitehouse Road crosses Marlborough Road, the longest street in South Oxford. It follows the route of the old railway embankment – its height made it safe from flooding once Oxford's first station had closed. This unassuming cluster of Victorian terraces and modern courts was once Oxford's station quarter. Grandpont station was a small wooden structure with a passenger platform, a waiting-room, goods shed and a track that led directly to the riverbank, where coal and goods could be loaded onto the boats. It would have been a centre for day-trippers on the surf and turf, boat-and-train excursions from Folly Bridge. As old filmreels are presented with atmospheric music, so I try to supply the noises and the smells. The sound- and nose-scape here would be an agri-industrial swirl: coal and gas, fertilizer, silage, manure (there's still a bit of that from the allotments); cows lowing, sheep bleating, pigs snuffling, hens yaffling; abattoir saws and meat being driven by cart, later van, out into the suburbs, down Abingdon way or up St Aldate's to the university's dining halls; the engines of trains and boats; the clatter of cargo scraping wharf or dropping into freight carriages.

When the station closed, this became Oxford's first football quarter. Outside the nursery school nearby, children are kicking a ball in the playground. Let them provide the soundtrack for me. The cries are a little over-enunciated – there's not much of the Oxford accent in areas like this – and there are no insults, chants or profanities (yet), but it's the smack of boot against ball that's universal. That'll do.

PLAQUE TO PLAQUE

The Whitehouse Road Ground was here until 1988, and it's difficult to imagine the scale of it now. In its place stands Hodges Court, a 1990s development with a plaque to the old stadium, and to H.F. Hodges, the player who scored the first goal in Oxford City's 1906 Amateur Cup win. It's on the side of the first house, beside a high window that today is crammed with children's party decorations that have just been taken down and piled on the windowsill against the glass – bunting, multicoloured lanterns and a little crown with the word 'Happy' on it. I take some pictures inside Hodges court, trying to find the angle from which one of the old photos on the South Oxford History website is taken. The stadium abutted St Matthew's Church on Marlborough Road, a church that looks just a little too big for the street. It too is full of history. Inside, there's a memorial plaque to a local man who died on the *Titanic*, and a brass memorial to the 66 men of Grandpont who died in World War I. The South Oxford History website links to a film and a project tracing their lives and connections to the area. The project and web pages are the work of historian Liz Woolley, who lives nearby, and whose work on Oxford's industrial history has been invaluable.[6] The scale of the war is often best expressed by the devastating microcosmic scale of its effect on people and community: of the 66 young men who died, more than a quarter of them lived, or had families who lived, on Marlborough Road. All that loss in a single street, all that pain happening long after and far away from where war 'happened'.

I find the old football ground – it's the forecourt of the new development, a few garages, some bins. Hodges Court is a quiet

little oasis accessible either from the side of Whitehouse Road or a tiny little door-sized underpass from Marlborough Road, the route I take as I leave. This is where Oxford City beat Germany 9-0 in 1909, and where, seventy years later, in 1979, World Cup legend Bobby Moore was fêted (briefly) as Oxford City's new manager.

As plaques go, the H.F. Hodges/Whitehouse Road Ground one is modest, especially in a city of plaques and memorials. *The first this, the last that, the discovery of X, the invention of Y....* There are divisions of plaques just as there are divisions of football and divisions of memory – national, civic, local, personal. There are the all-singing all-dancing blue plaques which English Heritage began in 1866, and to which there must, logically, also be a plaque: 'the location and recipient of the first plaque were decided here...'. Then there are the Oxfordshire Blue Plaques, created in 1999 by the Oxford Civic Society. I must pass a dozen plaques a day – every walk is a plaque-crawl: William Morris's on James Street, the Roger Bannister Four-Minute Mile plaque in Iffley Road, Olive Gibbs's on Osney Lane, and Annie Rogers, Oxford's first woman don, and founding fellow of my college, on St Giles. Then there's the plaque to the first use of penicillin on the wall of the Radcliffe Infirmary on Woodstock Road and the plaque to the Oxford Playhouse, where the likes of Gielgud, Tyrone Guthrie, Flora Robson and Margaret Rutherford trod the boards. Before that – and there's no plaque to this – it was Oxford's Big Game Museum. It's now the language centre.

Near my faculty is a plaque to the great also-ran, the painter

William Turner of Oxford – known, even in his own lifetime, as 'of Oxford' to distinguish him from his famous contemporary, J.M.W. Turner, whose views of Oxford are also better-known. Blisteringly outshone in his profession, even his name wasn't properly his until they'd added a localising provenance. I hear his voice: 'no, not *that* Turner... no... not *that* painter... no, not *that* painting ...'

This plaque in front of me, to Oxford's first but now second football club, which won an amateur championship a hundred and fifteen years ago, was mounted by Oxford City Council. Oxford United's plaque is in Headington, affixed to the wall of The Britannia pub on London Road opposite the site of the Manor Ground, and was unveiled last year with some media fanfare. I'm not sure why one football ground and one football club gets a city council plaque and the other gets an Oxfordshire blue plaque. Maybe memory itself is a matter of survival of the fittest? It's not even as if Oxford City are gone, though they are the poor relation: currently 12th in the National League South, the sixth tier of national football, their ground is now on Marsh Lane in Marston. The two football teams seem, to me at least, to have just as much history as each other, and equal amounts of past. But what the plaques are really saying is that one has more *present* than the other.

MEADOWS, MEADS AND COMMONS

The water that threatens South Oxford also protects it, because it keeps the developers at bay. It also keeps the place green, and makes this area of Oxford feel uncrowded and full of small treasures. No blocks of flats, everything proportionate. At the most, there's a converted loft not so much scraping the sky as tickling the belly of a passing cloud of mist. A few church spires. At the end of Whitehouse Road is Dean's Ham Meadow, another of Oxford's edgeland/nature reserve/city-green-belt urban unbuilt acreages. A little further, Spragglesea Mead, a name that needs to be the title of an anarchic children's programme. Greenery, allotments, places to walk and play and lie around. I'm more of an ambler than a rambler, but every variety of pedestrian motion is here: runners, joggers, power-walkers; hiking-boots, thermos-and-plastic-covered-OS-map walkers; wellies and dog-walkers; single athletes and group-fitness-outings; couples trying to get somewhere and couples trying not to. Then there's the person with the wrong shoes, zig-zagging their way between landmines of mud and puddle-swamps. Hello – yes, that's me.

On the way to the footbridge I see a place called SOAP. So tantalisingly close to SLOAP. A mother and two children are letting themselves in – there's a code to get through the gates. Another Oxford threshold in a city of secret places. I peer in and see an array of bright rides and carousels, zipwires and swings, all in mint condition and overlooked by a superb wooden castle with turrets and rope bridges. This really is a child's fantasy, a little world inside a world, tucked away off a small path. It's a Roald Dahl story in playground design, with a touch of Dahlian danger – just enough threat to make it exciting. I ask the lady what SOAP stands for. She asks me to guess. 'Secret Oxford's Absconding Portal'. She says yes, that's right. (Obviously it's South Oxford Adventure Playground.)

This is floodplain-greenery and rail-line wilderness. On the other side of a bright green footbridge lies Hogacre Common (another children's programme right there, or a location in Harry Potter). All around me are little streams or stagnant pools with insects. I'm surprised to see so many unpicked blackberries, shiny and bursting with juice. I eat them as I go. They're delicious, though I remember the old saying that after Michaelmas Day the Devil spits on them. That was 29 September, three weeks ago. The blackberries near my house in Aston's Eyot shrivelled and moulded over long ago. These bulging, railway-track blackberries are like high-season fruit – heavy and sweet, but tart too – and it's the end of October. I don't have a bag, but I'll come back and get them for Devil's Spit Jam.

Occasionally, a bright metal spike of fencing sticks out from the undergrowth and reminds me that the trains pass here. Electric generators and track-boxes are buzzing away in the foliage. Under the footbridge, as far as I can see, are freight wagons. Open containers of chippings. They're yellow, their sides rusty, their cargo grey stuff, ballast, gravel, stuff that looks like cat litter. If I were to judge from the contents of all the freight carriages I've seen over the years, it's chippings that keep the world turning. It's hard to tell whether they've been here a day or a year. Every now and then something flicks into life, an automated switch, a whirr, the faint tremble of a train passing far away, then it's quiet again. More walkers. A dog with a tennis ball that's almost split, its two halves held together, just, by its knit of green hairs. The dog drops it at my feet. I kick it (the ball), and the two halves go in two directions. The dog looks at me resentfully, the owner even more so. Many life-affirming stories start with conversations struck up over dogs on isolated paths. This isn't one of them.

Hogacre Common was once the Corpus Christi college sports ground. The lines and markings of tennis courts and cricket pitches are getting fainter as nature covers it, like ancient hill forts whose outlines are still just about visible from the air. The fencing of the courts is now perfect for keeping vandals and animals out of the ramshackle vegetable plots. The chard is growing colourfully on the baseline of one court, and there are polytunnels in the service boxes that still have tomatoes. There must be a microclimate here – juicy blackberries, Tuscan-looking tomatoes, kale and broccoli.... The other court is an old carpet court, and it's being used for grow bags, composting and gardening equipment: wheelbarrows and bathtub water-butts. Wooden pallets where the umpire sat. On the top of a small mound between the courts is the sports pavilion, now a community space, outside which the old cast-iron lawn-levelling rollers have rusted to a warm shade of fox fur. The universal jettisoned sofa lies outside – one day all the sofas and mattresses we've thrown out will come back reclaim their territory – and there's an odd raised corridor on a platform with a roof and green netting on the sides which has been transformed into a strawberry bed. You go up some steps, pick your strawberries, open a door that belongs to the bedroom of a house, and there's nothing on the other side but a three-foot drop back into the tall grass. So I go in – the strawberries are long-gone – then open the door and jump out. It's an invitation to be a child, just for a few moments. My favourite touch, however, is the way the tennis nets have been used to support plants and make bird-proof enclosures: the white vinyl headbands of the net are twisted around posts and have beans winding around them. This, I think, is how Ruskin would have liked to see sports grounds being used.

I'm not sure why the college handed it over – did the students get lost on their way? Or were they sick of playing their matches ankle-deep in Thames water? I don't know, but the place is being leased by South Oxford Renewables, who use it for education, beekeeping and school visits. There's even an orchard of recently-planted apples and pears. I leave this place of surreally-repurposed sports facilities and take the path through the adjacent sports ground, still in use, that belongs to Pembroke College. It's a bit of let-down after Hogacre Common. Of note, only a clock, which has stopped, and whose minute-hand has melted to a Dalí-esque twist.

THE LIDO, THE LAKE AND THE DEVIL'S BACKBONE

It sounds like a title C.S. Lewis thought up then decided against. Or an Arthurian legend.

After tasting the devil's blackberries, it seems fitting to rejoin Abingdon Road via the 'Devil's Backbone'. It's the name of the raised path that connects the village of South Hinksey to Abingdon Road, over two hundred years old. The name is more commonly used now for the dramatic metal footway that crosses Hinksey Lake and the railway track. This is the quickest route in from Hinksey, and when it was damaged by a lorry and closed for a month in 2018, the residents of the village were up in arms. Local councillors got involved. Articles appeared claiming South Hinksey had been 'cut off' from the city. Some *Schadenfreudean* observer in the comments section of the *Oxford Mail* article claimed it served the villagers right for abandoning their local shop.

Before I reach the Devil's Backbone, I get my bearings in the flood-plain landscape. More paths and more walkers, a few pylons, some disused pipes from the old waterworks to which I'm heading. In front of me, Hinksey Village; behind me, Botley. Linking them in the distance is a path called Electric Road, so-named because that's where the cables between South Hinksey and Osney substation are laid. We're not far from Ruskin's wheelbarrow, Jude Fawley's ripped shoe-leather and the scholar gypsy. We're not far from the ring road either, which I can hear on the other side of Hinksey village.

The Devil's Backbone is one of my favourite Oxford places. I can see why the bridge might look like the spiky, arched spine of some huge creature. I don't get the devil reference – to me it looks like the skeleton of a peaceful dinosaur that expired and left its bones to the community as a contribution to local infrastructure. It's the ancestor of the pylons, a cousin of the vaulted ceilings of Victorian railway stations. It has of course been photographed in all weathers and none. On a cold bright day with the water reflecting the sky beneath it, it has the industrial-sublime feel the romantic painters liked; in the snow it looks like a Christmas card view, an image of stillness and quiet despite the hundreds of trains passing nearby; in the autumn with the trees stripped bare and the water still, it looks spooky and sad, something out of *Don't Look Now*; on grey misty days it looks like it has been finger-sketched in window-breath, dissolving as you watch. On many days, it just looks normal – a footbridge you cross because you're trying to go somewhere. Some days that's all you want to do – get from A to B and not loiter loquaciously trying to describe it. Underneath me, more metal fences, and inside them more railway-sidings and sidelined freight. Railway sleepers, two-foot thick and twelve foot long, lie like dropped matches.

I try to get a photo of the bridge, the reservoir, the carriages and the lake, along with the roof and steeple of St John the Evangelist Church on Vicarage Road. It doesn't work – I can't get all the effects

in. That's just as well, because it's the failure of photography to capture this and so many other views, that made me want to write. There's no lens wide enough, so I just keep coming back.

WATER EVERYWHERE

I've said that water defines West and South Oxford, but in a very specific historical sense that's true here, because South Oxford is where the city's clean water came from. The first waterworks, built in 1694 just below Friar Bacon's Study, simply drew water from the river. Its successor, behind Folly Bridge on the St Aldate's side, closed in 1856 and was demolished to make Shirelake Close in the 1970s. Both of these were downstream of the St Ebbe's Gas Works, and provided, according to the historian Liz Woolley's invaluable guides to industrial Oxford, poor quality water. Bad drainage and dirty water contributed to deadly cholera outbreaks in Oxford's poorer areas, and the same Victorian scientists who built the great museums and laboratories were also instrumental in improving living conditions in the city and signing it up to the 1848 Health of Towns Act.

Water is life and livelihood. But here it's also leisure. Standing on the Devil's Backbone I can see that: the reservoir beneath my feet, at whose edges two men are birdwatching, was created by digging the gravel to make the rail embankment that's now part of Marlborough Road. It's called Hinksey Lake. It all connects up, and I'm about to see how, because on Lake Street the old/new state-of-the-art (in 1854) pumping station is today's South Oxford Community Centre.

I walk to the Oxford Lido, or Hinksey Pool, where I've swum many times, and where I used to take the children. Nothing beats swimming in warm water in cold weather, the tingle of the vying temperatures in the blood and along the skin. Today's Hinksey Park is the landscaped grounds of the old waterworks, and the pools were created from the old filter beds. The waterworks closed in 1934, and while much of the Victorian infrastructure was demolished, the park retains the flavour of what it was. The Lido was built in 1934 – a low, white, *art nouveau*-style structure of cubicles and changing rooms and undulatingly-shaped pools. It's not especially distinguished, but it's unusual for Oxford. There are children's paddling pools and fountains with wave machines, but all very discreet, very classy, very art deco. It opens between May and September, and it's closed now. I'm surprised to see the water still there. That's odd, wrong even: green and brackish, fronded with algae, the ducks and geese have claimed it for a few weeks before the migration instinct kicks in. At least they have somewhere to go. Unlike the grey heron, who never goes anywhere, and who stands at the edge today, peering into the empty, stagnant paddling-pool.[7]

I feel sadder than I expected to see the Lido like this. It's not a rational sadness – I'm just anxious it may never reopen. I'm so used to seeing places go, degrade, fall into what the nineteenth century French poets called *desuetude*, that I over-interpret signs like these. There must be an elegy for Oxford's lost bathing-spots, those closed or concreted-over open-air and open-secret places with their fantastic names: Parson's Pleasure, Tumbling Bay, Longbridges, Sunnymead. I know Hinksey Pool will open again next year (do I really?), but from where I'm standing, on the other side of the railings, it looks like a scene from a documentary about endings.

LITTLE PORTUGAL

I think of it as a holiday. I've never been to Portugal, so the nearest thing for me is Akiport, a café-supermarket with a terrace that swallows up the pavement on a small parade of shops on Abingdon Road. One side is a small crowded café with a TV perpetually showing sports: mostly football and motor-racing. Next door is the supermarket. If you count the terrace outside (you may as well – they use the whole pavement), it's micro-Portugal. In the café there's great coffee and a modest but specific range of food. The supermarket sells Portuguese and Brazilian food and wine, and has freezers full of octopus and fish, rissoles and dumplings. Vacuum-packed dried fish hangs from hooks. Behind the shop and café is a room with a pool table and another TV. The terrace is a microcosmos of expatriate life, of second and third-generation rootedness. I'm often there for a Saturday afternoon coffee. Today, as always, the scooters and motorbikers park up and call out their orders and chat outside; families meet and mingle, everyone knows everyone else, and if they don't, they soon will. A man in cowboy boots, a Liverpool scarf and a Stetson arrives at the supermarket on a mobility scooter. He's Oxford, I can hear from the accent, and has a regular order, because it's placed in the *pannier* of his scooter as soon as he arrives. He chats for a while then goes to the chemist next door, slaloming back home between the Akiport Café tables. The deliveries never come in one go, in one big lorry. They're always goods-specific, so the wine and beer arrive, the delivery man loads it into the shop, is offered a coffee, talks for a while, smokes, then goes; next up is the frozen food man – same scenario, different cigarette; crisps and biscuits and chocolate come a bit later. On it goes, a fizzing network of generations and cultures, jobs and languages.

GAS AND GEIST

I began this book with steam and I'll finish it with gas. My penchant is always for the industrial or the post-industrial, I can't help it. But I idealise it too. I end this book on the other side of the river from where I started – a bridge away from Oxford Station.

This would have been leaky, polluted, dirty water – not like the clean water up in Soapsud Island, where Oxford's washing was done. My idealised canals would have been toxic, full of industrial slurry; my towpaths dirty, shit-strewn and smoggy. I almost bought a house on Wytham Street, close to the Devil's Backbone, back in 1998. I was warned against it by tales of polluted gardens, arsenic in the soil, gasworks seepage and chemicals. It was probably a myth, but anyway, I lacked the imagination – I wanted to be on Cowley Road with the restaurants and the clubs, the pubs and the cafés. Not here, where there are more churches than pubs, and the only activity is a wholesome walk to the allotments or Hinksey. So I ended up in East Oxford all my adult professional life. But South Oxford is where I'd live if I had my time again – a phrase most commonly used by people who don't.

It's amazing to remember that the gas works were ten minutes from Christ Church and St Aldate's. Part of the hidden Oxford well-symbolised in the Mackenzie engraving I took out earlier, it wasn't despised by everyone. Not at all. Oxford was part of the industrial revolution, and it was a town where things were made: melted, smelted, burned, hammered. Machines came here – wheels and chimneys and engines and conveyor-belts – changed the landscape, swallowed populations, made new populations. Work was drawn here like iron filings to a magnet. Industrial history happened here, and its signs are everywhere.

Yes, people read books and got degrees, but the other Oxford was always here.

W.H. Auden loved it down here by the river, around the Oxford Gas, Light and Coke Company (which sounds like a very bad night out), where I've trudged in the wrong shoes and seen the rats, where I've kayaked and walked and swum. Rex Warner, one of Auden's contemporaries, remembers being taken by Auden 'on expeditions up foul-smelling tunnels in a canoe'. Auden 'was not really interested in nature unless nature was at work reclaiming old mines or derelict machinery'. In 'Letter to Lord Byron', his long poem which is also a personal manifesto-cum-autobiography (a bit early – he was only 29), Auden writes of his influences:

> But Eliot spoke the still unspoken word;
> For gasworks and dried tubers I forsook
> The clock at Grantchester, the English rook.

Some critics claim that Auden's reason for bringing his friends here was to illustrate Eliot's *Waste Land*. I disagree – nothing I've read in Auden suggests he read the industrial world in that apocalyptic way, or that he saw it as a cultural threat. On the contrary, I think the place I'm in now was – still is – a very Audenesque image of connections: routes, paths and waterways, between the parts of our lives and cultures that are presented to us as separate.

Lawrence Dale knew that when he imagined a new city that made a virtue of its connectedness, that broke down the barriers between the Oxfords. The gas that warms the room we sleep in, the electricity that lights the desk we read at, the farm that rears the animals we eat, the factories that make the tools we till the soil with, and the plant that made the cars that brought us here and let us escape from here. Auden is a poet of connectedness, where Eliot is the poet of disconnection. I don't think it was just the gasworks as an object or a symbol that attracted Auden, but its proximity to, and its involvement with, the city and university, the books and the libraries. Auden also knew that Oxford University likes to think of itself and its people as separate and splendidly aloof, especially from the city it grows out of. But, as Mackenzie's engraving shows us inadvertently, it takes a lot of shadows to support the city of light. Auden 'got' that, and this bankside towpath with an old gasworks bridge is where he got it.

STATION CODA

I'm at the station again. It's late, so it's the sirens of the freight trains I can hear, exulting in the endless track they have ahead of them, all those empty stations they can slice through while we sleep. Like the wild animals calling to get the measure of the jungle. It's dark, and time to go. As always, I approach the station and then turn back.

From the day I came here, I thought I'd leave. I didn't know.

Connoisseur of the noises things make
when they leave: the clip of heels on pavements,
the suitcases on rubber wheels;

a station pigeon's piebald underwing,
the bike chain's sticky grind.
A car chews through the gears,

a train burns through a sleeve of cable-sparks.
The barges clear their foghorn throats.
There are so many ways of going yet you stay.

Notes

1. Irma died while I was correcting the proofs of this book. Readers will get a sense of her life, and of her place in the community, from the *Oxford Mail* article https://www.oxford mail.co.uk/news/19243649.blackbird-leys-resident-philanthropist-dies-age-80/
2. 'Irma James talks about moving to Britain from St Vincent', *Museum of Oxford – City Stories*: https://museumofoxford.omeka.net/items/show/207
3. 'Ermine Rogers talks about moving to Britain from St Vincent', *Museum of Oxford – City Stories*: https://museumofoxford.omeka.net/exhibits/show/windrushyears/item/208
4. John Betjeman, *An Oxford University Chest* (Oxford: Oxford University Press, 1979), p. 8.
5 Lawrence Dale, *Towards a Plan for Oxford City* (London: Faber and Faber, 1944), p. 52.
6. As well as writing about Oxford and its people, Liz Woolley also writes and maintains the excellent South Oxford History Pages: http://www.southoxford.org/local-history-in-south-oxford
7. I later discover that this very heron is the subject of a poem by South Oxford resident Jamie McKendrick:'I feel the knowledge/ of that heron', he writes:'The world is a con', *The Years* (Todmorden, Arc, 2020), p. 7.

WORKS CONSULTED

Acland, Henry *Memoir on the Cholera in Oxford in the Year 1854*, Books on Demand, 2018

Attlee, James *Isolarion: A Different Oxford Journey*, And Other Stories, 2020 (1st ed. 2007)

Barbaresi, Rachel *Urbansuburban: Searching for St Ebbe's in the Suburbs*, https://drive.google.com/file/d/0Byrv1kt5GJn HdWl2SEl1UW5wbEU/view

Betjeman, John *An Oxford University Chest*, Oxford University Press, 1979 (1st ed. 1938)

Bowie, Duncan *Reform and Revolt in the City of Dreaming Spires: Radical, Socialist and Communist Politics in the City of Oxford 1830-1980*, University of Westminster Press, 2018

Brockliss, L.W.B. *The University of Oxford; A Brief History*, Bodleian Library, 2018

Cannan, Joanna *High Table*, Penguin, 1939

Chapman, Don, and Farr, Peter, *Images of Oxford*, Breedon Books/Oxford Mail, 1994

Collison, Peter *The Cutteslowe Walls: A Study in Social Class*, Faber and Faber, 1963

Colvin, Howard *Unbuilt Oxford*, Yale University Press, 1983

Compton, Hugh *The Oxford Canal*, David and Charles, 1977

Crispin, Edmund *The Case of the Gilded Fly*, Collins, 20117 (1st ed. 1944)

Crispin, Edmund *The Moving Toyshop*, Collins, 2015 (1st ed. 1946)

Curl, James Stevens *The Erosion of Oxford*, Oxford Illustrated Press, 1977

Dale, Lawrence *Towards a Plan for Oxford City*, Faber and Faber, 1944

Dexter, Colin *The Dead of Jericho*, Macmillan, 1981

Dibdin *Dirty Tricks*, Faber and Faber, 1999

Fenby, Charles *The Other Oxford*, Lund Humphries, 1970

Gibbs, Olive *'Our Olive': The Autobiography of Olive Gibbs*, Robert Dugdale, 1989

Graham, Malcolm, *A Century of Oxford*, Sutton, 1999

Graham, Malcolm *The Changing Faces of West Oxford*, Boyd, 1998

Graham, Malcolm *On Foot in Oxford*, Oxford City Libraries, 1974-1988

Graham, Malcolm *Oxford in the Great War*, Pen and Sword, 2014

Hardy, Thomas *Jude the Obscure*, Oxford University Press, 2008 (1st ed. 1895)

Heine, Bill *Hunting the Shark*, Oxford Folio, 2011

Hewison, Robert *Ruskin in Oxford: The Art of Education*, Clarendon

Press, 1996

Hibbert, Christopher *The Encyclopedia of Oxford*, Macmillan, 1988

Holmes, John *Temple of Science: The Pre-Raphaelites and the Oxford Museum of Natural History*, Bodleian Library, 2020

Kennedy, Julie *The Changing Faces of Summertown and Cutteslowe*, Boyd, 1995

Kennedy, Julie *The Changing Faces of Oxford City Centre*, Boyd, 1998

Larkin, Philip *Jill*, Faber and Faber, 2005 (1st ed. 1946)

MacCannell, Daniel *Oxford: Mapping the City*, Birlinn, 2016

Morris, Jan *Oxford*, Oxford University Press, 2001 (1st ed. 1965)

Morris, Jan *The Oxford Book of Oxford*, Oxford University Press, 1978

Newbigging, Carole *The Changing Faces of St Ebbe's and St Thomas*, 1 & 2, Boyd, 1997

Newbigging, Carole *The Changing Faces of Blackbird Leys*, Boyd, 2000

Newbigging, Carole *The Changing Faces of Marston*, 1 & 2, Boyd, 1996 & 1997

Newbigging, Carole, Shatford, Susanne, Williams, Trevor *The Changing Faces of Cowley*, Book 1, Boyd, 1994

Newbigging, Carole, and Williams, Trevor *The Changing Faces of Cowley*, Book 2, Boyd, 2002

Pevsner, Nikolaus, and Sherwood, Jennifer *Oxfordshire*, Penguin, 1979 (1st ed. 1974)

Pressnell, Jon *Morris: The Cars and The Company*, J.H. Haynes & Co., 2013

Pullman, Philip *Lyra's Oxford*, Doubleday, 2017 (1st ed. 2003)

Rice, Matthew *Oxford*, White Lion, 2019

Sayers, Dorothy L. *Gaudy Night*, Gollancz, 1935

Sharp, Thomas *Oxford Replanned*, Arthictectural Press, 1948

Spokes Symonds, Ann *The Changing Faces of Iffley*, Boyd, 1999

Spokes Symonds, Ann *The Changing Faces of Rose Hill*, Boyd, 2000

Spokes Symonds, Ann *The Changing Faces of North Oxford*, 1 & 2, Boyd, 1998

Stott, Martin *The Cowley Road Cookbook*, Signal Books, 2015

Taunt, Henry *The Thames of Henry Taunt*, ed. Susan Read, Sutton Publishing, 1989

Wain, John *Where the Rivers Meet*, Coronet, 1988

Waugh, Evelyn *Brideshead Revisited*, Chapman and Hall, 1945

Woolley, Liz *Oxford's Working Past: Walking Tours of Victorian and Edwardian Industrial Buildings*, Huxley Scientific Press, 2012

ONLINE RESOURCES

Oxfordshire History Centre
https://www.oxfordshire.gov.uk/residents/leisure-and-culture/history/oxfordshire-history-centre

Oxoniensa
https://oxoniensia.org/

Oxford History

http://oxfordhistory.org.uk/

Oxfordshire Local History Association
http://www.olha.org.uk/contact/

Local sites by area:

Cowley Road
https://www.cowleyroad.org/

Headington
http://www.headington.org.uk/

Iffley
http://www.iffleyhistory.org.uk/

Jericho
https://www.jerichocentre.org.uk/about_jericho/history

Marston
http://www.headington.org.uk/history/marston_history/index.htm

South Oxford
https://www.southoxfordhistory.org.uk/

Summertown
http://www.summertown.info/history.html

West Oxford
https://osneyisland.org.uk/
https://botleyhinksey.org.uk/

Local Historians, subject-specific blogs, sites and pages

Liz Woolley
http://lizwoolley.co.uk/

Life in the Floodplain (Joanna Innes)
https://jminnes.wordpress.com/about/

Queer Oxford
https://queeroxford.info/

Uncomfortable Oxford
https://www.uncomfortableoxford.co.uk/

John Eade's 'Where Thames Smooth Waters Glide'
https://thames.me.uk/index.htm

Simon Wenham
http://simonwenham.com/about-simon-wenham/

Oxford pages in *Municipal Dreams*:

https://municipaldreams.wordpress.com/2020/07/29/council-housing_in-oxford_part_i/

https://municipaldreams.wordpress.com/category/oxford/

Where Thames Smooth Waters Glide (Oxford Pages)

https://thames.mc.uk/s02430.htm

THE PHOTOGRAPHS

ACKNOWLEDGEMENTS

I've spent years walking around Oxford, much of the time accompanied by friends who made it come alive. Whether they lived here or were just passing, they had one thing in common: they didn't take Oxford at face-value, and they didn't believe all the stories it told about itself. They came to it at an angle, questioned it, turned it over and looked behind it, wondering what it might look like from the other side. They will see and hear themselves in these pages, and will know this book is theirs.

My thanks go to Peter Finch, the series editor, for his energy and enthusiasm, and for offering me the chance to make Oxford *Real*.

I owe equally large thanks to the people who write about Oxford and to the societies and institutions who preserve it.

In the first category, Oxford's local historians have written books and articles, and created online pages and resources, that have guided my walks and taught me about the connections between then and now. They make those connections dynamic: not just facts, but prompts to thinking and feeling. Oxford is lucky to have a wealth of online resources, history pages, and blogs, created by people who write well, have a sense of adventure and a sense of humour, and love where they live without idealising it. The websites and pages dedicated to specific areas of Oxford are of exceptional quality – newsletters, archives, oral history resources and photographic records. I have listed these in my bibliography. The Oxfordshire History Centre, a converted church on Temple Road, Cowley, has been invaluable.

In the second category, those of us who live in Oxford are not sufficiently aware of how much we owe to the Oxford Preservation Trust and the Oxford Civic Society. A great deal of what we owe is Oxford itself – literally, in many cases, as the reader will have gathered in this book. I also owe them thanks for the information they provide in their publications and web resources, for the quality of their analyses of questions of planning, and the events they run. I especially admire their respect for Oxford's social history and its heritage. Articulate, determined, and vigilant, they continue to keep watch over the delicate balance that Oxford, for all its wealth, prestige and centuries of history, depends upon. Actual places – 'real' places, I want to say – are only here because people fought for them, often against the odds. They know that the two forces that pose the greatest danger to Oxford are also the two forces that created it: changing and staying the same.

THE AUTHOR

Born in Tunisia in 1968, Patrick McGuinness is the author of two novels, *The Last Hundred Days*, which was longlisted for the Booker Prize, and won Wales Book of the Year and the Writers' Guild Award for Fiction, and *Throw Me To the Wolves*, which won the Encore Award. His memoir, *Other People's Countries*, about his childhood in post-industrial Belgium, also won Wales Book of the Year and the Duff Cooper Prize. He is also the author of two volumes of poetry (*The Canals of Mars* and *Jilted City*) and several academic books, and has written and presented several programmes for radio.

He is Professor of French and Comparative Literature at Oxford University, and a Fellow of the Royal Society of Literature.

INDEX